Abe Saperstein and
the American Basketball
League, 1960–1963

ALSO BY MURRY R. NELSON

*The National Basketball League:
A History, 1935–1949* (McFarland, 2009)

Abe Saperstein and the American Basketball League, 1960–1963

The Upstarts Who Shot for Three and Lost to the NBA

MURRY R. NELSON

McFarland & Company, Inc., Publishers
Jefferson, North Carolina, and London

LIBRARY OF CONGRESS CATALOGUING-IN-PUBLICATION DATA

Nelson, Murry R.
    Abe Saperstein and the American Basketball League, 1960–1963 : the upstarts who shot for three and lost to the NBA / Murry R. Nelson.
        p.   cm.
    Includes bibliographical references and index.

    ISBN 978-0-7864-7244-4
    softcover : acid free paper ♾

    1. American Basketball League — History. 2. Saperstein, Abe. I. Title.
GV885.515.A6N45 2013
796.323'64097309046—dc23
[B]   2013010284

BRITISH LIBRARY CATALOGUING DATA ARE AVAILABLE

© 2013 Murry R. Nelson. All rights reserved

No part of this book may be reproduced or transmitted in any form or by any means, electronic or mechanical, including photocopying or recording, or by any information storage and retrieval system, without permission in writing from the publisher.

On the cover: (top) Publicity photo of ABL Commissioner Abe Saperstein; (bottom) team photograph of the Pittsburgh Rens (both courtesy of the Dolph Briscoe Collection, University of Texas Archives)

Manufactured in the United States of America

McFarland & Company, Inc., Publishers
  Box 611, Jefferson, North Carolina 28640
    www.mcfarlandpub.com

To the players of the American
Basketball League, too soon forgotten

Table of Contents

Acknowledgments ix

Introduction: An American Basketball League Overview 1

One. The ABL — the "Run Up" 13

Two. The Formation of a New League, Rules, Constitution, Referees and More 29

Three. ABL Financing — Expectations, Hopes, Realities 37

Four. The Exiles and the Deserters 51

Five. The Coaches and the Starting Fives 70

Six. Chicago, Battleground of the ABL and the NBA 97

Seven. The 1961-1962 Season (First Half) 109

Eight. The 1961-1962 Season (Second Half) 125

Nine. The ABL Begins a Second Year, 1962-1963 139

Ten. The ABL, and Then What? 158

Appendix 1. Team Standings, 1961-1962 167

Appendix 2. ABL Scoring, 1961-1962 168

Appendix 3. Team Standings, 1962-1963 177

Table of Contents

Appendix 4. ABL Scoring, 1962-1963 178
*Appendix 5. ABL Most Valuable Player and
  All-League Teams, 1961-1962* 182

Chapter Notes 185
Bibliography 197
Index 207

Acknowledgments

This book started as a chapter in another volume, but thanks to Mike Domjan, an old college friend, I was able to access the necessary files on the American Basketball League at the Dolph Briscoe Center of the University of Texas Archives. That center contains the Abe Saperstein papers as part of the Joseph Anzivino Collection. I am indebted to the archivists there for their assistance in the acquisition of papers from the collection, as well as their permission to reproduce documents from the archive. The Saperstein Papers are well organized and indexed, allowing great access in person or through copies. My thanks to Vern Morrison and colleagues at Cleveland State University Libraries and Archives for the reproduction and use of photographs from the Cleveland Memory Collection.

Steve Ross was kind enough to do searches for legal cases, then provide them to me. He also read some of the chapters and provided useful feedback.

Carolyn Hastings was instrumental in the location of various players I was able to interview. She also provided the Cleveland Pipers audit material. Rich Macales also helped me locate players and other personnel to interview. Rich's encouragement in reading early drafts of chapters was greatly appreciated. Jose Padilla offered encouragement and suggestions. Matt Zeyzing, Bill Tosheff, Charlie Rosen, Seymour Smith and Neil Isaacs were also helpful in this endeavor. The alumni office at Tennessee State University also deserves to be recognized for their help in providing player information.

Those interviewed were great helps, despite recalling events and people from 50 years before. I thank John Barnhill, Bill Sharman, Monte Moore, Roger Kaiser, Kenny Sears, Hal Lear, Sylvester Blye and

Acknowledgments

Rossie Johnson, all of whom provided insights and anecdotes from the ABL.

The Interlibrary Loan staff at Pattee Library at Penn State University was helpful in obtaining newspapers as well as identifying papers that had been digitized and were available in that manner.

Jennifer Glasgow in the Department of Curriculum and Instruction at Penn State's College of Education was a great help in her copying of materials, re-formatting of data and overall clerical assistance. Ken Noel did great photography.

I also thank the various members of the North American Society for the Study of Sport History for feedback on early drafts of chapters for this volume. The web site of the Association for Professional Basketball Research and specifically, Robert Bradley, was also of great help; I want to acknowledge that assistance.

Finally, but most valued, my wife, Elizabeth, has been a great help in providing feedback and allowing me to spout off, at times, on the process and problems associated with this book. Her love and support continue to amaze me.

Introduction: An American Basketball League Overview

When I told people with a modicum of knowledge regarding professional basketball history that I was writing a book on the American Basketball League (ABL), there were a number of reactions, most of which indicated that there was very little familiarity with the subject. Some people immediately thought that the book was on the American Basketball Association (ABA), the league that existed from 1967 to 1976 before agreeing to disband in the latter year, with four of their teams, San Antonio, Indiana, the New York Nets and Denver, becoming members of the NBA. No, that wasn't the league I meant.

Some thought that I might be referring to the American Basketball League that began in 1925 and folded in 1933, later to return as a regional league, which became the Eastern League. That league had as members the Original Celtics for two years, years in which they dominated the league and were forced to disband for the good of the league. No, not that league.

And there were those who were totally perplexed, having no idea whatsoever who or what the American Basketball League might be. These people far outnumbered those who actually were aware of the league's brief existence, although even those folks were hard pressed to name a team or player in the ABL. And that is very sad, considering the effect that the ABL ultimately had on professional basketball and, later, by extension, on all of basketball, through the ABL's unique rules.

In the late 1950s Abe Saperstein may have been the most influential, if not the most powerful, person in professional basketball. That influence was a result of his ownership of the Harlem Globetrotters, the only consistently successful economic engine in professional basketball.

Introduction

No team could be assured of selling out a "game" (really a show/event) more than the Globetrotters. Such a realization had led to the NBA working with Saperstein through the 1950s in a cooperative arrangement that found the Globetrotters playing the opening games of many doubleheaders in which the second game was a clash of two NBA teams, most often in an NBA arena, but not always.

By the late 1950s the NBA had come to stand on its own two feet, but the league was now playing doubleheaders involving four NBA teams, and often playing NBA games in arenas other than those of the NBA. The league was still economically challenged; the draw of the Globetrotters was still greater than that of the NBA.

In August of 1960 Abe Saperstein and his partners formed the American Basketball League. Teams were drawn from the National Industrial Basketball League (NIBL), a semi-professional league, some independent professional teams and some that were formed for the new league season. The creation of the league was coincidental with the collapse of the NIBL,[1] and a number of players were drawn from that league.

On March 18, 1961, the league announced ownership and franchise locations. There would be eight teams in two four-team divisions. The East would be the Washington Tapers, the Pittsburgh Rens, the Cleveland Pipers and the Chicago Majors. The West would consist of the Kansas City Steers, the Los Angeles Jets, the San Francisco Saints and the Hawaii Chiefs. The key locations would be where the ABL would compete directly with the NBA — in L.A. and Chicago, where the NBA had located its first expansion franchise since the formation of the league in 1949. The Tapers would be owned by Harry Lynn of Washington, D.C., and would be a continuance, to a degree, of the Tuck Tapers of the NIBL, sponsored by the Technical Tape Corporation. Paul Cohen, the president of Technical Tape, would be a director of the team. The Rens chose a name to honor the great New York Renaissance teams of the 1920s–1940s and would be owned by Lenny Litman. The Pipers would be almost wholly formed from the Cleveland Pipers team of the NIBL and would be owned by George Steinbrenner and coached by John McClendon, longtime coach of Tennessee A&I and the first African American coach of a major professional, integrated basketball league. The Chicago Majors were initially assigned to Morrie Schneer as owner. There were financial problems, and Schneer dropped out almost immediately. The team ownership was swapped with the owner of the San Francisco Saints, Abe Saperstein, also the league commissioner, and George McKeon took over the San Francisco franchise. The Steers would be owned by Ken Krueger of St. Louis and coached by Jack McMahon, a former NBA player who had recently retired because of injuries. The Jets would be owned by Len Corbosiero and coached by Bill Sharman, late of the Celtics, who would also play a bit. The Hawaii franchise was owned by Art Kim. Kim had called his franchise the Hawaii Aliis, a name for Hawaiian royalty, but in June he informed the league that the name would be Chiefs. The reason Kim gave was that "members of the Hawaiian royalty had informed him that it was taboo to use the name of Aliis in conjunction with ordinary people as it could only be associated with the ancient Hawaiian royalty."[2]

One issue for all of the franchises was getting a decent venue in which to play. The Chicago Stadium was the best and biggest available in that city, and it was initially assumed that the NBA's new franchise, the Packers, would want to play there, but Saperstein had an edge in that pursuit, the Globetrotters. Were he to be denied the use of the stadium by the owner, Art Wirtz, he would no longer have his Globies appear there, where they regularly drew 15,000 to 18,000 fans.[3] Ultimately, Saperstein prevailed and the new NBA Chicago franchise would start off having to play in the International Amphitheatre, located by the city's stockyards and built, initially, for livestock exhibitions.

In April of 1961 Robert Sturman, law partner of Allan Bloch, league vice-commissioner, sent a memo to all clubs regarding contract types. One was a tryout contract, which gave the right of termination at any time during the training season. Form A contracts were binding and offered no right of termination (except for breach by the player). Form B gave right of termination if the player did not have "the ability to engage in League competition as a member of your team." Sturman went on to offer some tips on contractual signings and urged owners to contact him with questions or comments.[4]

There were those who believed that the ABL would never begin play or would fold within weeks, and some NBA owners were among that group. Walter Brown, the owner of the Boston Celtics, predicted a failure "by Christmas" and referred to the ABL as "a bunch of pirates." He was mostly concerned about Bill Sharman, who had quit the Celtics to coach,

Introduction

but had played and scored 26 points in the Los Angeles Jets' first two games.[5]

The ABL decided to experiment with new rules to make the game more appealing to fans. Their major alterations were:

1. A 3-point field goal from 25 feet
2. An 18-foot-wide center lane at its base in a trapezoidal shape.
3. A 30-second shot clock, rather than a 24-second one, on offense.
4. A split season with a first-half play-off, and the winner of that meeting the winner of the second-half play-offs for the championship in April.
5. Visiting teams would split gate receipts with the home team, a practice not followed in the NBA.
6. Unusual travel schedules that involved Hawaii and the creation of teams playing a series in order to keep travel costs more reasonable.

The Chicago situation. The NBA awarded a franchise to Dave Trager and his partners for the 1961-62 season, after what were claimed to be 15 months of negotiation with the NBA.[6] The team was unable to use Chicago Stadium and gained access to the International Amphitheatre at 42nd and Halsted for most of their home games, although like all NBA franchises at the time, regional games would be played at other venues such as Milwaukee to promote interest in the team and the NBA. Playing at the International Amphitheatre made a team name of "Packers" logical, since it reflected both the team's location (adjacent to the Union Stockyards) and heritage ("Hog Butcher for the world," as Carl Sandburg said in his poem, "Chicago" in 1916). The new team paid $200,000 to join the NBA, and each of the established teams were allowed to protect seven players as the Packers chose players off the other rosters, with no more than one per team. The new franchise then received the first pick in the NBA draft and six successive picks in the second round of the draft. The Packers were also hamstrung by a league proviso that did not allow them to trade any of the players drafted on NBA rosters without first securing the approval of four of the seven teams not involved in any potential transaction. (This was invoked in late November in a Packers–St. Louis Hawks trade.)[7]

The NBA Packers lost the venue battle, but won the first-draft pick battle. The Packers selected Walt Bellamy as the first NBA pick, and the Chicago Majors received him in a trade with the Cleveland Pipers after they procured him as their territorial pick.[8] Bellamy signed with the Packers, but Saperstein had a plan for enhancing his Chicago ABL roster that no other team could match. He would use the Globetrotters roster as a kind of "farm team" from which to select players for his ABL squad and then send ABL players to the Trotters or cut them lose as free agents. In addition, the Majors made a number of trades, as did most of the other ABL teams.

The Los Angeles situation. The Lakers had one season in Los Angeles in which to draw fans, and they had some great players to watch, most specifically Elgin Baylor and Jerry West, but the team finished second in the Western Division, with a record just under .500. It was clear that they would improve as their players gained more experience, and the next year they burst into first and remained there the entire season. The new Los Angeles Jets hoped that they could pull fans from the Lakers, but the Lakers had too much glitz, were too good a team and played in too good a venue to aid the Jets in their quest.

The Jets had an excellent roster, but there were financial problems on the part of owner Corbosiero; roster problems in that George Yardley, who had retired from the NBA, would play at home games, but few away games because of his engineering business; venue problems in playing at the Olympic Auditorium, which was not an arena fans would flock to. In addition, Los Angelenos don't have the same need to be indoors in the winter because of the weather, and professional basketball took quite a while to build interest there.

The Jets were a good team with Hal Lear (formerly of the NBA Warriors and an All-American at Temple), Bill Spivey (the seven-foot all-American from the early 1950s at Kentucky, blacklisted by the NBA for not reporting a bribe), Dan Swartz (the scoring leader from the defunct NIBL), Larry Friend (who had played in the NBA and starred at Cal), George Yardley (an NBA Hall of Famer who retired at 33) and Bill Sharman (another Hall of Famer who retired early from the Celtics to be the player-coach of the Jets). Nevertheless, the team drew only 33,957 for 16 home dates before rumors began flying of the team relocating to suburban Los Angeles (Long Beach or Pasadena) or even moving to Ft. Worth, Houston or Portland.[9] In mid–January, it was announced that

Introduction

the Jets' games scheduled for January 19 and 21 would be postponed, and the next day the Jets' league exit was announced. A league spokesman (unidentified, probably Saperstein, himself) also said that the Jets would reorganize for 1962-1963 and return to the league, probably in Long Beach, and that the players would "go out on option." This was viewed with skepticism by most media observers. The Jets had lost approximately $189,000 in the half season, and their owner, Len Corbosiero, was ill. Abe Saperstein claimed that his illness was the source of the withdrawal and that the team had plenty of money in the bank, but needed to "get their house in order."[10] It was at this time that Dave Trager, the Chicago Packers' owner, said that his club had lost $150,000 in the first half of the season and blamed it on the bad record of the team (9–31), bad weather and a bad schedule (only 12 home games) with an average of 3,370 per game. He said that they needed to average 4,500 to break even.

As noted, the Globetrotters would also serve as a gate attraction for ABL games, being the other team in ABL doubleheaders. The Trotters would play as part of doubleheaders in most, if not all, of the ABL cities to boost attendance across the league.

Without the "use" of the Globetrotters, the nine NBA teams played a number of doubleheaders with four NBA teams at one site, hoping to generate more interest and attendance for NBA games. There would also be the "home" games played at arenas or gymnasia throughout the NBA and ABL territories. Thus, the following sites had NBA games in 1961-62: Dayton, Hershey (PA), Milwaukee, Ft. Wayne, East Chicago (Washington High School), Providence, Utica, Rochester, Moline (IL), Indianapolis, Green Bay, Louisville, DePaul Alumni Gym in Chicago and Seattle. This was the *established* league; the new ABL played home games in Norfolk (VA), Steubenville (OH), Richmond, Muskegon (MI), Lansing (MI), Milwaukee, Rockford (IL), Wichita, Detroit, Columbus, Lorain (OH), Oklahoma City, Miami Beach, Oakland, Jacksonville, Ashtabula (OH), New Haven and Rochester. Some of these sites drew well, while others drew in the hundreds. Both leagues were struggling, but the new ABL was struggling more.

During the 1960-1961 season, the NBA had set a new attendance record with over 700,000, which is just under 2,500 per game. Attendance in 1961–1962 was much higher, but still less than 5,000 per game on

Introduction

average. The NBA had a small television contract with NBC for Sundays, but not all NBC-affiliated stations picked up the games. Most teams would lose money but were in better shape than the ABL, which had lower attendance, no television income and owners who did not have "deep pockets" to absorb losses for long.

The ABL's first season began with good crowds in Kansas City, Pittsburgh, Chicago and Cleveland and with adequate crowds in San Francisco and Hawaii. Washington and Los Angeles started with small crowds and things got worse. By the end of December there were rumors of the Tapers moving to Camden, a story denied by the owner Harry Lynn, also the owner of the Washington Coliseum where the team played. The rumor was only partly true, as the team moved to Commack, Long Island, within a week.[11] Lynn also yielded control of the team to Paul Cohen. Unfortunately, the move to Commack did not lead to increased attendance, with many "crowds" numbering in the hundreds, rather than thousands.

Player disputes. The ABL followed the lead of the new American Football League and contacted NBA players who might be interested in jumping to the new league. A number of players did so, since the NBA rosters, even after expanding, were still only 12, meaning that there would only be 108 active players in the NBA. In addition, some players who felt that they weren't playing enough or wanted to be in a different environment signed with the new league. The most noted were Dick Barnett of the Syracuse Nationals and Ken Sears from the New York Knicks, who signed with the Cleveland Pipers and San Francisco Saints, respectively. Barnett wanted to play more, and he wished to join former teammates and his former college coach from Tennessee A&I, John McClendon, on the Cleveland Pipers. Sears, a native of Northern California and college star at Santa Clara, wanted to return to the Bay Area. Both moves resulted in lawsuits, ultimately settled on behalf of the players allowing them to play in the ABL, unencumbered.

The ABL also signed players who had been blacklisted by the NBA for not reporting bribes in the wake of college basketball scandals of the period. Bill Spivey, mentioned earlier, was the first seven-footer in professional basketball and helped Los Angeles (and Hawaii after the Jets folded) greatly, finishing second in the league in scoring and third in rebounding. Tony Jackson, from St. Johns, played initially for

Introduction

the Tapers, then was traded to the Chicago Majors and led the league in three-point shots with 141. The biggest star, however, was Connie Hawkins, from Brooklyn, who had spent part of his freshman year at the University of Iowa. The 19-year-old (who turned 20 during the season) led the league in scoring, with over 27 points per game, was second in rebounding and was voted the most valuable player in the league. Despite his age, the league owners agreed to allow him to play as a "hardship case."[12]

Other top stars came from the NIBL or were rookies that the ABL managed to snag ahead of the NBA. The two most noted of the latter were Larry Siegfried from Ohio State, signed by the Pipers, and Bill Bridges of Kansas, signed by the Steers, and who led the league in rebounding.

The ABL gained early credibility by signing top coaches, most of whom had played or coached in the NBA. In the West, Kansas City selected Jack McMahon, a former Cincinnati Royal, forced to retire because of injury; the Jets chose Bill Sharman as player-coach; the Saints signed Phil Woolpert, the former University of San Francisco coach whose team won NCAA titles in 1955 and 1956; and Hawaii was led by Red Rocha, former BAA and NBA player. In the East, the Rens chose Neil Johnston, who had retired from the Warriors in 1959 at the age of 31; the Tapers selected Stan Stutz (*né* Stan Modzelewski), who had played in the Basketball Association of America (BAA); Chicago signed former Illini whiz kid and NBA guard, Andy Phillip; and the Pipers chose John McLendon, making him the first African American coach in a professional basketball league.

By December, the standings showed Kansas City as the top team in the West and Cleveland and Pittsburgh the top teams in the East. There were interesting events and actions during this period. Stan Musial signed on as a minority owner of the Steers; the ABL owners began discussing expansion when the season was barely a month old[13]; Neil Johnston returned to the court as a player for the Rens; Phil Woolpert was fired as coach of the Saints[14]; bad weather (which closed airports) forced teams to get to some games by renting cars; George Steinbrenner failed to pay his players one week because of cash flow problems and the players publicly complained and were defended by their coach, John McLendon, who "resigned" within a week under pressure; the Los Angeles Jets

Introduction

folded and their players were redistributed within the league; Steinbrenner signed Bill Sharman as the new Pipers coach.

As noted earlier, the Tapers moved to New York in early January, but there were other minor incidents that were interesting during that period. In San Francisco, the Steers lost to the Saints in a close contest, delayed, with five seconds left, when a teenager sneaked onto the floor at a time-out and absconded with the game ball. After finally finding another acceptable ball, the game resumed. Snowstorms delayed games in Kansas City, Wichita and Chicago. A player signed by the Steers was unable to play because his employer, the Fort Worth School District, prohibited their coaches from playing professional basketball, baseball or football.

The innovative play-offs (best two of three) set to begin on January 12 with all games played in the Eastern city, were rescheduled at the last minute to allow the first game to be played in the West. Kansas City defeated Cleveland in Game 1 in the Kansas City Municipal Auditorium. Tickets were $3 for boxes, $2 for lower balcony and $1 for upper balcony and 5,286 fans attended. Back in Cleveland, the Pipers won Game 2 before 4,276 fans, but the Steers came back to defeat the Pipers in Game 3 and claimed the First Half Title on January 14.[15]

The second half season began with just seven teams. The Tapers were strengthened by the addition of Dan Swartz and became a winning squad, despite their inability to draw fans. The Pipers started slowly, but as Dick Barnett rounded into scoring shape after being held out because of the legal restraints, they began winning again. Pittsburgh began to fade, despite Hawkins scoring more than 50 points in a game more than once. Chicago led the East most of the second half as Tony Jackson went on three-point shooting sprees, getting 12 in one game and more than 5 in a number of others.

In the West, the Steers and Saints played evenly and well most of the second half, while Hawaii was near .500. Hawaii played home games in Miami Beach, Oklahoma City, Jacksonville and Long Beach in order to lessen the travel burden for themselves and their opponents. When teams came to Hawaii, they usually played a three-game series with the Chiefs, and Hawaii would have 9-to-12-game home stands.

In early February, George Wilson, the owner of the Buffalo Bills football team, purchased the majority interest in the Pipers, but Stein-

Introduction

brenner remained as president of the team.[16] He then rehired John McClendon as vice president of personnel and public relations.

A few weeks later, the ABL owners met to decide if they should expel the Pipers because of their failure to comply with the ABL Constitution. They also discussed adding two franchises for 1962–63, probably in Portland and Dallas.[17] The Cleveland issues, involving communication with the league office, payment of gate receipts to the league and submission of financial reports were settled at the league meeting, but more troubles would arise with the Pipers at the end of the year.

Despite the ABL's stated intention to expand, some writers who followed the league saw continued difficulties unless the ABL could sign more impact players like Hawkins and Bridges. Attendance had not been phenomenal and recognition had been slow; the ABL was at a critical juncture.[18]

At the end of March the league announced a play-off structure as well as the all-league teams. The First Team consisted of Larry Staverman and Bill Bridges of the Kansas City Steers, Connie Hawkins of the Pittsburgh Rens, Dan Swartz of the New York Tapers and Dick Barnett of the Cleveland Pipers. The Second Team was Johnny Cox of the Pipers, Hershell Turner of the Chicago Majors, Kenny Sears of the San Francisco Saints, Bill Spivey of the Hawaii Chiefs and a tie for the tenth spot between Tony Jackson of Chicago and Nick Mantis of Kansas City.

As for the play-offs, the Steers would play the winner of a six-team tournament in which the Pipers and the Majors would have first-round byes. In the first round, the Tapers defeated the Chiefs, and the Saints topped the Rens, with both games being decided in overtime. New York then upset Chicago, and Cleveland topped San Francisco. The Tapers and Pipers then traveled to Kansas City, where they would play for the right to meet the Steers for the title. The Steers had drawn 99,000 fans for their home games, including one play-off contest, and the hope was that fans would flock to the final semi-final game, plus the finals contests.

In the Semi-Final, the Pipers defeated the Tapers 107 to 84, sending the Pipers into the best-of-five Finals. Games 1 and 2 went to the Steers, with Bridges and Staverman leading in scoring and rebounding. Then the series shifted to Cleveland, where the Pipers won two close games.

Introduction

The first drew almost 8,000 fans since it was coupled with a Globetrotters game. Bridges continued his hot shooting, but Dick Barnett and Connie Dierking led Cleveland to victories.

Then more uncertainty and controversy arose. Steinbrenner and Pittsburgh owner Len Litman claimed that the fifth game was to be played in the East. Saperstein said there was a misunderstanding and that it was to be played in the West. Steinbrenner declared that the Pipers would not play in Kansas City and wanted a neutral site, like St. Louis. The Pipers failed to come to Kansas City for the game on April 9, but they finally agreed and arrived the next day for the game in Kansas City. Unfortunately, the game had to be played in the Rockhurst College gym because the Municipal Auditorium had been previously booked. Steinbrenner complained that the gym only held 4,000, but the game only drew 3,000. Cleveland, led by Barnett and Dierking, won once again and were the first ABL champions.

The season had proven that a second major professional basketball league could appeal to fans, particularly those in cities that had no NBA team. Almost all of the teams lost money; any successful league would have to have owners who were patient and had deep pockets from other enterprises. The new rules, particularly the three-point shot, proved to be very popular with fans, despite the fact that "traditionalists" said that there was no room in the game for such "gimmicks." There were enough good players to make for a top game, although it was difficult to compare it to the NBA just then. ABL teams issued challenges to the NBA, but the NBA, wisely, did not respond, feeling that doing so in any manner would legitimize the ABL. Saperstein and the other owners looked forward to a 1962-1963 season with an expanded league, more publicity and respect and, they hoped, some sort of television contract. Little of that would materialize, and the league would struggle to stay afloat in 1962-63 and would ultimately fail.

One

The ABL — the "Run Up"

The post-war period brought renewed and excited interest in professional sports, most particularly major league baseball and football. The All-American Football Conference began in 1946 and merged with the NFL in 1949 as the National-American Football League. This was one of the first indicators that there was room for other professional leagues, under the right conditions. In addition it was important to note that professional football was far less popular than major league baseball in terms of both total attendance and professed favorites. In 1960 a Gallup poll indicated that baseball was still the most popular sport by far, with 34 percent ranking it first, 21 percent naming football and 10 percent basketball.[1] In the immediate post-war period, baseball's popularity was even higher although there was not the same "official" designation.

During the early 1950s, major league baseball enjoyed great growth in popularity, but that was not always followed by box office success, often because of the location or condition of the baseball stadiums. Nowhere was this more evident than in New York where the New York Giants and the Brooklyn Dodgers were the top teams in the National League. From 1951 to 1956, either the Dodgers or the Giants won the National League pennant. The Giants, however, were not an attractive draw. Their park, the Polo Grounds, was located just north of Central Park in the Morningside Heights area of Manhattan. The ballpark was built in 1883 and was in need of significant renovation, if not replacement. Owner Horace Stoneham wanted the city to assist, and the city fathers of New York were not terribly interested. The attendance for the Giants was last in the league in both 1956 and 1957, despite the fact that the Giants had won the World Championship in 1954 and had the most exciting player in the game in Willie Mays.

The Dodgers had the second or third best attendance in the league (behind the new darling, Milwaukee), but Ebbets Field was tiny, bound in by the Flatbush neighborhood, and had almost no parking. As Dodger fans moved to Long Island, attendance looked to be going in the wrong direction. Owner Walter O'Malley wanted the city to assist him in building a new park in the Atlantic Yards area of Brooklyn, but Robert Moses wanted a park at the Flushing Meadows area and neither would budge. O'Malley was swayed by the city of Los Angeles to relocate there and convinced his friend Stoneham to move his team to San Francisco to carry their traditional rivalry to California. Thus, in August of 1957, it was announced that the Giants would move to San Francisco. It was the lead headline in all the New York daily papers. The Dodger announcement followed in September.[2]

The move of the two franchises was a significant blow to New York City, both in pride and economics. Almost immediately there was a call from many in the city for National League expansion in order to bring a franchise back to the city. The major leagues were not initially eager for expansion, fearing that their product would be diluted and attendance would suffer. The indecisiveness made for a perfect time for an old baseball warrior, Branch Rickey, to step into the breach. Rickey hoped to start a third major league, and he set about lining up wealthy backers interested in such an endeavor. These included Joan Whitney Payson and George Herbert Walker, Jr., initial owners of the New York Mets in 1962; Jack Kent Cooke in Toronto; Craig Cullinan in Houston; Edwin "Big Ed" Johnson in Denver; and folks from Minneapolis connected to Hamms Beer.[3]

Rickey was maneuvering to make his Continental League a third major league, and the established major leagues did their best to forestall that while seeming to support his plan. Most of the intended owners wanted to be in the major leagues and would (and did) abandon the Continental League once major league baseball was forced to expand in order to prevent the formation of the new league. Nevertheless, the league argued for changes in major league structure that would have "saved" the majors from themselves, contended Michael Shapiro. These actions included revenue sharing and a league television contract, rather than individual team controls.

To the major league owners this was anathema, and they managed to repel this onslaught, helping baseball to fall behind football in popularity and revenue. Interestingly, the notions were adapted and adopted by the founders of the American Football League (AFL), which came to birth in 1960. Lamar Hunt, the most influential league founder, openly acknowledged that the idea for revenue sharing and centralized media control came from Rickey and the Continental League. Hunt said, "I met Mr. Rickey only once (during a planning session regarding the Continental League) and I do recall hearing his idea about sharing TV revenue for the proposed Continental League.... I did copy this idea in relation to the start of the Football League."[4]

The success of the American Football League was largely a result of this innovation. Teams could thrive in any city, no matter what the size (reasonably speaking), and this was illustrated in the success of Oakland, Kansas City and Buffalo, for example. The television contract with ABC not only ensured the success of the AFL; it also created a renaissance in that network, making it the leader in television sports.

The AFL model was based on many of the Rickey/Continental League ideas, but the AFL managed to create better "buzz" for the league by doing some things that the Continental League only dreamed of doing. First was the aforementioned television contract. It was true mutualism as the two parties both needed what the other could provide. For the AFL, it was exposure; for ABC, it was a sports product that would draw an audience.

Rickey had argued that fans wanted competition, close contests and good play. It didn't matter if the Continental League teams were initially inferior to the American or National League teams. Parity would come, Rickey asserted, in a few years. Meanwhile his league would build with young players who would emerge as stars. This was the thinking adopted by the AFL. There would be a competitive league that was entertaining. This latter notion was largely brought about by an emphasis on and innovations in offense, a high level of scoring to excite the viewer.

The plan worked to perfection for the AFL as the high-scoring offenses brought in viewers and allowed ABC to raise revenue rates for their ads. Ultimately, of course, this led to the great merger of the AFL/NFL in 1966, which ended the AFL's independence but solidified the AFL teams and their futures in the NFL pantheon.

A second, though less hyped, action that helped the AFL win new converts and viewers was the contract with Fleer gum, by which Fleer brought out sets of AFL trading cards beginning in 1960. The typical card collector of that era was in the 8–12 years age range, which meant getting new young fans who might also influence and interest parents (mostly dads) in watching the AFL on television. Again, this was a great example of mutualism, as Topps gum had locked up the NFL players until that time, and Fleer was searching for a product to promote their sales. The AFL sought exposure, and this was a focused and useful product for them.

The AFL also chose to be in cities that were largely untouched by pro football and, in some cases, by any of the major leagues. These "aspirational cities" saw themselves as big league, and having a major professional franchise would solidify that claim. This was not a totally new strategy, but it was well carried out by the AFL, modeling, at least in part, on the Continental League. The latter league had been premised on an anchor franchise in New York, which worked perfectly after the abandonment of the Giants and Dodgers. The other anticipated teams were in Denver, Houston, Minneapolis/St. Paul, Toronto, Miami, Atlanta, Buffalo and Dallas, none of which had major league baseball franchises. All, save Buffalo, have them today.

The AFL had anchor teams in two NFL cities, New York and Los Angeles. The other cities were all without NFL teams and, but for Boston, none had a major professional franchise in 1960. These were Buffalo, Houston, Dallas, Denver and Oakland. Dallas moved within two years to Kansas City, where they became firmly ensconced as the Chiefs. The Los Angeles franchise moved in 1961 to San Diego where the Chargers have resided since.[5]

It was with this history and contemporary action that Abe Saperstein formed the American Basketball League in 1960. Saperstein always had contingency plans to maximize his revenue streams. As owner of the Harlem Globetrotters, with at least two different squads, he had a team playing every day somewhere in the world. He also was one of the key reasons that the NBA was able to pay its bills from the formation of the league in 1949 through the 1950s, as he had the Globetrotters play doubleheaders before many NBA games, often doubling or tripling the average attendance figures for those games.

Saperstein was also a vice president of the Philadelphia Warriors, an original (1946) Basketball Association of America (BAA) franchise

One. The ABL — the "Run Up"

that became a founding franchise in the NBA. Because of that and his financial aid to the league, he was expectant of a franchise in the NBA, when the league chose to expand. The story was that he was promised the first West Coast franchise, but when the Lakers moved from Minneapolis to Los Angeles in April of 1960, Saperstein felt betrayed and began his own league. This is an often-told tale, but not completely true.

Saperstein was planning a new league before the Lakers' move was announced. Whether he would have abandoned those plans if he had been given the option of a new West Coast franchise is moot. What is clear is that as early as the spring of 1959, Saperstein was trying to put together a new professional basketball league, believing that the NBA was not ready to either expand or shift a franchise to the West Coast. After a series of phone calls, he sent letters to a number of persons around the country raising the possibility of a new pro basketball league. Replying to Saperstein's letter of April 20, 1959, Harry Glickman (who would later become one of the founders of the Portland Trailblazers in 1970) replied to Saperstein that he would be interested in a meeting to discuss Saperstein's proposal for another league. He agreed to attend a meeting in Los Angeles in May on the subject.[6]

Saperstein responded two days later with thanks for Glickman agreeing to meet and reiterating that such a new league would provide "interesting and topflight basketball."

There is no archival record of the meeting, but it was mentioned in some West Coast newspapers. Glickman sent these on to Saperstein, and he responded with thanks, as well as anticipation of an upcoming meeting with Maurice Podoloff, NBA commissioner. In a brief night letter sent three days later, Saperstein said, "Internal rift NBA makes getting anything concrete done only remote possibility. Fellow will need to be super salesman but will continue old college try."[7]

So Saperstein was going to have to work both sides of the street, that is, seeking NBA expansion and a franchise in that manner and also planning a new league, were his efforts at an expansion franchise for the West Coast to fail. Glickman wrote to Saperstein in July, inquiring as to progress with Podoloff as well as to voice his support for a new league.

> Abe, I have given much careful thought to the matter of professional basketball and I am becoming more convinced than ever that your proposal for a new league has more merit than affiliating with the NBA.... The only draw-

back would be the competition for a handful of "name" players. I agree with your contention that there are plenty of players available to fill out a league of eight clubs. We could organize this league properly and profit by the many mistakes that the NBA has made in the past and continues to make at the present time. With your direction and leadership, I believe that such a league would be a tremendous success.[8]

Saperstein, still on the Globetrotters' tour of Europe and Russia in early August, wrote back to Glickman, from "somewhere in the Pyrenees Mountains." He noted that not much had happened in regard to the NBA and he still believed that a new league was the solution, but he was on tour for three more weeks and couldn't do much until returning. He suggested that he call Glickman since it was better than trying to get all of his thoughts down on paper.[9] Saperstein's letter of September 2 provided both a litany of events from the Globetrotter tour as well as a disappointing comment on the proposed new league: "We had a bit of difficulty rounding up six clubs for a new league ... will keep you abreast of the situation in the interim."[10]

Another note to Glickman on September 8 indicated that the NBA was only interested in expanding to San Francisco and Los Angeles and was confident of a group in L.A. Saperstein felt that they'd be overpaying for a franchise (at $100,000 to $150,000 and no players in return), but no one asked him. Thus, he retained his belief in the "need and desire for a well organized new league in the professional basketball field."[11]

Things seemed to cool regarding a new league, as Saperstein got busier with his Globetrotters and their upcoming tours. He noted in late October, "We are still fooling around with the development of a new league," but that was all he said in that regard.[12]

In an undated (but judging by internal references, probably written in mid–December of 1959) letter to Robert Smith, a prominent oil executive in Houston, Saperstein says, "In recent months ... the thought of a new league (professional) has dawned in my mind ... and there certainly is a need for something along those lines."[13]

Saperstein went on to describe the problems he saw with the NBA, which included too much scoring, too little team play and uneven financial allocation of gate receipts. Saperstein also noted that he had discussed such a league with groups in Los Angeles, San Francisco, Portland (Oregon) and Chicago and needed only two more cities to make his circuit a reality. He saw Kansas City as a possibility after visiting there. He then tried to mollify concerns about the lack of a proper fieldhouse in Houston that such a team could utilize.

The likely cost of such a franchise would be $250,000, but Saperstein felt that television revenue could immediately offset some of this and claimed that "an opposing network has indicated that they would be interested in a new circuit."[14]

Saperstein saw time being of the essence in order to get arrangements under way for the 1960-1961 season and offered to visit Smith again to solidify his interest or to entertain Smith in Chicago. Just after the first of the year, Saperstein sent another note soliciting interest in the new league and again pushed Smith for a quick decision, but Smith's reply of two days later was brief and opaque.[15]

After returning from a Globetrotter tour of Europe, Saperstein wrote to Smith again on January 24 and again asked if there was any interest in a pro basketball franchise in Houston in the future. Then, on February 15, Saperstein tried again, noting, "We are now under the hammer as far as time goes."[16]

Smith replied that the city was in a "state of flux in relation to a stadium or I might say including all sports ... and even at this time the people that hold the franchise in the International League and the ones that have the franchise for the Continental League are unable to work out their affairs so we don't know what to do at this time."[17]

Saperstein's reply of February 27, 1960, indicated that he was moving on, but he noted, "Should any interest develop (to your knowledge) in the field of professional basketball ... would feel honored in being apprised of that fact as it develops."[18]

Smith's reply of March 7 noted that politics had now entered into the issues there, and he was skeptical of any pursuit of basketball at that time. He did note that there was a lot of interest in a Continental League baseball franchise.[19]

Saperstein traveled with the Globetrotters on many, if not most, of their tours and checked into his Chicago office between tours. He continued to use his traveling to visit cities that might be interested in a new franchise for his unannounced league and corresponded with individuals in a number of cities.

In July of 1959 Saperstein sent a telegram from the Hotel Ukraine in Russia (not specified, but likely Kiev) to Kirk Kerkorian, who then was the owner of a small flying service in Los Angeles, which made most of its revenue flying gamblers on charters from Los Angeles to Las Vegas.[20] Judging by the cryptic contents, Saperstein had already raised the issue of professional basketball in the San Francisco Bay area, which would somehow involve Kerkorian. The telegram noted, "Have group now interested Bay area professional basketball activities."[21]

Saperstein followed this telegram up about three weeks later with a letter from Switzerland in which he elaborated on his vision for basketball on the West Coast.

> Concerning pro basketball in the Bay area.... I have felt that the Pacific Coast was certainly ready for this type of sport ... as they were for big league baseball and football. As far as this writer is concerned, I made initial overtures for a Los Angeles franchise with a group largely headed by people in the Los Angeles Rams football organization ... and when the current National Basketball Association took very little notice of expansion of this kind ... made efforts to form a new circuit of Los Angeles, San Francisco, Portland, Chicago and a couple of other cities.

But the couple of other cities which included Denver, Houston, Mexico City and Kansas City just were not ready for this sort of thing.

In conferences with Maurice Podoloff, president of the NBA, in May and June of 1959, he advised,

> If I could get two "solid" groups in Los Angeles and San Francisco, they would be interested in taking in the two groups for the season after next [1960-1961] ... and asked that applications be made ... and consequently I made one for the Los Angeles group.
> One has to be made for a San Francisco group ... and Al [Weill, a mutual friend] indicated that you were interested.... At any rate it is high time that the "ball is started rolling."[22]

Saperstein sent a follow-up telegram to Kerkorian in August, noting that he had received a letter regarding the Bay Area franchise and that he would be back in his Chicago office in early September. In a later telegram from Chicago, Saperstein advised Kerkorian of his travel to New York, San Francisco and Los Angeles within the next two weeks to discuss the "professional basketball picture" and said he looked forward to getting together with him.[23] Kerkorian replied and Saperstein responded to that telegram, and they were scheduled to meet on September 14 and/or 15 in Los Angeles.

There was no follow-up record of this meeting or this topic again until March of 1960 when Saperstein sent a note to four interested persons regarding the creation and organization of a new basketball league. Obviously there were discussions among each of them and Saperstein, but there is no archival record of such meetings, indicating that most of it must have been carried out by telephone. The recipients of the Saperstein letter were, besides Kerkorian, Isadore Bronstein of Buffalo, Henry Konysky of Hollywood and Phil Fox or Stan Stutz of the Technical Tape Company of New Rochelle, New York. Saperstein's letter said, after months of discussions, "Am moving ahead with recently discussed informal get together in Chicago for purposes of solidifying the many ideas and suggestions in this particular field. Date is March 24th at private club Fritzel's Restaurant and if need be carryover until day following.... Hope that you or a representative will be on hand."[24]

Kerkorian did not attend the proposed meeting, as indicated by a note from Saperstein's staffer, Marie Linehan, who apparently took a phone call from him on March 22, wherein Kerkorian said that he was in bed with flu but that Saperstein should call him advising developments between 3 and 4 p.m. on Thursday (the 24th).[25]

Apparently the meeting went well, judging by Saperstein's letter to Kerkorian, Bronstein and Harry Glickman of Portland, sent on March 25. He called the meeting "highly satisfactory" and noted that there was representation in person or proxy by people from Washington, Buffalo, Cleveland, Chicago, Portland, Los Angeles, and San Francisco, plus a New York group interested in a Kansas City or Houston franchise. There were, he claimed, also "worthy possible franchise inquiries" from Baltimore, Toledo and Honolulu. The minutes would be rushed to them, and a follow-up meeting was scheduled for April 21 at a site to be determined. Saperstein said that he would be in touch with all interested parties by phone periodically.[26]

That same day (March 25) Saperstein also sent a similar note to Sid Goldberg of Toledo (who had been involved with the Toledo franchise of the National Basketball League in the 1940s) and Hyman Tatelbaum of Baltimore (treasurer of the Baltimore Bullets basketball team of the Eastern Professional Basketball League [EPBL], who had sent a telegram of interest on March 23). Saperstein said that each interested party needed to produce financial proposals, details, objectives and a yes or no answer for the April 21 meeting.[27]

Tatelbaum did not attend the April 21 meeting but wrote to Saperstein in May asking to discuss the new league with Saperstein the next time he was in New York. Saperstein replied that he probably would not be in New York again before mid–August. He closed in an uncharacteristically short manner: "Any discussions about recently organized American Basketball League would have to come by letter for the time being."[28] This was very unusual for Saperstein and he clearly was disturbed by the manner in which he must have perceived that he was being "jerked around" by Tatelbaum. He didn't have time for games like that and would not pursue anything more with Tatelbaum and the Bullets for the time being.

Sid Goldberg had sent a telegram of interest on March 23 in which he said that he headed a group wanting entrance to the new league and that they had available to them two excellent facilities—the sports arena and Toledo University, both with capacities of 8,000. A later letter indicated that the group was not financially ready, but hoped to start as a farm team if the league was successfully begun.[29]

Harry Glickman sent a note of acknowledgment concerning the minutes of the March 24, 1960, meeting. He also enclosed a six-page memorandum, which "outlines my thoughts about some of the items which were discussed at the Chicago meeting and some which I would like to have discussed at the next meeting." He went on to say that he had investigated a lease for the venue that the Portland team would use, although details would have to wait until Portland formally entered the ABL when it was formed.[30]

Glickman's memo was the most thoughtful generated by the notion of the new league. He made ten major points. First, he agreed that there was room for such a new league. Second, he thought there was sufficient talent to stock such a league, although a bidding war with the NBA for top "names" seemed inevitable. Third, he opposed starting in 1960-1961, since there should be more time to plan, plus Portland could not join until 1961-1962 since the venue was booked already. He felt that most clubs would run into this problem. He also felt that the NBA was not going to expand and L.A. was a key city to the ABL's success. He fully agreed that wise draft selections would be vital to the league's success and suggested that the league employ a head scout for the league as a whole. He also strongly supported territorial draft selections and described why and how he would implement this process.

He was very supportive of another system for allocating gate revenues than the NBA's home team keeps all. Glickman described a system whereby the home team kept 60 percent, and 40 percent went to the league office to cover officiating salaries and expenses, league office operating expenses, and traveling expenses of each club, with the balance to be equally divided among the eight clubs. He also thought that the league entry fee should be $15,000, rather than $10,000.

Glickman also presented ideas for the scheduling of the eight clubs, a topic not covered in the meeting minutes. From this we can see that the Eastern teams would be Buffalo, Cleveland, Chicago and Washington while the Western would be Los Angeles, Kansas City or Houston, Portland and San Francisco. He suggested that play-offs be limited to division winners. In that regard, he saw a shorter season (68 games from mid–November to mid–March) superior to a longer season. He urged that Saperstein share his comments with the other prospective owners.[31]

Saperstein responded a few days later, noting that he had sent out the proposals to all interested parties. He went on to say that he felt it imperative to begin in 1960-1961, even if only six clubs could begin that year. He was now going to push to ascertain if there was financial backing for all the supposedly interested parties. Glickman replied three days later with some absolutes. First, Portland would not join for the 1960-1961 season. He suggested that Portland join the ABL as a charter member, but not begin play until 1961-1962. He looked forward to the meeting in Chicago on April 21.[32]

After Glickman's statement of non-entry for 1960-1961, Saperstein wrote to suggest that Glickman not waste his time by attending the meeting on the 21st. The league needed to begin in 1960 or the "entire picture as it exists at the moment will completely change in another season."[33]

After the meeting on April 21, 1960, in Chicago there was a press release announcing the new league. Particulars of the new circuit were still sketchy, but it would include at least six teams—Chicago, San Francisco, Los Angeles, Cleveland, Kansas City and Washington, D.C. Two other teams were to be selected from among Pittsburgh, Vancouver,

Portland and Honolulu. No mention was made of Glickman's decision to not enter in 1960-1961. Backers for the L.A. team included Bing Crosby and Len Corbosiero while the Kansas City team sought local backers, with Phil Fox of New York being the initial awardee of the franchise.[34]

Saperstein wanted to shore up the league members, but he was also a realist, even when there were what seemed to be earnest pursuits of a league franchise. Robert Siegel of Cincinnati wrote to Saperstein in April of 1960 seeking a franchise for Indianapolis. Siegel describes an interesting history of pursuing professional basketball, beginning in 1956 when he managed to get the NBA to play a game in Cincinnati between the Rochester Royals and the Fort Wayne Pistons. The Royals, owned by Les Harrison and his brother, were on the block, as Rochester was no longer providing a sufficient revenue stream for the Harrisons, who had no other income source. After the successful game in Cincinnati, the Harrisons removed the team from the market and moved to Cincinnati in 1957. Two years later, the Harrisons ended up selling the team anyway, and Siegel, according to his letter, "went to New York ready, willing and able to purchase from the Harrisons. However the league preferred Mr. Thomas Wood, who owns the Cincinnati Gardens."

Siegel then goes on to bemoan the mismanagement of the Royals by Wood and his partners, as well as Siegel's continued efforts to gain a new franchise for Indianapolis from the NBA in which he had been continually rebuffed. He asserted that Oscar Robertson would be the nucleus of such a team; Siegel had employed him in the summer and entertained Oscar in his home. He then assured Saperstein that this discussion would be confidential and that he had the financial means to purchase a team for the new league.[35]

Saperstein immediately replied, thanking Siegel, but asserting that "over a period of many years ... Indianapolis just hasn't been too kind to professional basketball operations." He did say that he would submit Siegel's letter to the ABL partners, but that was just another way of saying no way, since Saperstein made almost all the important decisions.[36]

Siegel would not let it go and wrote back agreeing with Saperstein, but noting that the key to the success of pro basketball in any city was "management," which he had, and that he'd like to discuss the issue further. Saperstein wrote back saying that the league owners ("the fellows") "feel that they will go along with what they have gotten together at the moment.... Certainly appreciated your advice and your general thoughts."[37]

At that same time Saperstein was working all of his contacts to find a franchisee for Kansas City, "but all groups were shying away from Kaysee." It appeared that Kansas City would not be a part of the new league (despite the award of a franchise to Phil Fox), but ultimately Ken Krueger of St. Louis came forward and was accepted as owner for a Kansas City franchise.

In April of 1960, a potential offer came from New York City, which would have had media cachet. Benjamin Stern, who had talked with Saperstein via telephone, said that he desired to "undertake the franchise in this enterprise since we feel that the need and the timing is right at this moment." Stern said that the key man in his syndicate was Leo Merson, formerly of Long Island University and widely experienced in professional athletics.[38]

Saperstein was not very sanguine regarding Stern's pursuit, reiterating a key point that he had, apparently, made by phone, regarding the lack of a good venue other than Madison Square Garden. He felt that a Brooklyn project might have a chance, but he called it at best a long chance. He did go on to suggest that if the syndicate had the money and the desire, they might be interested in pursuing a franchise for some other part of the country. Saperstein got no reply and wired Stern on April 20, asking if he or a representative planned to attend the April 21 meeting in Chicago, but there is no record of further efforts on Stern's part.[39]

Inquiries continued to come to Saperstein regarding the new league. Melvin Davis of Wichita wrote in early April, seeking a possible entry. This was tied to the fact that the Vickers Oilers of Wichita announced their withdrawal from the NIBL the day before Davis sent his letter. He made a case for his city, based on the venue; the attendance at past Vickers games; the possibility of their Vickers coach, Alex Hannum, being available; the quality of the players available in the area; and the general support for basketball in the area. Saperstein sent two follow-up wires to Davis, which went unanswered, after which one of Saperstein's colleagues called Davis, only to find him on vacation in Florida. The determination was that this was just something that he wanted to "play" with. Harry, one of Saperstein's colleagues, felt the inquiry was "a dud."[40]

Davis returned from Florida and sent a letter to Saperstein in early May. He decried Kansas City as a pro basketball town and extolled Wichita, though Davis had done some further investigation and noted, "My enthusiasm for this endeavor has cooled some." He did say he'd be interested still if a workable plan might be outlined. Saperstein replied with his standard "Thanks for your ideas. We'll stick with our current plan and will get back to you if anything of interest to you might arise."[41]

Seymour Smith, a sportswriter for the *Baltimore Morning Sun* and a friend of Saperstein's, sent a telegram on April 21 asking if Baltimore had a spot in future ABL plans. He also inquired if the player pool for the ABL would include Eastern League stars Spivey, King, Lear, and so forth. and asked to be on Saperstein's mailing list. Saperstein got back to him the next day, saying first that no one had expressed serious interest in Baltimore as a league member and, second, there didn't seem to be any pursuit of Eastern League stars at present, but he thought it very possible.[42]

A San Diego group wrote at the same time expressing interest in an ABL franchise and seeking information from Saperstein. He replied with encouragement, but seeking more information on a possible venue and some financial data from the group. The reply from San Diego came almost three weeks later noting that the group was hopeful of playing in a new, state-constructed pavilion due to open in February of 1961. By the time the letter arrived, Saperstein was on the road again, and Marie Linehan sent an acknowledgment, saying that the letter would be held for Saperstein's return with a copy sent to him in London on tour with the Globetrotters. Saperstein replied from London that the plan was for an eight-team league with three on the West Coast. Los Angeles, San Francisco and Portland were the designated and interested sites. If any were to be found wanting, he would get back to the people in San Diego.[43]

Saperstein updated Glickman in May regarding the league, saying that he would release a statement to the press that week noting that the league would not begin until 1961-1962. As Glickman had assumed, too many venues were already tied up for 1960-1961 to make such a start for the league feasible. League entries for 1961-1962 were now to be Cleveland, Pittsburgh, Washington, Chicago, Los Angeles, San Francisco,

One. The ABL — the "Run Up"

Portland and either Salt Lake City or Vancouver. Kansas City had been dropped from the plan. Glickman was pleased by the new turn of events and welcomed Saperstein's visit to Portland (and other league cities) soon.[44]

Saperstein's press release appeared in various papers May 11–14, and Glickman wrote a letter of excited response on May 17 in which he said that the announcement was "met with tremendous enthusiasm among the press and public ... [and] we made banner headlines on the front page of the *Oregon Journal*." Glickman went on to encourage immediate planning for the 1961-1962 schedule in order to get the most desirable

Abe Saperstein pictured on a 1948 tour with the Harlem Globetrotters. Left to right, front row: Ducky Moore, Ermer Robinson, Sam Wheeler, Boid Buie; back row: Abe Saperstein, Babe Pressley, John Netherly, Ted Strong, W.S. Welch (traveling secretary). Ermer Robinson was the business manager of the Chicago Majors from 1961 to 1962 and the coach of the Oakland Oaks from 1962 to 1963 (author collection).

dates in the chosen venues. A brief note from Saperstein to Glickman and Harry Lynn, president of the Uline Arena in Washington and prospective owner of the D.C. franchise, emphasized that Saperstein would stay close to the league formation wherever he was and he would maintain regular contact with them regarding maintenance of publicity and local interest.[45]

Over the next year, Saperstein would have to shore up the franchises; collect the $10,000 in earnest money from each party; devise a schedule; initiate a college draft as well as sign other players, most notably from the National Industrial Basketball League which collapsed after the 1961 season; and secure referees. He visited each franchise location over the next few months and two franchise changes were made. Portland dropped out.

Kansas City reappeared on the radar with Ken Krueger as its financial and administrative leader. Also reappearing was Honolulu, backed by Art Kim. Kim, a Hawaiian of Korean descent, had had something to do with the Washington Generals, according to Terry Pluto.[46] Thus, he was seen as knowledgeable about basketball operations. He would have been well known to Saperstein since the Generals were one of the regular Globetrotter opponents starting from about 1953. Pluto's speculative assertion was incorrect. The Hawaii Chiefs' 1961-1962 official program says that Kim was league director and head official of the Honolulu Senior League during World War II. He then coached in high school as well as an all-star team that played the Harlem Globetrotters, and "this started his association with the fabulous Abe Saperstein."[47]

Two

The Formation of a New League, Rules, Constitution, Referees and More

Once the ABL had its eight teams, Saperstein started in at his usual enterprises, that is, doing three things (or more) at once. He needed to devise rules, organize a draft and free agent signings, and get a league schedule at the same time that he was both running the Globetrotters and getting his own franchise (initially San Francisco, later Chicago) up and running. He elicited input from his many friends across the country — sportswriters, entrepreneurs, sports administrators and observers. Don Murphy, a Chicago acquaintance, sent suggestions regarding franchise operations. Most pertained to stadium seating, playing dates, franchise sponsorship by locals and travel. Some were simply too offbeat to be seriously examined, such as playing most of the ABL games in the afternoon in order to attract businessmen and fill local daytime television schedules. One, however, must have struck a chord with Saperstein, the aspect of reducing travel costs. Murphy suggested playing two games in a row in the same town, which would also enhance publicity focus, which worked well in baseball. This resonated with Saperstein, especially with the "problem" of Hawaii being such a far distance to travel for just a game.[1] Ultimately, what was adopted was a system similar to what the old National Basketball League had adopted in 1948-1949 when Denver entered the league and the next closest city was Waterloo, Iowa. In the NBL that year teams would travel to Denver for two or three games, while Denver had a seven- or eight-game home stand. The downside for them was that the Denver team then had eight games or longer road trips.²

A major difference in 1961 was that teams were now flying to many more contests, rather than taking trains as most had done in the 1940s and early 1950s. Obviously, the improved air travel made a team in Hawaii much more feasible than it had ever been before.

Saperstein was also trying to contend with sniping at the new league from various quarters, and he sometimes responded in a less-than-polite manner. He complained to his friend, Seymour Smith, about knocking his new league, but Smith, hurt rather than chastened, responded to Saperstein with a note of clarification. In it he said that it was not he (Smith) that was questioning the character and quality of the new league, but rather someone (not named) in Baltimore who saw accusations of the new ABL raiding the Baltimore Bullets' roster as good publicity for the Bullets, who were "in desperate need of publicity."

Smith went on to say that they (at the *Baltimore Morning Sun*) had actually been giving the league very favorable publicity and that Buddy Jeannette (the current Bullets coach) was interested in coaching in the ABL. Smith also mentioned players whom he thought would be interested in getting a chance to play in the ABL. These included Guy Sparrow, Herschell Turner, and three others—McCann, Scott and Turmon—as well as Kelly Coleman, whom the new Chicago NBA team had contacted.³

Saperstein followed up with a request for addresses/phone numbers for both Sparrow and Turner, and Smith complied. Saperstein went off to Europe again and wrote to Smith in June from Budapest, but was mesmerized by his visit to Auschwitz and mentioned little about basketball.⁴

Earlier in the spring, the ABL draft had been held and yielded these top players for the various teams. Walt Bellamy was the number-one choice by Cleveland, and he was traded to the Chicago Majors for Hank Whitney, the Majors' territorial pick out of Iowa State. Bellamy, however, was also the top pick of the NBA draft, taken by the new Chicago expansion franchise, and he chose to sign with the NBA's Chicago Packers. The top pick for the Majors (at #3) whom they were able to sign and who made their team was John Wessels from Illinois. Cleveland signed their top pick, Larry Siegfried from 1960 NCAA champion Ohio State. Pittsburgh drafted and signed Tony Jackson, whom they traded to the D.C. Tapers and who later was traded to the Chicago Majors. Jackson had been implicated in the college basketball scandals of that time, accused of not reporting a bribe to "shave points" on his St. John's team. He had been "blacklisted" by the NBA. Washington had selected Doug Moe, also named in these same scandals, but he chose not to sign with the ABL. The Tapers also selected and signed Roger Kaiser from Georgia Tech, a good shooter, considered too short and slow for the NBA, although he had gone to training camp with Chicago. Kansas City drafted and signed Bill Bridges from Kansas University, while neither Los Angeles nor Hawaii signed a top college pick. The L.A. Jets had selected Rafer Johnson, the Olympic decathlon champion in 1960, but that was more a public relations stunt than a serious pursuit.[5]

Most of the ABL rosters would be filled out by former NIBL players, former Eastern League players and former NBA players who had been cut or, in a few instances, were signed to competitive contracts by the ABL. These latter signings almost always ended up in court, and some were accompanied by injunctions that prevented the former NBA player from playing in the ABL until settlements had been reached by the courts. Former NBA players who were signed after not getting an NBA contract for 1961-1962 included Gene Tormohlen and Larry Staverman of the Kansas City Steers, Archie Dees of Cleveland, Connie Dierking of Washington, and Hal Lear and George Yardley of Los Angeles. Yardley had actually retired a year earlier, but would play for L.A. only on home stands, so he could continue his "day job" as a mechanical engineer. Other former NBA players signed by the ABL included Nathaniel "Sweetwater" Clifton for Chicago as well as Mike Farmer and Kenny Sears of the San Francisco Saints, both of whom were still being pursued by their former NBA teams. Dick Barnett was also the object of the Cleveland Pipers and the Syracuse Nationals. Besides Jackson, the other top players signed by the ABL and blacklisted by the NBA were Connie Hawkins and Bill Spivey. Spivey, an All-American player at Kentucky, had been implicated in, but never convicted of, "point shaving" in the early 1950s and had played pro ball in the Eastern League for ten years. Hawkins was just 19 and had never played for the University of Iowa, but he was tainted by not reporting a bribe when he was a freshman at Iowa (and not eligible for the varsity).

Saperstein, meanwhile, was working on a league constitution, which was presented to the league owners in the spring of 1961, amended in the summer, and approved as amended in July of 1961. The document is 26 pages long. Most of it is standard constitutional fare, but there were instances that needed to be explicated because of the unusual situation facing the start-up of the league. Saperstein was elected commissioner and Alan Bloch (league attorney) was elected both deputy commissioner and secretary treasurer. These would only be allowed for two years since both had stock in the Chicago Majors. The constitution prohibited the commissioner and deputy commissioner from having a proprietary interest in any league team, but Saperstein and Bloch were exempted for the first two years of the league, after which the Board of Directors could vote to make them choose one or the other.[6] A number of the constitutional sections reflected discussions that Saperstein had with colleagues in the prior two years, especially Harry Glickman. Gate receipts from the games were to be split 20 percent to the visiting team and 5 percent to the league with the remainder to the home team. The Pittsburgh situation was such that the 5 percent requirement was eliminated before the season started, and this did not bode well for the league.[7] It was raised by the Pittsburgh management, and Saperstein supported the waiver in a note sent in July from Bruges, Belgium, by Allan Bloch.[8]

At a meeting in Chicago on August 3, 1961, the American Basketball League was officially organized with eight teams and eight designated directors, one from each club.[9] By this time, there had been a switch in ownership for the Chicago and San Francisco franchises. Originally, Saperstein had taken the San Francisco franchise, but he then traded his franchise to George McKeon for the Chicago franchise. There is no explanation in the Saperstein papers, but in 1970 the action was explained in a tax case that Saperstein (and subsequently his heirs) had brought. (Saperstein died in 1966 at age 65.) In the case, Saperstein's heirs petitioned to have his loans to the ABL during the 1961-1962 life of the league declared business debts (and they subsequently were), rather than non-business debts. The court summarized how Saperstein became the Chicago owner.

> The ABL had its share of organizational problems in the winter of 1960. Morrie Shneer, executive vice-president of Son-Mark Industries, Inc. (hereinafter Son-Mark), which had agreed to take over the Chicago franchise, notified Abe Saperstein in mid–December 1960 that Son-Mark would not be able to operate the Chicago franchise due to unforeseen factors, including inability to secure an adequate playing site. Since the original plan for the 1961-62 season entailed eight ABL teams, it was considered important to

Two. The Formation of a New League

locate someone to take over the franchise which Morrie Shneer and Son-Mark had declined.

Although petitioner had been interested in obtaining the ABL San Francisco franchise, his attorneys suggested that it would be in the better interests of the ABL to leave the San Francisco franchise in the hands of local representation. Since Morrie Shneer and Son-Mark had already declined the Chicago franchise as of December, 1960, petitioner was advised by his attorney in January 1961 to "move into the Chicago picture" where there would be opposition from a newly established NBA team.[10]

All teams were required to deposit $20,000 with the league, and for each subsequent year the amount was to be $25,000, these amounts being for league expenses. In addition, the Honolulu club was required to pay each visiting club $1,729 for each trip to Hawaii to "compensate for a portion of the additional transportation charges incurred."[11]

Article XXVI, "Offers to Students," stated that clubs may make offers to students only after a student had attained his senior year (in college) and after the end of the regular season. This mirrored the NBA rule, but there would arise a need for an exception with Connie Hawkins, who had been expelled from Iowa and whom no colleges would recruit after the 1960-1961 season.

Article XXXI prohibited any ABL club stockholder, officer, director or employee from having any stock or financial interest in any other club, directly or indirectly. That rule would come up in the future of the league.

One of the most vital pursuits was finding referees for the new league. On June 24, 1961, Saperstein contacted Phil Fox about being referee-in-chief. Two days later, Fox wrote to Saperstein outlining his desired salary as well as his intended officiating procedures for the ABL. Fox asked for $6,000 per year, plus traveling expenses. He also described his plan to "sectionalize" officials and keep costs to a minimum. Depending on experience he intended to offer $40 to $60 per game plus 10 cents a mile. He was confident of attaining capable referees at these salaries.[12]

Before Fox was announced as referee-in-chief, there were discussions in the ABL office regarding various aspects of officiating. Notes were taken, although they are unsigned and dated August 2, 1961, and were probably part of discussions with the coaches held in Chicago over three days. There is a note that the notes should be sent to Phil Fox. In these notes a number of details as to rules and equipment were decided. A Spalding ball with narrow seams would be used, as the coaches had selected. Only Jack McMahon (Steers) dissented. Referees and rules, as well as conduct were discussed. McMahon noted that the league lacked stars and had to keep players in line from the start. Phil Brownstein of the league office noted that coaches can make or break officials. John McLendon of the Pipers said to remember that fans come to see players, not coaches, something the NBA doesn't seem to believe. Phil Woolpert of the Saints agreed and said that the ABL should keep their game different from the NBA and not ape their rules. Regarding the three-point shot, Woolpert presented his view of the court and how to measure the distance, suggesting 25 feet from the board and 23'9" from the center of the hoop.

The group adopted, at McLendon's suggestion, the college rule of one foot in between the offensive and defensive players on the free throw line. They vetoed the suggestion of three 15-minute periods and agreed to discuss it at another time. The coaches adopted the 30-second clock unanimously. They tabled the use of hands on defense, but agreed that scoring should be at more of a premium. Four 12-minute periods were agreed upon as was the five team foul limit per quarter before a bonus free throw would be awarded. They also agreed that an offensive foul would be a personal foul, not a team foul, as had been in the rules in some jurisdictions.

The meeting ended at 6:15 and continued the next morning (August 3) at 10:30. Technical fouls were discussed regarding their definition and use as a team foul or not. Only players in the game would be allowed to shoot the technical foul, which would always be one shot. Double fouls were clarified as well as number of times out. The group was undecided as to the use of the zone defense and decided to refer the decision to Saperstein, who called in the next day with a "no" vote. One question deadlocked the coaches at 3–3, and Phil Fox was to poll the two coaches (Neil Johnston of Pittsburgh and Elmer Ripley of Washington)[13] not in attendance as to their thoughts. Finally, there was agreement that no coach would criticize any referee in the press.[14]

Who was Phil Fox? According to his own summary, sent to Saperstein, Fox had been a referee in professional basketball for over 20 years, beginning in the original American Basketball League, which existed from 1925 to 1931, then the reorganized American Basketball League from 1937 to 1946. He was an official in the National Basketball League from 1946 to 1948 and in the Basketball Association of America from 1948 to 1949, when the new NBA was formed, and he officiated in the

Two. The Formation of a New League

NBA from 1949 to 1955. He also refereed at many Globetrotter–College All Star games, so Saperstein was very familiar with Fox.[15]

Fox was hired and began his duties, almost immediately finding referees and assigning them to games that were being scheduled by Saperstein for the league. Fox was praised by Saperstein for being "high on the rules innovations we contemplate for bringing the game back to the fans and restoring a semblance of defense."[16] These included the three-point shot, the trapezoidal lane and the 30-second possession clock.

Fox submitted a working budget in August with estimated total officiating costs for November — 48 assignments from Washington to Pittsburgh to Cleveland to Chicago to Kansas City, a total of $8,000 — which he broke out into fees and per diem for hotel, food, and in-city transportation. All that was missing were the actual transportation costs. He also included a list of "A" and "B" referees, the former being the most experienced and the latter young men who "had a basic schooling in both college and semi-professional ball." He made an estimate for West Coast refereeing costs and expressed concern over the Hawaii situation, but he expected to hear from Art Kim regarding recommendations for five local referees.[17]

Abe Saperstein (left) and Art Kim, the owner of the Hawaii Chiefs, as shown here in a Hawaii Chiefs program (courtesy Dolph Briscoe Collection, University of Texas Archives).

In October, Fox sent his referees an assignment schedule for November, ABL rule books, officials' cards for game reports and a description of game uniforms (black or blue trousers, black shoes, black shirts with gold stripes and a pocket-sized ABL emblem).[18]

Fox soon followed up with a second memo to referees, which contained the December schedule and some admonitions/tips such as "enforce technical fouls and close supervision of coaches and players," and to "call home team officials at least two hours before game, stating that you are referee for a game." This was followed by "*PLEASE* [sic] do not reveal your name." Apparently, there was a need for secrecy because of gamblers and betting lines, one must assume. The memo also stated that transportation was to be reimbursed at $.15 rather than $.10 per mile, as initially proposed. Fox had established his office in New York City, but expense requests were to be sent to the league office in Chicago.[19]

Fox's memo #3 was on "Disciplinary Code" and has a handwritten date of December 20, 1961. The memo specifies the amount of fines for technicals and ejections ($50 for first ejection, $100 for second and $500 for third) as well as flagrant fouls ($25 for first offense, $100 for second, $250 for third). Flagrant fouls are defined, game protest rules are explicated and all fines are designated as contributions to the Commissioner's Office for worthy national charities.[20]

The rules sent to all officials had a two-page "highlight" of adopted rule changes, including the "Olympic key" changed from 12 to 18 feet, the three-point shot and where lines should be on the court. There also was a suggested signal for recognizing the making of such a shot. These included a red flashing light or a gun with blanks, with the exact method to be left to the discretion of the home team. There would be a 30-second clock, four 12-minute quarters and the use of the college rule on defining goal tending. There were also some differences on fouls and free throws.[21] Much of this came from the coaches' meetings described above.

There would be fine-tuning left, but by September 1, the American Basketball League had eight teams with full rosters, eight venues, a corps of referees led by Phil Fox and a schedule for November and December contests. A television contract had not been successfully executed and publicity was uneven. The big question was, would the fans turn out in these cities to see pro basketball? No amount of speculation would be sufficient; November would tell the tale.

Three

ABL Financing — Expectations, Hopes, Realities

Where does a new league start? As noted earlier, Saperstein began soliciting in 1959 and by 1960 had agreements for a new league. The intended franchisees agreed that a better start time would be 1961-1962, so that gave the league a chance to develop a working constitution and a plan for hiring players and referees, as well as securing venues. The league would also get fees from each franchise to maintain an office and staff.

After a series of meetings, the league set a fee of $20,000 as the amount to be a league member. The constitution maintained that this would rise to $25,000 the next year and remain at that level in subsequent years. These monies would also be the security deposits for the teams.[1] As it turned out, the actual entry fee was closer to $10,000 for year 1 of the league.

These monies would start up a league office, although the staff was already on board and working. Saperstein merely increased the workload of Marie Linehan and the Harlem Globetrotters staff to include the new ABL. At some point, new personnel would be hired, but only as many as were truly warranted since the league was anticipating losing money for at least the first year.

Teams would hire a staff and players. The league would hire referees. Phil Fox, a former referee in various leagues going back to the American Basketball League of the early 1930s, would be the supervisor of officials. He requested a salary of $6,000, plus traveling expenses[2]. Fox dictated a league uniform for referees, some of which would be the referee's responsibility and some the league/various teams'. "Our uniforms will be the black or blue trouser, black shoe and referee's shirts will be obtained at the club's home games and returned after game (jersey will be black and gold stripes with pocket sized ABL emblem)."[3]

Referee expenses would be paid at the rate of $15 per diem (but only when an overnight stay was necessary), and this would include hotel, food and other incidental expenses. They would also receive $.15 per mile, which would include full transportation, round trip, including gas, oil, food, and so on. If air travel was necessary, referees were to book passage via tourist class.[4]

The total officiating costs anticipated were $8,000, with fees totaling $4,800 and travel/per diems at $3,200.[5] This may have ended up as a lesser expense after Los Angeles left the league in mid-season, but there is no evidence to indicate that slight decrease.

Also in this memo was a schedule of fines, which would be rare, under the strictures provided. Two technical fouls in a game for a player or coach brought a fine of $50. A second instance led to a fine of $100 and a third, $500. No more were specified, the obvious assumption being that no one would be stupid enough to do this more than three times. Flagrant fouls were also detailed as to fining structure, with $25 for a first, $100 for a second and $250 for a third. The player would also be disqualified from the game upon such a foul. The money was to go to worthy national charities rather than expenses in the league office.[6]

Net gate receipts would be distributed with the following formula, 20 to the visiting team, 5 percent to the league and the remainder to the home team. The NBA's formula at that time did not provide for any money to the visiting team, making visits by the top teams vital to the weaker franchises in the NBA like Detroit and Cincinnati and the new Chicago franchise.[7] The ABL planned a lot of doubleheaders, and the three visiting teams would get 11 percent of the net and the league 5 percent, in such instances. In addition, all radio, television and newspaper revenue would have 5 percent go to the league and the remainder to the eight clubs in equal shares.[8]

Because of the unusual circumstances of having a Hawaiian franchise, a special article was placed in the constitution addressing these extra expenses. Teams would visit Hawaii and stay about a week, playing at least three games there to make the visit cost effective. The Honolulu franchise would pay each visiting club $1,729 at the end of the club's trip to Hawaii. Each visiting club would play a non–Honolulu game with no

38

Three. ABL Financing — Expectations, Hopes, Realities

shared receipts, although the Honolulu club would "defray all traveling expenses of the visiting club to and from such games."[9] The Honolulu franchise would get no similar aid from the other clubs when they (Honolulu) visited the mainland.

There were no salary caps for players, but there were guidelines, apparently discussed, but not included in written documents. The range seemed to be from $4,500 to $15,000 per year, which was actually six months, paid at the end of each month, beginning in November. There were exceptions. The pattern and exceptions will be more fully described. What was clearly prescribed was roster size. From the beginning of pre-season training camp, 12 could be rostered. After the first month, no more than 10, nor less than 8, could be on a team roster, with no more than 15 in reserve (and likely not paid). The smaller rosters would, of course, keep payments for salaries lower.[10]

As indicated, there were no limits on salaries, but the range was $4,500 to $15,000. Roger Kaiser was at the top of that pay scale, and he noted that one other teammate was far beyond it.

> The Chicago team (the Packers) drafted me (in the fourth round,) but the ABL offered more money. I was getting between $11 and $12 thousand, which I think was third on the team. Gene Conley got $20 thousand, I think. He was a veteran player as well as a pitcher for the Red Sox.[11]

Another exception was Kenny Sears, who had signed after playing for the New York Knicks for six years and averaging between 13 and 21 points per game during that time. Sears had played college ball at Santa Clara and was from Watsonville in Northern California, so the ABL's San Francisco Saints hoped to sign him and attract a fan base interested in local heroes.

> I was unhappy in New York. I thought that I was one of the best shooters and maybe the best player on the team (Willie Naulls and Richie Guerin were the other top players on a Knick squad that had only won 21 games in 1960-1961) and I wasn't playing as much as I thought I should have. Then they wanted to cut my pay. I was young and we didn't have agents in those days. So, I go to the Knicks offices at Madison Square Garden and go upstairs and talk to one of the executives about my contract and he says that they want to offer me 25 percent LESS than the previous year. I had been in contact with the Saints and they said that I didn't have to sign another contract with the Knicks because of the Sherman Anti-Trust Act, which I knew nothing about. So, the executive asks me to sign right then and I said that I

wanted to think about it. I already knew that I was not going to sign it. He got really upset with me, but I left. When I signed with San Francisco, their lawyer said that I didn't have to worry; they would take care of any efforts that the Knicks might make to pursue me in court. They sued me for a million dollars! I had to go up to San Francisco once for a deposition, but that was it. The suit was finally dropped by the Knicks. I didn't pay anything, although I ended up having to return to them in 1962 when I went back to the NBA.[12]

Even in 2011 Sears was reluctant to reveal his salary, but he was surprised that Conley was getting so much. He indicated that it was in the neighborhood of Kaiser's and that he (Sears) was able to buy a house and a car. He also revealed a very unusual payment method. "I was paid up front for two years. The money was escrowed and I drew on that. When the league folded I gave the remainder back. I don't know that I had to, but I did."[13]

Another player who was highly paid was Hal Lear who had come out of Temple with much acclaim in 1956, but played only briefly with the hometown Warriors before heading for the Eastern League, which was a weekend league, as well as a job with the city of Philadelphia. Lear felt that the quota of blacks had prevented Philadelphia from keeping him as the second African American on the team (in addition to Jackie Moore). Lear was seen as an accomplished player by new coach Bill Sharman, who would be a great asset in Los Angeles and was signed for $20,000.[14]

Herb Lee was signed by Saperstein to his Chicago Majors team for $4,500, but was traded to Hawaii for George Price on November 28, 1961. Price was getting $6,500 from the Chiefs. The trade differences were broken out into monthly salaries and rounded off to the end of the month, and the subsequent switch of salaries was made on that basis. Lee ended up being Hawaii's third leading scorer and didn't miss a game. Clearly, Hawaii got the better of this deal. Later, Price's contract negotiations for the next season provide a window on this process.

About a dozen contracts are included in the Saperstein papers, and these may be utilized to see how certain owners paid their players, although conclusions have to be taken *cum grano salis*. Five players on the Kansas City Steers received salaries of $6,000 to $10,000. The lowest amount went to a player who failed to make the roster, so it is likely that he received no more than one month of salary. Of the two players at

Three. ABL Financing — Expectations, Hopes, Realities

$7,000, one failed to make the roster and the other (Bryce Vann) was a regular, but not a starter, and averaged seven points per game. Larry Staverman received $9,000 and also made the first all-league team after averaging 17.5 points per game. Win Wilfong was paid $10,000, was a starter in most games and averaged seven points per game and was second on the team in assists per game. It is likely that no one received more than this on the Steers. Their top scorer and rebounder, Bill Bridges, was a rookie from the University of Kansas and was African American. He likely received no more than $8,000 in salary.

The contracts of three Cleveland Pipers were included. These ran from $6,000 to $11,000. The former two players did not make the roster, but Johnny Cox, an all-American player from Kentucky in 1958-1959 and an NIBL star for the Pipers in the prior two years, received the higher salary. He ended up having the highest scoring average on the team, 18.5 points per game for more than 50 games. Dick Barnett, who played in 50 games and was the subject of an ABL-NBA signing battle, averaged 26 points per game and likely received at least as much as Cox, probably $20,000, which turned out to be well spent. Barnett had averaged about 14 points per game in his two years in Syracuse with the Nationals. John Barnhill, who had played with the Pipers in the NIBL in 1960-1961 after a year of military service following graduation from Tennessee A&I, was paid $6,500 to $7,000.[15]

John Wessels of the Chicago Majors received $6,000 as a salary and played the entire season, averaging 9.9 points per game. Charles Raslow signed for $4,500, but failed to get out of training camp. Herschell Turner, whose contract is not included, is mentioned in a memo the next season as refusing to sign his contract for the same salary as he had received in 1961-1962, when he averaged 16 points per game. Added was a comment: "Here again ... bread cast on the waters, by the other owners in the way of disproportionate salary figures which hit astronomical highs ... is coming back to haunt."[16] For some comparison, the median family income in 1962 was around $6,000, so most of the ABL players were largely at that level or above slightly.[17] Some, like Sears, Conley and Barnett, as noted, and other key selections, were doing as well or better than NBA counterparts. To provide some contemporary context, the median family income for 2009 was $50,000 and the average NBA player received more than $3.4 million.

Leonard Koppett notes that the top stars in the NBA were making as much as $50,000, but even the best all-around player, Oscar Robertson, was only making $33,000 per year as part of a three-year $100,000 contract signed before he began his pro career.[18] Thus, $20,000 was an excellent wage for some lesser lights of the NBA, where the minimum salary was around $5,000.

In a later note it was mentioned that the teams in the ABL hoped to average about $4,000 per game in gate receipts. The Chicago Majors were promoting package deals, as all the ABL teams surely were. The Majors offered 18 home games in box seats for $60, $3.33 per game, as opposed to the $4 individual price. For mezzanine reserved, the price was $45 for 18 games, an average of $2.50 a game versus the individual price of $3. Balcony seats were unreserved and sold for $1.25 to $2.00 each.[19] To get a net of $4,000, the Majors needed around 2,500 fans a game. They didn't come close, nor did any other team.

It would be most instructive to examine the details of assets and liabilities to see how ABL clubs managed their finances. Such details are offered in an audit of the Pittsburgh Rens conducted by Jerome Davis, CPA, and presented to the Board of Directors of the Pittsburgh Sports Corporation in May of 1962. The auditors found nothing untoward in the operation of the Rens, only that they lost a lot of money. In fact, the Rens and the Steers most likely came the closest to breaking even in 1961-1962, although that wasn't saying a whole lot.[20] The Rens lost $94,532. Their income was $140,985, with $126,400 coming from gate receipts, or about $3,200 per game. They got $14,350 from advertising receipts, probably the bulk of that coming from program advertising. Miscellaneous income was less than $250. Thus, the team had two sources of income, both related to having people at the stadium. (It should be noted that the Rens were on local television at least a dozen times, but there seems to have been no revenue generated for the team, itself, from this enterprise.)

Expenses were more varied. Player salaries were $80,000 for eight regular rostered players with at least 65 games. Two players played 41 and 21 games and six others played 1 to 15 games. Average salary was probably around $7,000, as hypothesized earlier. This also is reinforced by the statements of Connie Hawkins, who said that he received $6,500 salary on the Rens.[21] Rentals were $49,000, and that would have been

Three. ABL Financing — Expectations, Hopes, Realities

largely for the stadium.[22] Travel was $44,000. League expenses were $12,000, office salaries were $10,000 and advertising $7,700. Total expenses were just under $236,000. There was little to cut in the expense department, since it can be assumed that the teams were already getting by as cheaply as possible. The key was obviously increasing revenues.[23]

A more limited, but still useful report was an audit of the Cleveland Pipers done in June of 1962, possibly as a prelude to Steinbrenner either selling the team or getting additional investors. Issued in August 1962, the audit, done by the auditing firm of Ernst & Ernst, notes assets of $3,789, mostly in furniture and insurance deposits. Liabilities are $254,672, comprised of expenses, taxes, accounts payable and notes payable to stockholders on demand.[24]

George Steinbrenner sent a letter to all stockholders regarding the audit and attached expenditures for July and August of 1962, at a time when he expected to be entering the NBA. Only two players' salaries or expenses were listed as expenditures for that period. One was Connie Dierking (misspelled as "Connie Durking") with a July salary of $1,235, indicating that he had a contract that extended beyond the basketball season, which almost none of the other players had. (It also meant that Dierking might have been paid just under $15,000 for the year.) The other was Jerry Lucas, whose representative received $2,500, as well as expenses paid directly to Lucas of $514.31. Total expenses for those two months were just over $35,000 with the largest payment to the IRS of $14,364.[25]

In a report to the league owners, not prepared by Saperstein, but very likely prepared by George Steinbrenner, it is stated that the teams averaged $1,500 in gate receipts per game and that every owner was in the red "to the tune of at least $100,000 and most are closer to $150,000."[26] With that in mind, they had Arthur Anderson & Associates do a survey to help improve planning and implementation for 1962-1963. The memo also mentions that they (Anderson) did a similar survey for the NIBL the year before (probably for the 1960-1961 season, since it was the NIBL's last) and Cleveland was part of that, so this makes Steinbrenner's involvement more likely.

The Anderson recommendations focused first on scheduling, which included league organization. The report said that two, four or preferably five team divisions with only 50 games would be a better organization.

Games would only be from December to March, teams would play only in their division and there would be no games on Mondays or Tuesdays. Buses could be chartered that carried both teams. Salaries could be cut by two-thirds because the number of games would be cut by that amount.

Officials needed to be better, and the league would have to pay top dollar to engage them. They need to be assigned from the league office, not gotten by each individual club. The Globetrotters should be billed in each city at least three and possibly four of their home dates. The league needs to get some superstars and pay them to stay in the league. This was seen as one of the two key factors in success. The other was television, and there needed to be a national television package. "This must be the prime objective of Abe during the summer," and the report recommends ABC as the network where the chances were best.

Eight, no more than ten, players to a team should be the goal. An executive assistant to the commissioner was necessary, one who could act in Abe's absence. Uniform game times must be in place, and a much better P.R. effort was necessary. The report closed by saying that they had to act that spring, not in September, and they should be prepared to move on this platform at their spring meeting. Thus, the date for this report was probably late February or March 1962.[27]

This report was probably the precursor to a formal report presented by Steinbrenner at the Annual Meeting in Chicago, March 24–25. This was entitled "Proposed Standard Operating Procedure for the American Basketball League 1962-1963 Season." First was a request for a full-time commissioner to "relieve Abe of this burden." Second was the recommendation for league-assigned officials, but allowing league members to "blackball" any official on the list. There would be eight officials, four substitutes and they would be employed full time by the league.

The two divisions were recommended, and it is interesting to see what cities were intended at that time. The East remained the same as 1961-1962, but the West was to be Dallas replacing Los Angeles, and Hawaii would continue, as would San Francisco. Fifty-six games were proposed for each team, and ten men would be on a roster with only nine dressing per game. All travel would be handled by a travel agency for the league.

An increased bond ($50,000) would be required from each team.

Three. ABL Financing — Expectations, Hopes, Realities

Visiting teams gate receipts would be reduced from 20 percent to 10 percent or $750, whichever was greater. Television was seen as a must. Greater exposure in national magazines and news media was needed, but T.V. was a must. "Name" ballplayers needed to be obtained through the draft and/or independent signings.[28]

Television Efforts

It was obvious that the league needed exposure. What were their efforts? Saperstein had good relations with television executives because the Globetrotters were a great draw in person and almost as good on television. Thus, his inquiries would be responded to at the highest levels, rather than by some lower-level plebian. In early May, Saperstein had Marie Linehan try to set up a meeting with Bill McPhail at CBS Sports, but the week that Saperstein requested for the meeting was Derby week. McPhail had representatives from across the network and the nation in for meetings on Thursday and Friday; then he would leave for the Kentucky Derby on Saturday.[29] No meeting was possible, and Saperstein continued on to London, where he cabled McPhail indicating his interest in some sort of network package for the new ABL.[30] Having no reply, Saperstein cabled McPhail once again, a week later, this time from Scotland, in reference to a possible television package for the new league. A letter from Jack Dolph reached Saperstein's office and expressed regrets from CBS. Marie Linehan, on May 17, cabled Saperstein in Scotland with Dolph/McPhail's regrets regarding possible ABL telecasting.[31] Saperstein followed up to McPhail with a letter of thanks for the consideration on May 18.

Saperstein, busy with the Globetrotter European tour that summer, hired Lester Malitz as an agent to try to get the ABL a television package. In August, Malitz contacted ABC and its vice president for sports programs, Chet Simmons, seeking to get the ABL All-Star game included as part of the *Wide World of Sports* series that had been announced as commencing in January 1962. Malitz's letter provided the date and location of the game and the possible stars who would appear. Since the league hadn't begun as of yet, he pushed five top former NBA players— Bill Sharman, Nat "Sweetwater" Clifton, Dick Barnett, Mike Farmer and Kenny Sears— as well as Bill Spivey and Larry Siegfried (whom he calls Siegrief), recently graduated from Ohio State, as being in the game and promised that "new stars will arise as League play commences." Malitz also noted the ABL's rule innovations and looked forward to discussing a slot with Simmons.[32]

The NBA, meanwhile, had a television contract (with NBC) as early as 1955, albeit one that was not providing a lot of income, nor as much exposure as the NBA or the network would have liked. Ben Rader describes the way that television has transformed sports in his 1984 volume, *In Its Own Image*.[33] There he discusses the earliest television packages for each of the major sports and how it altered the structure and vitality of the professional leagues (as well as college sports). Basketball came to major network exposure later and was initially much less successful than either baseball or football. Surprisingly, Rader begins his analysis of NBA basketball and network television with the NBA's 1965 pact with ABC, but the NBA had the earlier agreement with NBC, one that had low ratings and was not retained after 1963.

In the 1961-1962 season, NBC broadcast games on Saturday afternoon at 2:30 or 3:00 Eastern time, beginning on October 28 and ending March 10, with a total of 17 games. Every team appeared at least twice and three teams were shown five times. There is no discernable pattern, but there seems to have been an effort to expose the entire league. This may have been a mistake, with bottom-dwelling teams appearing too often. Combining that with the competition from college football and, later in the season, regionally produced college basketball, the NBC NBA telecasts were hardly moneymakers and may have been money losers. The networks were just beginning their efforts to fill weekend afternoons with sporting events and there was a lot of experimentation. The NBA package was not picked up by many of the NBC affiliates, as was their right, choosing instead to show either local programming or some other purchased package. Atlanta's NBC station showed movies in the time slot in the fall and, in the winter/spring showed bowling and wrestling. Most other southern stations were similar in this respect. The Los Angeles station carried the games live at 11:30 a.m., competing against children's television and college football. Pittsburgh carried the NBA games, and occasionally channel 11 (semi-affiliated with CBS) carried a Rens game. So both the Rens and the San Francisco Saints had small television packages. This was the sad state of professional basketball on television at the time.

Three. ABL Financing — Expectations, Hopes, Realities

An accurate snapshot of the success of NBA basketball on television at the time is provided by the Nielsen ratings quoted in a letter from Lester Malitz on December 21, 1961. There he notes that the December 2 game of the Chicago Packers and Syracuse Nationals reached just under 1.2 million homes and had a 2.5 percent rating and a 9.1 share with 95 stations showing the game. Contrast that with NCAA football on ABC which drew 7.5 million and had a 15.9 percent rating and a 54.8 share as this program was carried on 216 stations. Of interest was also the observation that NBC broadcast the NBA on November 25 without sponsorship, indicating that no ratings were possible and that the network allowed the affiliate stations to sell the commercial time locally. A further comparison with the NFL ratings on Sunday, December 3, showed that the NFL, broadcast on 169 stations, was seen in 7 million homes, had a 15.1 percent rating and a 47.9 share of the audience.

Malitz went on to speak in dollars, asking how much would a sponsor pay for commercials. With a number of figures, Malitz notes that a sponsor would need a minimum audience of at least 3 million homes or a 6.0 percent rating for economy of purchase, something the NBA was far short of. Thus, an ABL network package was not likely, but Malitz suggests seeing how the NBA does in January, after football ends[34].

It was at this time that ABC stumbled into the success of *The Wide World of Sports*, initially just filler, because they had no other sports contracts.[35] Once ABC grew in stature with the concomitant rise of Roone Arledge, they became much more savvy at acquiring sports programming, and the acquisition of the NBA contract in 1965 contrasted greatly with NBC's earlier contract. ABC showed the NBA on Sunday afternoons in what became euphemistically termed the Celtic–76er game of the week since one or the other team, with stars Bill Russell and/or Wilt Chamberlain, was shown nearly every Sunday.

In 1961, however, this was not the case. A number of teams, most notably the New York Knicks, the Boston Celtics, the Philadelphia Warriors and the Chicago Packers had limited local broadcast packages. The Packers were broadcast on WGN, a local channel that later was transformed into one of the two "superstations," along with WTCG (later TBS). The Packers and WGN broadcast ten games, all on Saturday nights. One had to be a real die-hard NBA fan in Chicago to watch both NBC (WMAQ) and WGN on Saturday afternoons and evenings. Judging by the Packers' lack of success on the court and at the box office, the television exposure may have been as much a negative as a positive.[36]

Still, Saperstein and his ABL longed for any exposure, and they were contacted by a San Francisco company, which hoped to handle radio broadcast coordination for league members. The company, Franklin Mieuli & Associates, would provide sportscasters, an engineer as well as feed the broadcast via phone lines or package it on tape and air express it for delayed broadcast. The company did many major league baseball and NFL football teams. A problem for ABL teams was getting initial radio broadcast coverage, so there is no record of any replies to Mieuli, other than the contract that he had with the local ABL team, the San Francisco Saints, mentioned earlier.[37]

Lester Malitz continued to pursue a television contract for the ABL and reported his work to Saperstein in late October. He had tried to interest Chet Simmons, then at ABC, but got no agreement on any package, however minimal. He also contacted Jack Dolph and Bill McPhail at CBS, but McPhail was "quite discouraging," noting that CBS would continue to show the Globetrotters as part of their *Sunday Sports Spectacular* and would pick up the Coaches All-Star Game were they to want more basketball in that series. Further meetings were unproductive.[38]

Malitz kept at it and reported to Saperstein regularly, though with negative results. Saperstein would reply with thanks and encouragement. The Globetrotters were taped in Washington in late December, and the director of business affairs/sports for CBS Television wrote to Saperstein, thanking him and saying how well things went at the taping (which would be shown sometime during the Christmas season). Saperstein's reply to that letter also included another request for consideration of the ABL on a CBS show. He noted

> While most of the teams have broken no records at the box office in the early season ... still, press and everyone who has seen their new style of play has been most appreciative ... and the reception has been magnificent. It certainly seems to me that it would well warrant an exposure of this kind.[39]

Malitz and Saperstein did not communicate, it seems, for the rest of the ABL season, but in April Saperstein sent the same exact letter

Three. ABL Financing— Expectations, Hopes, Realities

(other than a final personal paragraph) to Malitz, Martin Carmichael of CBS and Don Taffner of Paramount Pictures wherein Saperstein extolled the ABL's first year and hoped that a television package for 1962-1963 might be possible.[40]

Obviously, that television package failed to come together, despite Steinbrenner's additional lament and encouragement at the league meeting in March of 1962. With the instability of the league and the lack of television coverage and financial support, the ABL's days were numbered.

Some might question why the league's finances rose or fell on the television package, but the ABL had been based on the AFL model discussed in an earlier chapter, including a national television contract, a competitive league and eventual absorption/co-existence in some manner with the NBA. None of these key aspects of the league's foundation occurred. The NBA was barely hanging on financially, despite an increased gate. The owners were fortunate in that many had hockey teams and/or arenas to keep their revenues flowing.

Basketball, despite its great national popularity at the high school and college level, simply didn't have the interest of most sports aficionados. In fact, college basketball and its NCAA tournament would not be really great moneymakers until 1979 when Bird and Indiana State met Magic and Michigan State in the NCAA Finals. That also carried into the NBA, but in the early 1960s the NBA gate was abysmally low, as will be noted in later chapters. The NBA was forced to offer doubleheaders to try to attract a bigger gate; only in New York was there relatively consistent revenue from the ticket sales, and that would have been much better if the Knicks had not been so awful. Chicago, Cincinnati, Los Angeles, Detroit, Syracuse and St. Louis were barely making ends meet. Three of those teams relocated in search of better gate, and one, Los Angeles, had just moved in that effort. It would take television to bring in the fans to the live game. Only Philadelphia and Boston could get by with ticket sales, and then just barely. Philadelphia, of course, also relocated to San Francisco in another year. Despite Boston's success as five-time champion, they hardly ever had a sellout.

Thus, the NBA strategy was not to outbid the ABL for players, but to wait for the ABL to collapse and fight the ABL in court cases to retrieve their players. Even there the effort was halfhearted since the players were not their stars, and the risk of drawn out court cases (and concomitant spending for legal fees) was not attractive. All of the cases were settled out of court, with the former NBA players being allowed to play in the ABL. It was a kind of war of attrition that the NBA was confident it could win by bleeding the ABL of more funds.

Four

The Exiles and the Deserters

When the ABL began formation, it was obvious that the best professional basketball players were in the NBA, so the basic strategy was to draft top talent from the colleges, raid the NBA for players underpaid or unsatisfied with lack of playing time or find talented players that had somehow been omitted by the NBA. The collapse of the NIBL allowed whole teams like the Pipers and many individual players to enter the league. At this time there was very little quality play outside the U.S. and the ability to find such talent was nearly impossible and financially prohibitive, so the search in the latter category would be limited to the United States.

There were a number of semi-pro and lower-level professional leagues, but media coverage was nearly non-existent, necessitating in-person scouting or the use of "bird dogs," that is, people who sought out hidden talent and reported to major clubs in return for financial rewards or other perks. There were at least three quality players performing in some of these leagues, but they had a taint on them, all being connected, at least indirectly, to point shaving or gambling scandals that had rocked college basketball in the early 1950s and, again, ten years later. Of the "tainted" players, three, Connie Hawkins, Tony Jackson and Bill Spivey, stood out.

Connie Hawkins

Hawkins was a high school star of mammoth proportions at Boys High School in Brooklyn, New York. As a sophomore his team went to the city public league finals, before being upset, but Hawkins played only a few minutes. He was 6'3", 140 pounds and not strong enough to play much for the Kangaroos. During the summer of 1958, Hawkins grew two inches and gained about 25 pounds and his game became sharper and stronger. He and his neighborhood buddies played together on the local schoolyard, but they would also travel the city to play against other top city players in high school and college. One of those players whom they challenged was Tony Jackson of Brooklyn's Jefferson High and, later, St. John's University.[1]

Hawkins began to excel at basketball, but he was an academic disaster. He could hardly read, and little attention was paid to his academic needs in his high school, or at home, where his brothers usually were watching television and his mother was busy in the kitchen. As Hawkins' play improved, teachers at Boys High felt pressured to pass him, although he often endured their taunts in class for his shortcomings in the classroom. Hawkins' junior year saw Boys again a dominant team and him playing as a starter, scoring about 12 points a game. They won the city championship, played in Madison Square Garden, and Hawkins had 15 points and was a force on the backboards. The big star of the team, Bill Burwell, was voted the top player in the city and accepted a scholarship to the University of Illinois, where he became an All–Big Ten player. It was assumed that Hawkins would follow a similar path.

Led by Hawkins, Boys High went undefeated his senior year, but barely edged Wingate High and Roger Brown, 62–59, in the city semifinals, a game where Hawkins fouled out and was outscored by Roger Brown, 39–18. In the finals, Columbus High stalled, hoping to keep the game close and steal a victory. Hawkins had two points in the 21–15 game, but was still named top player in the city and, a few weeks later, First Team on the Parade All-American squad.[2] He then was named Most Valuable Player in an All-American High School game played in Jersey City in late June. Not having committed college plans, Hawkins was inundated with offers, although he was still a student with enormous academic needs. Since his junior year, recruiters had come calling at Boys High, and many provided under-the-table money. Hawkins, who had almost nothing, was, at first surprised and unsure, but soon grew to expect some payments for their visits.[3]

Hawkins was still tremendously underprepared for college, and a kindly English teacher, Nathan Mazer, offered to tutor him, tying to get him up to some level of acceptance for college classes. With Mazer's

Four. The Exiles and the Deserters

assistance, Hawkins managed to get his reading level up to 11th grade and his IQ score from 65 to 113. Mazer saw that Hawkins was intelligent, but had not been exposed to any process of analyzing a word problem in any way. Having only read comic books, he could not recognize words in print that he knew orally. Mazer's work with him made him much better, but the challenge of college work would still be nearly overwhelming.[4]

Hawkins' college choices came down to Colorado and Iowa. Both assured him that he'd do well and they were both going to pay him a good salary, under the table, for non-existent jobs, such as checking the Boulder football stadium for algae once a day. He decided to accept a summer 1960 "trial" in Colorado, which would include his brother, Earl, accompanying him and also getting his schooling paid for. It was a disaster, as Hawkins again felt like the class dummy and received almost no academic assistance. He and his brother returned to Brooklyn after less than a month when Earl threatened a football player with a gun. Earl was told to leave town, and Connie left with him.[5]

Hawkins then got back in touch with the Iowa people, and they set up a nice package for him that assured him $150 a month, which seems ridiculously small, but for Hawkins, it was $150 that he had never had on a regular basis. He arrived in Iowa City in September of 1960. Freshmen were not eligible for varsity play, so he would play only intersquad games on a good freshmen team and seek to adjust to college, or at least that was the plan. In the one game against the varsity, Hawkins outscored and outplayed All–Big Ten star, Don Nelson.

Hawkins had at least two tutors, but the academics were simply too much for him. He passed nothing but PE classes first semester and likely would have been ineligible for varsity basketball had he not been expelled from school in late April. Hawkins had been befriended by Jack Molinas, a well-known former player who had been tossed from the NBA for gambling on games and attempted point shaving. He was a lawyer and still played ball at lots of playgrounds and befriended lots of great players. He treated them to meals and provided a little spending money; he also introduced some to his partner, another gambler named Joe Hacken. Aside from that, Hawkins had little contact with either man. Nevertheless, he never told anyone in any authority about his contacts with them, since it didn't mean anything to him, although he did borrow $200 from Molinas when he was in dire straits financially.

Abe Saperstein and the American Basketball League

Investigators from the district attorney's office in Brooklyn visited Hawkins in April of 1961 and questioned him about his ties to gamblers. Hawkins was confused and panicked, and things got worse when he was taken back to New York and kept in a hotel for eight days and questioned. Frightened and completely lost in a jumble of words and terms, Hawkins agreed to things that were not true and was later named in four counts of a grand jury indictment of Joe Hacken, as an intermediary. When he returned to Iowa after two weeks, Coach Sharm Scheurmann told him he was too far behind and said he should withdraw from school. He did, after much anguish and with no support from the Iowa coaches. His date of withdrawal was May 10, 1961, the day that he testified before the grand jury in New York.[6]

Hawkins was just short of his 19th birthday and had no basketball future in an NCAA school or, subsequently, the NBA who blacklisted him for being named in the Hacken indictment.

That summer, Hawkins played in the Rucker league and with some neighborhood friends in various tournaments, but he had no real future until Lenny Litman called and asked if he'd try out for the Pittsburgh Rens. In the fall, Hawkins was given a tryout and Coach Neil Johnston said he could be the greatest ever, so Litman signed him. His class had not graduated, but he was declared a hardship signing. The district attorney's office in Brooklyn said that he was not going to be indicted, and that was enough for the ABL. Ultimately, it would not be for the NBA.

Hawkins played with the Globetrotters after the collapse of the ABL. During his years with the Globetrotters, Hawkins filed a $6 million suit against the NBA for unfairly barring him from playing in the league. He then signed with the Pittsburgh Pipers when the American Basketball Association began in 1967 and led the league in scoring and was voted Most Valuable Player for the year and the play-offs. The Pipers won the first ABA championship with a record of 54–24, and Hawkins averaged 26.8 points and 13.5 rebounds for the season.

In 1968-1969 the Pipers moved to Minneapolis, but injuries ruined their season. Hawkins averaged over 30 points a game, but played in only 47 games as he suffered a severe knee injury, something that would plague him for the rest of his career. Following that season, the NBA offered to settle Hawkins' suit for $1.3 million, and he accepted, then

Four. The Exiles and the Deserters

signed with the expansion Phoenix Suns, who had received his rights from the NBA, for the next season.

Hawkins was rookie of the year in 1969-1970 with the Phoenix Suns, a second-year expansion team. He scored 24.6 points per game, and grabbed 10.4 rebounds per game, and the Suns improved by 23 games from the prior year, making the play-offs, but losing in the first round. In three more full seasons at Phoenix, Hawkins averaged between 16 and 21 points per game, but his knees became more and more unsteady. He was traded to the Lakers and played with them for nearly two years before finishing in Atlanta in 1976 at the age of 33, with NBA averages of 18.7 points and 8.8 rebounds per game. He was an NBA All-Star from 1970 to 1973 and, despite his knee problems, still had impressive enough credentials to get elected to the Hall of Fame in 1992. For many years he worked in community relations for the Suns. He was diagnosed with colon cancer in about 2007 but was said to be cancer free in 2009. Recent indications are that the cancer may have returned.[7]

Tony Jackson

Tony Jackson was a high school shooting star at Jefferson High School in Brooklyn, where he scored over 1,400 points, graduating in 1957. Kenny Sears recalled going to see him play in Brooklyn in high school when Sears was with the Knicks. "He [Jackson] was that heralded. He was a great shooter there."[8]

Jackson enrolled at St. John's in New York and started on the varsity as a sophomore, beginning in the fall of 1958. He averaged 20 points and 15.4 rebounds per game, and St. John's won both the Holiday Festival and the NIT, going 20–6 for the year. Jackson was the MVP of both tournaments. He set a school record with 27 rebounds in one game and was the leader of Coach Joe Lapchick's Redmen. Lapchick had coached St. John's from 1937 to 1947 before going to the new pro league, the BAA, which became part of the NBA after the merger with the NBL in 1949. Lapchick's terrible stomach problems made returning to the college ranks seem less stressful, and he returned to St. John's in 1957. Having Jackson made his return that much easier.

In 1959-1960 Jackson was named an All-American, as he averaged 21.2 points and 12.9 rebounds per game for the 17–8 squad. The next season Jackson was on the cover of many basketball annuals, as well as the subject of an extensive article ("The Sport Special") in *Sport Magazine* in December of 1960. His pre-season hype proved to be justified as he averaged 22 points and 10.7 rebounds per game as St. John's went 20–5, losing in the first round of the NCAA tourney to Wake Forest, 97–74. This was a team that was more than just Jackson. The center was Leroy Ellis, who played in the NBA for 14 seasons, and another guard, a transfer from Boston College, was Kevin Loughery, who played 11 years in the NBA.

Jackson finished his career at St. John's with a 21.1 average and was the school's leading rebounder (now third) with 991 rebounds. He was a two-time All-American and recipient of the Haggerty Award as the top college player in the New York metropolitan area for the 1960-1961 season.[9]

At some point during the season a gambler called Jackson and offered him money to shave points. Jackson had met the guy in a park playground once and considered the offer a joke and never reported it. Nor did he ever hear from the guy again. Ultimately, he was named in one of the indictments that came out of the Brooklyn district attorney's office in 1961. The New York Knicks of the NBA had drafted Jackson with the first pick of the third round, but they were told by NBA commissioner Maurice Podoloff not to sign him because of the betting scandal. He was then drafted and signed by the Pittsburgh Rens, then traded to the Washington Tapers in October 1961, but soon ended up on the Chicago Majors as their top outside shooting threat.

After the ABL folded, Jackson played in various semi-pro leagues before hooking on with the American Basketball Association in its inaugural season, 1967-1968, playing for the New Jersey Americans. He averaged 19 points and nearly 7 rebounds a game and played in the ABA All-Star game, where he set an ABA record by making 24 free throws in that contest. The next year he played for the Houston Mavericks, and his average dropped to 12 per game. He was shipped to Minnesota at the end of the season, played one game and finished up the season back with the New York Nets, where he played three games and scored just one point. He was then out of the league at age 28. Jackson worked in recreational programs in New York City and played at times in the Eastern League on weekends. He died in Brooklyn at age 65 in 2005.[10]

Four. The Exiles and the Deserters

Bill Spivey

Unlike Jackson and Hawkins, Spivey was not a recent college graduate. He had been a star for the Kentucky Wildcats before graduating in 1952. Spivey was born in 1929, in Lakeland, Florida, but his family moved to Georgia when he was a boy. By the time he was in high school in Macon (Jordan High School), he was over 6'9" tall and became the top star in the state. He accepted a scholarship to Kentucky to play under the fabled Baron of the Bluegrass, Adolph Rupp, and enrolled in the fall of 1948 as Kentucky's first seven-footer. Kentucky was the defending national champions, having won Rupp's first NCAA title with a team that included a number of 1948 Olympians. Rupp was named Olympic coach, and his team practiced in Lexington, allowing Spivey the chance to square off against top players.

Spivey played on the freshman team since players were not eligible for varsity status until sophomore year. Kentucky repeated as NCAA champions but lost most of the squad in 1949 to graduation. The team had been led by Alex Groza and Ralph Beard, both of whom would be implicated in the point-shaving scandals that were revealed, and pursued, in 1951. The belief was that Kentucky would be much weaker in 1950, but Rupp rebuilt the team around Spivey and they went 25–4, but the NCAA chose no teams from the Southeastern Conference for its eight-team field that year, and the Wildcats accepted an NIT bid. There they met CCNY in the first round in the Beavers' amazing runs to both the NIT and NCAA titles. Kentucky lost 89–50, but Spivey was named 1st team all–SEC and 3rd team All-American.

The next season (1950-1951) the Wildcats, led by Spivey, went 28–2, losing games by one and four points, and were invited to the NCAA tournament, newly expanded to 16 teams. Kentucky beat Louisville, St. John's, Illinois and Kansas State to claim Rupp's third NCAA title in four years. Spivey was named 1st team all–SEC as well as 1st team All-American and was the Helms Player of the Year. He averaged 19.2 points per game after averaging 19.3 his sophomore year.[11] Rebound stats were not rigorously kept at that time, but he did snare 21 in the 1951 championship game, along with his 22 points.

It was at this point that the rumors of point shaving became deafening and players from many of the top teams in the New York area—

CCNY, LIU, Manhattan — were initially implicated. After that, players from other top squads outside the metropolitan New York area were named, including Bradley and Kentucky. Spivey was one of those investigated. Spivey missed the first half of the 1951-1952 season with a knee injury, then was held out from joining the team pending the point-shaving investigation. He never played for Kentucky again.

Beard, Groza and Dale Barnstable, Spivey's Kentucky teammates in 1949, were all charged and confessed to point shaving. In February of 1952, Spivey testified before the grand jury in New York and denied any knowledge of point shaving. Nevertheless, the University of Kentucky barred him from playing again on March 2, saying evidence pointed to his agreeing to accept bribes from a known gambler in 1950 and engaging in point shaving. In April he was indicted by the grand jury for perjury, saying that he had lied under oath during his testimony in February.

In June 1952, Spivey was arrested and charged with perjury, and his trial commenced in January 1953. Both Jack West (a gambler) and Jim Line (a teammate) testified that Spivey was in on game fixes[12], but Spivey denied the charges, of both perjury and taking any bribe money and the jury voted 9–3 for acquittal, making a hung jury. The government declined to reinstate the charges, and they were dropped later in 1953. In addition to Kentucky's ban, Maurice Podoloff, commissioner of the NBA, also banned Spivey for life, despite the fact that he had not been convicted of any of the charges. The NBA was just a few years old and feared that any taint would harm the fragile status of the league that was barely getting by financially as it was.

In October, Spivey played briefly for the Elmira Colonels of the American Basketball League, scoring 32 and 21 points in two games before the league voted to disband rather than allow Spivey, Beard, Groza and Sherman White (from LIU) to play in the league and "taint" it. The latter three were playing for the New Jersey Titans. Spivey then played for a barnstorming team, the Detroit Vagabonds.

Spivey played three years for Harlem Globetrotter "foils," the Boston Whirlwinds, the House of David and the Washington Generals before playing for another barnstorming team, the New York Olympians, later renamed the Kentucky Colonels. He was in the dregs of professional basketball. Some regularity emerged in 1957 when Spivey became a regular player in the Eastern Basketball League, beginning with the Wilkes-Barre Barons, whom he led to two consecutive EBL titles. He continued to play for the EBL in 1959-1960 and 1960-1961, but for the Baltimore Bullets, leading them to the EBL championship in 1960-1961 and setting an EBL scoring record with 36.3 points per game in 1959-1960.[13]

In 1959 Spivey signed a contract with the Cincinnati Royals, which Podoloff voided, so in 1960 Spivey sued the NBA and Maurice Podoloff for $800,000, seeking entry into the league. He was convinced that he could still play top-level pro basketball. The case was settled, eventually, for $10,000, claimed Spivey.

When Saperstein formed the ABL, Spivey was eager to play. Though now 32, he had been the MVP of the various leagues where he had recently played and sought to display his talent on a larger stage. After the small cities of New Jersey and Pennsylvania, the prospect of playing in metropolises like Los Angeles, Chicago and Washington was thrilling. That would, of course, not last long. Spivey was paid around $15,000 for the 1961-1962 season, certainly better than EBL salaries, where many of the players had other jobs to actually support themselves and their families.

When the ABL died, Spivey returned to the EBL, playing for the Scranton Miners, for whom he then played for five seasons, retiring in 1968, one month short of his 38th birthday. Spivey never recovered from the scandals that caused his life to change. He was a businessman in Kentucky and ran for the Democratic nomination for lieutenant governor in 1983. In the early 1990s he was involved in an auto accident, from which he never fully recovered, leaving him often in great pain. An operation was botched and resulted in him receiving some money in a settlement. After vacationing in Costa Rica he moved there in 1993. He died in May of 1995 at the age of 66 in his apartment in Quepos, Costa Rica, of what were termed natural causes.

Sylvester Blye

To a lesser but still crippling degree, Sylvester (Sy) Blye was also an exile. Blye was born in New York City in 1938 and attended Ben Franklin High School, graduating in 1957. He played on various playground teams with Jack Molinas, who later gained infamy for fixing games both as a player and a gambler. He was murdered in 1975 in Los Angeles in what many speculated was a mob hit. Blye was close to Molinas and that association eventually tainted him enough to lead to an NBA ban.

Before the NBA blacklist, Blye was declared ineligible for college competition. Blye had accepted a scholarship offer from Seattle University, a top program at the time, where Elgin Baylor attained All-American status after averaging over 31 points per game in two seasons there. He left in 1957, shortly before Blye's arrival on campus.

In need of money, Blye was playing at Seattle in his first year as well as for the professional Harlem Clowns basketball team. Blye played under an assumed name, hoping to keep college officials from finding out about his professional playing and thus retaining his eligibility. According to Blye, a picture of him playing with the team in Canada was sent by someone to the NCAA, and he was declared ineligible. According to Roger Kaiser, Blye was playing in Canada and someone asked him for an autograph and he signed his own name, which led to his being exposed and losing his eligibility.[14]

After that, Blye played in various leagues around New York and was a regular at the Rucker League in the summer. He is in the Rucker League Hall of Fame. One day he was asked by a man whose car was stuck to assist him and was offered $500 to help the man get his car started. Blye knew little about cars but rounded up some guys from a local store that got the car going, but they wouldn't take any money. The man was Paul Cohen, who was the president of the Technical Tape Company. Cohen invited Blye to his birthday party, which, coincidentally, was the same day as Blye's (February 14), and they ended up as friends.

Cohen had a team in the National Industrial Basketball League, the Tuck Tapers, and Blye became a star on that team. Later the team entered the ABL, when the NIBL folded after the 1960-1961 season.

Blye played with the Tapers until the ABL folded, then played in the Eastern League and went to work for Cohen at Technical Tape, the second-largest tape company in the United States, rising to become a vice president and a special assistant to Cohen. He later started some of his own businesses and retired in 1998, and he now lives in West Virginia. After Blye signed a big bonus contract with the Lakers in about 1960, Maurice Podoloff banned him because of his association with Molinas, with whom Blye played on Eastern League and barnstorming teams.

Four. The Exiles and the Deserters

Despite this, Blye led a successful life and is happy in retirement, but still bothered by his inability to ever "show his stuff" in the NBA.

The Deserters

A number of NBA players jumped to the ABL when it formed in 1961. Some went for more playing time; all wanted more money. The NBA didn't seem to mind losing guys at the end of the bench like Gene Tormohlen, Larry Staverman, Jim Palmer or Gene Conley, but the losses of young starters like Kenny Sears, Dick Barnett and veterans Bill Sharman and George Yardley stung. The NBA went to court seeking to enjoin Barnett and Sears from playing in the ABL, and the Celtics also sought damages from Sharman. Yardley had retired in 1960 to join an engineering firm in California and came out of retirement to play part time for the Los Angeles Jets at the age of 33. He had retired at 31 after scoring 20.2 points per game for the Syracuse Nationals, so he certainly could have helped them had he stayed in the NBA.

Kenny Sears

Ken Sears was the New York Knicks' number one pick out of Santa Clara University in 1955. He was 6'9", but barely 200 pounds, and his strength lay in his shooting, particularly from the outside. He joined a good Knicks team that had been 38–34 in 1954-1955, and managed to displace Nat "Sweetwater" Clifton as a starter by mid-season. Sears averaged 12.8 points and 8.8 rebounds per game and was one of the top rookies in the league. The next year the Knicks were a .500 team and Sears improved to 14.8 points per game, topped only by Harry Gallatin's 15. In 1957-1958 Sears led the team in scoring with 18.6, ninth in the league. He also snared 10.9 rebounds per game, second on the team, and he failed to miss a game in two straight years. The Knicks, however, were always just short of the play-offs until 1958-1959, when they went 40–32 for second in the East. Sears led in scoring with 21.0, seventh in the league, and was second to Willie Naulls in rebounds. A rookie teammate of his was Mike Farmer from the University of San Francisco. The Knicks lost two straight in the best-of-three play-off series.

The Knicks declined markedly the next year, and Carl Braun, who missed 28 games with a back injury, became player-coach in January of 1960. The team finished at 27–48, but Sears still averaged 18.5 points per game and 13.7 rebounds per game, the latter sixth in the league. Then in 1960 he was injured and missed 30 games and averaged only 14.4 points per game. Braun also reduced his playing time to 27 minutes per game.

The San Francisco Saints contacted Sears during the summer of 1961 and expressed their interest in signing him, but he returned to New York to negotiate a contract. There he was told that they wanted to cut his salary 25 percent. Sears was pretty steamed. As he noted, "I thought that I was one of the best shooters and maybe the best player on the team, and I wasn't playing as much as I thought I should have.... They wanted me to sign right there, and I said that I wanted to think about it."[15]

Instead, Sears called back to the Saints, and they told him that he could sign with them without fear of reprisal; they would handle any legal action that might be taken. And they did. The Knicks sued him for $175,000, but all he ever had to do in that regard was go to San Francisco for a deposition. The suit was eventually dropped after the judge denied the Knicks' request for a temporary injunction preventing Sears from playing in the ABL. The Saints also asked if he knew of any teammates that they should pursue. He suggested Mike Farmer.

> Mike Farmer and I were close. We were both Northern California boys and played on the Knicks together and lived on Long Island. We would often drive into the games in the city together. Our wives were friends also. So when I signed with the Saints ... I suggested Mike since he wasn't that happy in New York either.[16]

Sears made second team all ABL, but once the league was in trouble, he returned to the NBA for the 1962-1963 season. The Knicks still held his rights, so he played there for 29 games before he and Willie Naulls were traded to the Warriors, who had relocated to San Francisco, for Tom Gola, a Philadelphian, unhappy on the West Coast. As Sears explained,

> The Warriors now had Wilt Chamberlain. They got me because they wanted to get some shooters at forward who would keep defenses from collapsing on Wilt. So they got me and Willie Naulls. We were both good shooters, but despite that, when the ball went in to Wilt, he didn't throw it back out!

Four. The Exiles and the Deserters

Sears averaged just 5.3 points per game for the Knicks in 15.6 minutes per game before he was traded to the Warriors. There, his average improved only a bit to 6.1 in less than 15 minutes of playing time per game. The next year he played just 10 minutes per game, averaged only 3.3 points and 1.8 rebounds per game and was through at the age of 30. As he recalled in a 2001 interview with *Sports Illustrated*,

> The game passed me up.... It became very physical, a lot of pushing and shoving and I didn't weigh much. A rebound was something I never saw unless it bounced right to me.[17]

Sears returned to Watsonville, where he owned a bar, then spent 26 years selling and renting recreational vehicles.

Mike Farmer

Mike Farmer was born in Oklahoma, but his family moved to California when he was a youngster and he attended Richmond High School in Richmond, California, just across the Bay from San Francisco. He then attended the University of San Francisco and played on the Bill Russell–led teams that had a 55-game win streak in 1954–1956. Farmer started his sophomore year in 1955-1956 and was the leading scorer in the 1956 semi-final game against SMU with 18 points. The streak went five games into 1956-1957 before USF lost, but they ended the season 18–6 and were the winners of the West Coast Conference. In the NCAA tourney, USF won the West Regional before losing in the Final Four to Kansas and Wilt Chamberlain. Farmer was the team's leading scorer both that year and the next (1957-1958), when they went 25–1. USF was upset by Seattle and Elgin Baylor in the second round of the NCAA tournament, but Farmer was named West Coast Conference Player of the Year for the second straight year.

Farmer was the number-one draft pick of the New York Knicks (third overall) in the 1958 draft and scored 6.0 points and had 4.4 rebounds per game that year for a 40–32 team. The next year the Knicks fell to 27–48, but Farmer improved slightly to 7.4 points and 5.3 rebounds per game. He played two games for the Knicks in 1960-1961 before being sold to the Cincinnati Royals where he became an occasional starter, averaging 7.3 points and 6.3 rebounds per game. He was not thrilled with living in Cincinnati and only playing 23 minutes per game, so he was very responsive to the interest of the San Francisco Saints.

Farmer returned to the NBA for the 1962-1963 season, playing in 80 games for the St. Louis Hawks, who had purchased his rights from the Royals. He played three full years for the Hawks, then he was cut, nine games into the 1965-1966 season. He averaged 6.7 points and 4.6 rebounds for his NBA career. In 1966-1967 he was hired, at age 31, to coach the Baltimore Bullets, but he was fired after a 1–8 start.

In 1987 Farmer completed his degree requirement and was a USF assistant basketball coach from 1986 to 1990. He then continued as a physical education teacher and assistant coach of men's golf until his retirement. His number (17) was retired by USF in a ceremony in 2000.[18]

Dick Barnett

Dick Barnett was raised in Gary, Indiana, and he was a top player for Gary Roosevelt High School. He played alongside Wilson Eison, who was voted Mr. Basketball in the state and went on to Purdue, where he was an All–Big Ten player. Roosevelt, led by Eison and Barnett, went to the state championship game, but lost 97–74 to Crispus Attucks, led by Oscar Robertson.[19] Both teams were all black, and either winner would have been the first all black team to win a state basketball championship. Barnett went on to Tennessee A&I, coached by John McLendon. They won three consecutive NAIA (National Association of Intercollegiate Athletics) championships, and Barnett was voted MVP of the championship in both 1958 and 1959. Barnett scored 3,209 points in college, an average of 32.1 points per game. He was the first-round pick (fourth overall) of the Syracuse Nationals.

In 1959-1960 Barnett missed 18 games due to military service, but in 57 games, he scored 12.4 points per game, sixth on the team, which went 45–30. The next year Barnett was the first guard off the bench and averaged 16.9 points per game, third on the team, in just 27 minutes of playing time per game. The Nats went 38–41, and Barnett was convinced that had he played more, the team would have had a better record. Thus, when the ABL began operations and Cleveland was to be coached by McLendon, he was eager to jump to the new league. He wanted more playing time and more money, and he would get both in Cleveland (his salary was $13,000). He would also team with former A&I teammates Ben Warley, John Barnhill and Rossie Johnson.

Barnett's ABL career was delayed by the Nationals enjoining him from playing in the new league, but he joined the Pipers after 30 games, when the court case was resolved in his favor. He averaged 26.2 points per game in 50 games and was named First Team All ABL. He also was just six assists from leading the team, despite playing 25 fewer games than the team leader, John Barnhill.

After the 1961-1962 season, Barnett thought that the ABL was shaky and expressed a desire to return to the NBA. The Nationals, who still held his rights, sold him to the Lakers in September of 1962. He became a starter at the other guard spot, opposite Jerry West, and averaged 18 points and 2.8 assists per game for the 53–27 Lakers. The next year he upped his numbers to 18.4 points and 3.1 assists per game. His averages dropped the next year, 1964-1965, to 13.8 and 2.1, and he was traded to the New York Knicks in October of 1965.

Barnett's career flourished with the Knicks. In seven seasons he averaged between 12 and 23 points per game, and the Knicks won two NBA championships. The 1972-1973 championship season was his last full season with the club and he only played in 51 games, averaging 3.8 per game. The next season he played in just five games and retired at the age of 37, with over 15,000 points in the NBA and an overall average of 15.8 for his career.

Barnett ended up returning to graduate school and received a Ph.D. in management from Fordham University. For many years he taught sports management at Saint John's University, before retiring in 2009. He founded Sports Scope (Center for the Study and Research of Athletes and Sport in American Society) and is CEO of this non-profit, which focuses on the education and social development of youth. He was elected to the Tennessee, Indiana and College Basketball halls of fame.

George Yardley

Yardley attended Stanford University after starring in basketball and volleyball at Newport Harbor High School in Newport Beach, California. He enrolled at Stanford to pursue engineering and was the only player on the basketball team not on scholarship, since his family was wealthy enough to pay the tuition. Yardley started for two years at Stanford, and his 16.9 points per game average in his senior year led the Pacific Coast Conference. He graduated in 1950 with a degree in engineering. He was drafted in 1950 by the Fort Wayne Pistons, but chose to play AAU (Amateur Athletic Union) basketball in order to retain his amateur standings since he hoped to make the 1952 Olympic basketball team. Unfortunately he broke his hand in a game in 1952 and was unable to try out for the Olympic team.

Thus in 1953, Yardley signed with the Pistons after rejecting their initial offer of $6,000 and finally got $9,500 for his first season of play. He was an occasional starter by the end of his rookie season, in which he averaged 9.0 points and 6.5 rebounds a game. The next year Yardley led the team in scoring with 17.3 and was second in rebounding with 9.9 per game, leading the Pistons to the Western Division title. After topping the Lakers, the Pistons lost to the Syracuse Nationals, four games to three in the NBA Finals, losing the last game by one point. The Pistons repeated as Western Division champions in 1956, and Yardley was the leading scorer and rebounder. Despite losing in the NBA Finals to the Philadelphia Warriors, Yardley led the Pistons with 23.0 and 13.9 rebounds per game in the play-offs. Two years later Yardley became the first NBA player to score 2,000 points in a season, averaging 27.8 per game, but the Pistons were declining, finishing under .500 for the second year in a row.

The Pistons continued their decline the next season, and after 46 games, Yardley was traded to Syracuse. He only averaged 19.8 for the year, but in the play-offs, he averaged 25.1, second on the team to the 28.2 of Dolph Schayes, but the Celtics defeated them in seven close games. In 1959-1960 Yardley scored 20.5 points per game and teamed with Schayes (who averaged 22.5) to lead the Nationals to a 45–30 record, but they had an early exit in the play-offs. Yardley was making the top salary on the team, $25,000, but at 31 he retired, fulfilling a promise he had made to his wife that he would return to California when their oldest child reached school age.

After a number of years of working for an engineering firm in Southern California during the offseason, Yardley began his own company upon retirement, selling mechanical engineering equipment. When the Los Angeles Jets came calling, he was adamant in his desire to not leave the state, and he make road trips only to San Francisco. The ABL approved this condition in November 1961 by a vote of 7–1. When the Jets went out of business in December, he returned to his firm and left pro basketball behind. Yardley invented and patented a seal for the liquid oxygen fuel tank on the Atlas-Titan rocket.

In 1996 George Yardley was enshrined in the Naismith Basketball Hall of Fame. In 2003 he was diagnosed with amyotrophic lateral sclerosis (ALS) and became a fund-raiser for the disease. Before dying in August of 2004, he raised over $120,000 for the ALS Association.

Bill Sharman

Bill Sharman was born in Abilene, Texas, but moved to the central California city of Porterville when still in school. After high school he attended the University of Southern California and was drafted in the second round by the Washington Capitols, but he signed initially with the Brooklyn Dodgers to play baseball. He made it to the Dodgers in late 1951 but never appeared in a game, although he remained in their farm system through 1955.

Sharman joined the Capitols for the 1950-1951 season and scored 12.2 points per game in 31 games before the team folded, and he went to the Fort Wayne Pistons in the dispersal draft. He never played in a game for the Pistons because of military service, and they traded him to the Boston Celtics in April 1951 for Chuck Share. He was the third guard in 1951-1952, scoring 10.7 points per game for a 39–27 Celtics club. The next season he moved into a starting position alongside Bob Cousy and upped his scoring to 16.2 points per game, led the league in free throw percentage and was fourth in field goal percentage, the only guard in the league to shoot better than 41 percent.

For the next three years, Sharman and Cousy were a deadly shooting and passing combination for a good, but not great, Celtics team. Sharman continued to lead the league in free throw shooting and increased his average to 19.9 points per game in 1955-1956. The team had great scoring, but lacked a presence in the middle. This was, of course, rectified by the acquisition of Bill Russell. The Celtics and Sharman won championships four of the next five years before Sharman chose to retire in 1961. He left the NBA with an average of 17.8 points per game and a free throw percentage of .883, best in the league's history, since broken by Rick Barry.

Sharman returned to Southern California and was sought as the coach of the Los Angeles Jets, but when he said he would be a player-coach, at age 35, Walter Brown and the Celtics sued him to prevent him from playing in the ABL. Sharman won that suit (as well as one against the Utah Stars, whom he coached in the ABA in 1971 in order to sign as the coach of the Lakers).

After the Jets folded, he was the coach of the champion Cleveland Pipers, replacing John McLendon, then coached at Los Angeles State and worked for Tidewater Oil (Flying A gasoline), putting on basketball clinics as part of the company's community relations program. He also sued (and won) to enforce his contract with the Jets after they had dissolved.[20]

In 1966 he was hired as coach of the San Francisco Warriors and had an 87–76 record in two years. He was let go by the Warriors and

Left to right: Ben Warley, John Barnhill and Jack Adams of the Cleveland Pipers (The Cleveland Press Collection, Michael Schwartz Library, Cleveland State University).

Four. The Exiles and the Deserters

immediately signed as coach of the Los Angeles Stars of the new American Basketball Association (ABA), leading them to a two-year record of 76–86. In his first year, Ben Warley, from his Cleveland Pipers team, scored 14.4 points per game for the Stars. The team moved to Salt Lake City for 1970-1971 and added Zelmo Beatty to their roster, after he had been enjoined from playing the prior season by a court order because of jumping from the Atlanta Hawks. The Stars went 57–27 and won the ABA championship. Sharman was voted Coach of the Year in the league but was eager to return to southern California.

In Sharman's first year as coach of the Lakers, he led them to a record of 69–13 and a record 33-game winning streak. They won the NBA championship, and Sharman was voted NBA Coach of the Year. He remained the Lakers' coach through the 1975-1976 season and finished his coaching career with 466 wins and 353 losses. In 1976 he was inducted into the Naismith Memorial Basketball Hall of Fame as a player, and in 2004 he was inducted as a coach. Sharman is the only coach to win league championships in the ABL, ABA and NBA. He is one of three members of the Hall of Fame as both a coach and player (John Wooden and Lenny Wilkins are the others). As of 2012 he lives with his wife, Joyce, in Southern California.

As noted earlier, there were other "deserters," including Connie Dierking, Archie Dees, Jim Palmer, Maury King and Larry Friend. Some made it back to the NBA; others did not, either by choice or the decision of others. Friend, for example, decided not to seek another basketball position, instead going into banking and being very successful at it. In 1984 he founded his own investment banking firm, Friend, Weinress and Frankson Inc., locating it in Irvine. He was president of the firm when he died in February of 1998 of prostate cancer.[21]

Five

The Coaches and the Starting Fives

The ABL gave a number of coaches and players an opportunity to begin a career that in many cases led to the National Basketball Association, but it also was a venue for former NBA or even National Basketball League or Basketball Association of America (BAA) coaches or players to extend their professional careers before moving into other fields. The experience that these personnel gained would serve many of them well as they continued lives within the basketball arena.

Chicago Majors

The Chicago Majors had a most unusual, yet familiar structure in their organization. Not only did Abe Saperstein move players back and forth between the Harlem Globetrotters and the Majors, but he also moved a number of his former Globetrotters into administrative positions within the Majors' organization. The business manager of the Majors was Ermer Robinson. Originally from San Diego, he had tried out for the team in 1946, following his discharge from the army after World War II. During the war he had played AAU ball while stationed at Fort Warren in Cheyenne, Wyoming. Robinson was soon a starter because of his intelligent play and accurate set shot and was a star in the 1948 contests against the Minneapolis Lakers. In the first, played in Chicago Stadium before almost 18,000 fans on February 19, he scored 17 points, including the game winner as the clock expired in the 61–59 Globetrotter victory. He played with the Trotters until around 1953, when he began coaching one of their squads, occasionally playing.

Five. The Coaches and the Starting Fives

When San Francisco's franchise moved to Oakland for the 1962-1963 season, Robinson was named the new coach. Since later revelations showed that Saperstein was controlling at least two franchises during that season, it is reasonable to assume that he heavily influenced the hiring of Robinson for the Oakland team. Following the collapse of the league, Robinson was as scout for Saperstein, then did the same for the Oakland franchise of the newly formed American Basketball Association for 1967-1968. Robinson died in 1982 at age 60 in San Diego of cancer of the larynx.

Also part of the Majors staff was Inman Jackson, one of the all-time great Globetrotters, who served as equipment director. Jackson was the greatest star of the Globetrotters in the 1930s, first appearing on that squad on December 5, 1930.[1] He made his last appearance as a player on the team in 1943. Jackson served the Globetrotters in various capacities for the rest of Saperstein's life. When Saperstein died unexpectedly at age 63 in March of 1966, Jackson was one of three (Marie Linehan and Saperstein's sister were the others) to receive 4 percent of his estate (close to $100,000 each). Jackson, himself, died in April 1973 at age 65.[2]

The coach of the Majors was Andy Phillip, captain of the original University of Illinois "whiz kids" of the 1940s, who won the Big Ten championship in 1942 and 1943, losing only one game each year. Phillip was named National Player of the Year in 1943. Phillip then enlisted in the Marines and returned to graduate at Illinois after World War II and played in the 1946-1947 season. He was then drafted and played for the Chicago Stags of the BAA for two years, finishing third and second in the league in assists, while scoring at a 10.8 and 12.2 point per game clip, respectively. Phillip remained on the Stags after the BAA/NBL merger formed the NBA and led the league in assists for its first two years, scoring 11.7 and 11.2 points per game. The Stags folded after the 1949-1950 season and Phillip was obtained by the Philadelphia Warriors in the dispersal draft in October of 1950.[3] In November of 1952, he was sold to the Fort Wayne Pistons and remained with them until August of 1956 when he was claimed on waivers by the Boston Celtics, with whom he played through the 1957-1958 season, retiring at age 36. He retired as a five-time All Star.

In 1958 he was hired by Ben Kerner to coach the St. Louis Hawks, who were defending NBA champions, but he and Kerner did not get along and Phillip was fired after 10 games with a record of 6–4, and was replaced by "Easy Ed" Macauley. Phillip moved to Palm Springs, California, and operated a restaurant and got into real estate. Phillip jumped at the chance to return to professional basketball and compiled a 39–44 record in 1961-1962, but his biggest highlight that year was probably his election to the Naismith Memorial Basketball Hall of Fame.

For the 1962-1963 season, Saperstein named Ron Sobieszczyk, who played as Ron Sobie, as the player coach. In 1961-1962 Sobie came out of retirement at age 27 to play for the Majors in eight games. Sobie had played at DePaul from 1953 to 1956, breaking George Mikan's scoring records there. He was then drafted by Detroit, but traded to the Knicks before the season began. He ruptured a blood vessel early in his second year in the league, and it ultimately led to his exit from the league after just one game in the 1959-1960 season.[4]

Sobie averaged 13.5 points per game in his brief tenure in 1961-1962. In 1962-1963, he played in all 28 games before the league folded, averaging 12.6 points per game, third on the team behind Kelly Coleman and Tony Jackson. His coaching record was 8–20. He also played for the Washington Generals, one of the Globetrotters' "traveling opponents," in 1960, leading to his ascension to the ABL. In later years he owned Sobie's Bar and Grill in Cicero, Illinois. He died in 2009.

The Majors started six men in various combinations during the 1961-1962 year. Tony Jackson, once he was obtained from Washington, was the leading scorer and a regular starter. The others were Herschell Turner, Kelly Coleman, Bob Wilkinson, Hank Whitney and John Wessels. Nat "Sweetwater" Clifton, on the down side of his playing career with the Trotters and Knicks, was also a spot starter when needed.

Herschell Turner was a 6'3" guard from Indianapolis, Indiana, who had starred at the University of Nebraska. He was drafted in the sixth round of the 1960 NBA draft by the Syracuse Nationals. After being cut by the Nationals, he played with Baltimore of the Eastern League, then was signed by the Majors for 1961-1962. During that season he averaged 16.5 points per game and led the team in assists with 190. He was named Second Team All League. The next season his scoring dropped to 9.0 per game, as he was no longer a regular starter, losing his spot to player-coach Ron Sobie.

After the ABL folded, Turner played in various leagues until he hooked on with the ABA in its first season, 1967-1968. He played nine games for the Pittsburgh Pipers before being traded to the Anaheim Amigos. He averaged just over three points per game for the year and was

Five. The Coaches and the Starting Fives

out of the league after that season. He played for the Globetrotters at times during the 1960s.

Kelly Coleman, from Wayland, Kentucky, was the first Mr. Basketball in the state of Kentucky in 1956, and he set records unlikely to be broken in high school. He averaged 47 points a game his senior year and 33.6 for 127 games in high school. He was seen as comparable to Oscar Robertson and Jerry West, high school graduates that same year and the top players in Indiana and West Virginia, respectively. After graduating from Wayland High School, he attended Kentucky Wesleyan, where he averaged 30.7 points per game and was named a Little All-American. He had planned to attend either West Virginia or Kentucky, but the NCAA barred him from West Virginia after allegations of recruiting improprieties on the part of West Virginia emerged after a complaint was filed by the University of Kentucky. Coleman refused to attend Kentucky after that.

Initially drafted by the New York Knicks as the 11th pick in 1960, he failed to make the team and played with Baltimore of the Eastern League in 1960. In 1961-1962 he was third on the Chicago Majors in scoring with 14.2 points per game, and he was second on the team in rebounds, despite his 6'3" size. The next year, he led the team with 19.0 points per game in the 28-game attenuated season. Following the ABL collapse, Coleman played briefly in the Eastern League again, then returned to Kentucky.

Bob Wilkinson was a 6'1" guard from the University of Indiana, who had played AAU ball for the Denver-Chicago (D-C) Truckers. He scored 10.9 points per game in 1961-1962, but was traded to Oakland for the next season. He averaged just 5.5 points per game, then, left pro basketball to pursue a position in marketing, in which he had his degree from Indiana.

Hank Whitney, a 6'7" forward, was from Brooklyn and played ball at Iowa State. He was initially drafted in 1961 by Syracuse of the NBA and the Los Angeles Jets, and he chose to sign with the latter. He came to the Majors in a trade early in the season and was a solid scorer (9.1 points per game), as well as the leading rebounder on the team by far with 662 (9.0 rebounds per game). Whitney was out of the league the next year, playing in the Eastern League, and then reappeared when the American Basketball Association began in 1967. He played with the New Jersey Americans that year (averaging a double-double, 16.0 points per game and 12.8 rebounds per game) and then was traded in mid-season the next year to the Houston Mavericks. He ended his ABA career with

Carolina in 1969-1970, averaging 9.0 points and 7.6 rebounds per game in the three seasons.

John Wessels, a 6'8" center/forward was from Rockford, Illinois, and had been co-captain of the 1960-1961 University of Illinois team and was an All–Big Ten selection. He was first signed by Cleveland, but was obtained by Chicago with the expectation that he would have local attraction because of his high school and college affiliations. He was an average rebounder, averaging 5 per game in 1961-1962 and 9.9 points per game. He was reluctant to sign for 1962-1963, leaving pro basketball.

Cleveland Pipers

John McLendon, as noted earlier, was the first African American coach in a major professional league, the ABL. He also was the first African American coach in the American Basketball Association. McLendon had graduated from the University of Kansas in 1936 and had worked with Dr. James Naismith, the inventor of basketball, who died in 1939. After graduation, McLendon obtained a master's degree at the university, then began college coaching, first briefly at Kansas Vocational School, then for fifteen years at North Carolina Central, then at Tennessee A&I from 1954 to 1959. He won three straight NAIA national championships and in 1959 agreed to accept the position of coach of the Cleveland Pipers who were an AAU team joining the National Industrial Basketball League. In the team's second season, they won the NIBL title, then won the weeklong AAU Tournament held in Denver in the spring of 1961.[5] In 1961 the NIBL collapsed and the Pipers joined the newly formed ABL.

After the demise of the ABL, McLendon returned to college coaching at Kentucky State University, where he went 50–29 in two years, then Cleveland State, where he was 27–42 in three years. His overall collegiate coaching record was 522 wins and 165 losses. In 1969 McLendon was named the coach of the Denver Rockets of the American Basketball Association and he was 9–19 when he was abruptly fired. He then worked for Converse as a "basketball ambassador" for the next 20 years. He was elected to the Naismith Memorial Basketball Hall of Fame as a contributor in 1979.

STARTING FIVE

At the end of the season, the Pipers started three players who had played for McLendon at Tennessee A&I, but one was Dick Barnett, who

Five. The Coaches and the Starting Fives

was only able to play the last 50 games. (A fourth A&I player, Rossie Johnson, came off the bench.) Before Barnett joined the club, rookie Larry Siegfried started, but came off he bench after Barnett joined the team. Siegfried was a heralded signing for the ABL, having started for Ohio State, who had won the NCAA championship in 1960, then lost in the finals to Cincinnati in 1961. Because of Jerry Lucas and John Havlicek, Siegfried was less well known, but still was a First Team All–Big Ten player. He was drafted in the first round of the NBA draft by Cincinnati but signed with Cleveland, partly because it was closer to his home in Shelby, Ohio, and also because the Pipers offered more money.

During his rookie year Siegfried averaged 9.0 points per game. When the Pipers folded, his rights were acquired by the St. Louis Hawks of the NBA, who cut him in training camp. He sat out the year, teaching high school, then was invited to the Boston Celtics training camp in 1963 at the urging of former OSU teammate John Havlicek. Over the next seven years, Siegfried helped the Celtics to five NBA championships, and in five of those years, he averaged in double figures in scoring, as either a starter or the first guard off the bench. In May of 1970, he was left unprotected by the Celtics in the expansion draft and taken by the new Portland Trail Blazers, who immediately traded him to the San Diego Rockets for Jim Barnett. In 1970-1971 he averaged 8.0 points per game for the Rockets as the third guard behind Stu Lantz and Calvin Murphy. He also led the team in assists with 6.5 per game. The next year he began the season with the Rockets, who had moved to Houston, but was traded, along with Don Adams, to Atlanta in November of 1971 for John Vallely and Jim Davis. After playing only 16 minutes a game and averaging 3.3 points per game, Siegfried chose to retire at the age of 33. He coached for three years, then left basketball and was a counselor and motivational speaker in his later years. He died suddenly of a heart attack in October of 2010 at the age of 71.

Dick Barnett, the top Piper scorer was discussed earlier. His two Tennessee A&I teammates, John Barnhill and Ben Warley were also starters. Both were drafted in 1959, Barnhill by the Hawks and Warley by the Syracuse Nationals, but chose to play on the Pipers of the NIBL with McLendon as coach. As a Piper, Barnhill averaged 11.3 points per game in 1961-1962, then, was signed by the Hawks for the 1962-1963 season. He was a starter in his first year, then, came off the bench as third guard for two years, averaging 7 to 11 points per game in those years. In December of 1965, he was traded to the Pistons for Joe Caldwell. At the end of the season he was drafted by the new Chicago Bulls but was sold by the Bulls to the Baltimore Bullets just before the start of the 1966-1967 season. He averaged eight points per game, but was drafted, again, at the end of the season, this time by the expansion San Diego Rockets. There he scored nearly ten points a game, but was made available for another expansion the next year and went to the Phoenix Suns for the 1968-1969 season, but he was cut before the season began. In January of 1969 he was signed as a free agent by the Bullets once again, and he played in 30 games for them but was dropped at the end of the year.

Barnhill signed with Indiana of the ABA for 1969-1970 and played with them the entire season, averaging 11 points a game during the season for the ABA champion Pacers. Midway through the next season he was traded to Denver, where he averaged 11.4 points per game for a high-scoring team that finished fifth in the division. Barnhill was not offered a contract for the next year and went back to Indiana as a free agent, where he finished his playing career and retired at the age of 34.

Ben Warley, as noted, also played with the Pipers and for McLendon from graduation until the team folded. He then played for Syracuse in 1962-1963 and remained on that team for the next three years, although the franchise relocated to Philadelphia and became the 76ers for the 1963-1964 season. In October of 1965 he was sold to the Bullets and played there for two seasons. Except for one season, Warley never played more than 17 minutes per game in his NBA career, and he chose to jump to the ABA in 1967 rather than go to the Seattle Supersonics, who had drafted him in the expansion draft. He played with Anaheim, Los Angeles and Denver in three years and in the first two averaged 17 and 14 points per game respectively. He retired in 1970 at the age of 33.

Johnny Cox played 80 games for the Pipers in 1961-1962 and averaged 18.5 points per game; he was named Second Team All League. Cox was a 6'4" guard who had been an All-American at Kentucky and drafted by the Knicks in 1959. He did not make the squad and signed with the Cleveland Sweeny Pipers of the NIBL, where he was the Rookie of the Year. A franchise shift made him a free agent, and he signed with the Akron Goodyears for 1960-1961. He went to the Chicago Zephyrs in 1962-1963, where he averaged 7.3 points per game as the third guard on a 25–55 team. The coach was Jack McMahon, who had coached Kansas City in the ABL the year before and likely saw enough of Cox to want him on his club. He was one of the all-time greats at Kentucky, but never achieved much in the pro ranks.

The Pipers obtained Connie Dierking in an early season trade with the Tapers, and Dierking was the key to their limited inside game, averaging nearly 12 points a game. Dierking had been Syracuse's first-round pick in 1958 out of the University of Cincinnati and had signed with the Syracuse Nationals, which put him closer to his home in Long Island, New York. After the ABL collapse, Dierking returned to the NBA in 1963 and played for the Philadelphia 76ers and was traded to the San Francisco Warriors in January of 1965 in the trade that brought Wilt Chamberlain back to Philadelphia. Before the next season began, he was traded by the Warriors to Cincinnati in October of 1965. There he found a home, back in the city where he had starred in college. He played for the Royals for five years and averaged better than 16 points and 8 rebounds his last three years there. He was traded back to Philadelphia one game into the 1970-1971 season and finished his NBA playing career there, averaging 10 points and nearly 7 rebounds per game for his career. He retired to Cincinnati at age 34 and still lives in that area.

Hawaii Kings

The Hawaii Kings hired Ephraim "Red" Rocha as their first (and only) coach. Rocha was a native of Hawaii who had attended Oregon State University and was known as "the Thin Man" because of his 6'9", 185 pound build. He was drafted by the Toronto Huskies of the Basketball Association of America in the second round of the 1947 draft, but was assigned to the St. Louis Bombers when the Huskies left the league. He was on St. Louis for three years, two in the BAA and one as they transitioned to the NBA. St. Louis folded after the 1950 season, and Rocha was taken by Baltimore in the dispersal draft and played for them for one season. Then he was traded to Syracuse, where he played four years as their starting center before being sold to the Fort Wayne Pistons in October of 1956. He played one season for Fort Wayne as a backup center and only averaged 5.3 points per game, the first time in his pro career that he failed to average in double figures.

He retired at the end of the season with a pro average of 10.9 points per game and 6.6 rebounds per game. He was the first Hawaiian player in the NBA. Rocha became the Pistons' coach in December when Charley Eckman resigned. He guided the team to a 24–23 record and into the play-offs, where they defeated Cincinnati in the first round and lost to St. Louis in the Western Division finals. The next year they went only 28–44 and in 1959-1960 they were 13–21 when he was fired by owner Fred Zollner and replaced with Dick McGuire.

Rocha returned to Oregon State as an assistant coach under his former coach, "Slats" Gill, then returned to the pro ranks as coach of the Kings with the creation of the ABL. The next year Rocha remained in Hawaii as the coach of the University of Hawaii Rainbow Warriors from 1963–1973. He later moved back to Corvallis and died there in 2010.

For the 1962-1963 season, the Kings moved to Long Beach, and their coach was Al Brightman, who had finished the prior season as coach of the San Francisco Saints and gone 23–24. With Long Beach he had a record of 16–8, good for second to the Kansas City Steers. Brightman was from Long Beach and had gone to Long Beach State (and Morris Harvey College) in the 1940s, then served in World War II before playing one year for the Boston Celtics in the first year of the Basketball Association of America (1946-1947). He was player coach for Seattle of the short-lived Pacific Coast Professional Basketball League in 1947–48, before becoming the baseball and basketball coach of the University of Seattle from 1949 to 1956. After coaching in the ABL, Brightman coached at a number of high schools in California before being hired to coach the Anaheim Amigos of the ABA in 1967 where he was 12–24 before being let go in mid-season. He died in 1992 at age 68.[6]

Starting Five

Hawaii had six top starters during the season, the sixth being Bill Spivey, who became their leading scorer and rebounder after coming to the Chiefs when the L.A. Jets ceased operations in December of 1961. Despite Spivey's addition, Hawaii finished in last place in both halves of the season, a likely result of the difficulties of playing eight- game home stands, followed by twelve-game road trips, with occasional "home" games being played at various locations on the mainland.

The second leading scorer (15.3 points per game) was 6'1" guard Frank Burgess, who had been All Air Force in the 1950s after leaving

Five. The Coaches and the Starting Fives

Arkansas A&M (now University of Arkansas at Pine Bluff) after his first year. After leaving the Air Force he enrolled at Gonzaga University in Spokane, Washington, and became the school's all-time leading scorer (which he still is). In his senior year (1960-1961) he averaged 32 points a game to lead the nation and scored 52 in one game. Burgess was an All-American in both his junior and senior seasons and upon graduation was drafted by both the Chiefs and the Los Angeles Lakers (third round). He signed with the ABL and after the Chiefs moved to Long Beach the next year, he decided to enroll at the Gonzaga School of Law, from which he received his law degree in 1966. After 11 years of private practice, Burgess became a judge or magistrate at various levels with a year out as regional counsel for the Department of Housing and Urban Development in 1980–81. In 1993 he was named to the U.S. Federal Court for the Western District of Washington by President Clinton. Burgess was the second African American ever named to that court. He died in March of 2010 at age 75.

Jeff Cohen was a 6'7" All-American forward from William and Mary who scored more than 2,000 points and grabbed more than 1,000 rebounds in college. He was drafted in the second round of the NBA draft by the Chicago Packers, but signed, instead, with the ABL. He averaged 10.8 points per game for the Chiefs in 1961-1962. Following the Chiefs' move to Long Beach, Cohen ended up on the Chicago Majors for 1962-1963. There he averaged 12.5 points per game and was the team's third leading rebounder (8.0 rebounds per game) at the time the league disbanded. He died in Switzerland in 1978, and his jersey was retired by William and Mary in 1990.

Dave Mills, 6'7" from the University of Seattle, where he was a freshman when Elgin Baylor was a senior, was an eighth-round pick in the NBA draft by Syracuse, but signed with the ABL. He scored 13 points per game for the Chiefs and was their second leading rebounder (to Spivey). The next year, Mills played for Oakland and scored 7.3 points per game. He was not signed by the NBA or the ABA and left pro basketball.

Govoner Vaughn was from Edwardsville, Illinois and played at the University of Illinois, where he led the Big Ten in free throw shooting his senior year (1959-1960). He was one of the first African Americans to be a starter at the University (along with former high school teammate, Manny Jackson, now the president of the Harlem Globetrotters). Vaughn played with the Globetrotters for a year before signing with the ABL, where he started with Chicago and then was traded to Hawaii. He averaged 10.5 points per game, then, played for Oakland the next year, averaging 5.5 points per game. Vaughn coached, went into real estate and eventually back to the Globetrotters as a manager when Jackson bought the team in the early 2000s.

Herb Lee, who scored 14.2 points per game, also was second in assists, but failed to continue in the ABL after 1962. A 6'0" guard, he had played at the University of Indiana, graduating in 1960. Lee Harman had been the Los Angeles High School Player of the year in 1953-1954. In 1961-1962 he scored 8.3 points per game, led the Chiefs in assists with 226 (3.2 per game), played nine games the next season with the Chiefs, then left the league. He had come out of Oregon State, a 6' guard, graduating in 1959 and was drafted by the St. Louis Hawks in the fourth round. He left pro ball after that season.

In Long Beach in 1962, Spivey was joined by new starters, Ben Warley from the Pipers, Ron Horn, Charlie Hadden and a former sixth man in Hawaii, Grady McCollum. Horn was drafted by the St. Louis Hawks from Indiana in 1961, played three games and was cut and signed with the Saints in the ABL. He averaged 8.5 for them in a backup role, then averaged 18.7 for the Chiefs in 1962-1963. When the league folded he managed to hook on with the Lakers for the remainder of the year and averaged 2.6 points a game. He played for various minor league teams until 1967 when he played one game for the ABA's Denver Rockets. He died in 2002 at age 64. Grady McCollum, from Western Illinois University, played with the Globetrotters and the Pipers in both the NIBL and in the ABL. He averaged 9.8 for the Chiefs in 1961-1962 and 11.2 in 1962-1963. Charlie Hadden played with the Los Angeles Jets in 1961-1962, averaging 2.5 points per game before the team ceased operations. He averaged 10.4 for the Chiefs in 1962-1963.

Kansas City Steers

The Steers hired Jack McMahon as their coach, despite the fact that he had no head coaching experience. He had been a all-city guard at St. Michaels in New York City, then played at St. John's, graduating in 1952, and was drafted by the Rochester Royals. For the next seven years he was a solid guard for the Royals, and then the St. Louis Hawks, to whom he

Five. The Coaches and the Starting Fives

was traded during the 1955-1956 season. He hurt his knee during the 1959-1960 season when he was a player–assistant coach for the Hawks and retired as a player after that season. He worked as a scout and adviser to owner Ben Kerner of the Hawks the next season, then was hired by the Steers in 1960 and began to help develop the team for the 1961-1962 season.

McMahon left the league and went to the Chicago Zephyrs for 1962-1963 as head coach, but resigned at mid-season with a record of 12–26. He replaced Charley Wolf as Cincinnati Royals head coach for 1963-1964 and led the team to a second-place finish in the West with a 55–25 mark. He remained as coach of the Royals through the 1966-1967 season, when he was let go. He was hired by the San Diego Rockets and remained as coach for two years, before being fired in December of 1969, when their record was 9–17. He returned as a head coach the next year with the Pittsburgh Condors of the American Basketball Association and went 36–48, then was fired ten games into the 1971-1972 season. From 1974 to 1986 he was the director of player personnel and an assistant coach of the Philadelphia 76ers. McMahon died in 1989 at age 60.[7]

STARTING FIVE

The Steers had the best overall record in the league, and four of their players went on to the NBA. By far their best player was Bill Bridges, the rookie forward out of Kansas. Originally from Hobbs, New Mexico, he completed his college years by being named MVP of the Big Eight Christmas Tourney and being named an All-American. A rugged rebounder and scorer from Kansas, Bridges was not selected in the NBA draft until the third round by the Chicago Packers; he was seen as undersized at 6'5" and 225 pounds. Instead, he signed with the Steers where he was a First Team All ABL player. He averaged 21.4 points per game and 13.4 rebounds per game. Only he and Connie Hawkins snared more than 1,000 rebounds in 1961-1962. The next season, he scored 29.2 points per game which led the league, as did his 15.0 rebounds per game, at the time the ABL ceased operations.

Bridges was then signed by the St. Louis Hawks, who had traded for him in June of 1962, and played the rest of 1962-1963 with them and seven more years after that, during which time he was named to three All Star teams (1967, 1968, 1970). From 1965 to 1972, Bridges was in the top ten of

NBA rebounders each year. In November of 1971, shortly after the season began, Bridges was traded to the Philadelphia 76ers, where he played for one season before the 76ers traded him to the Lakers in November of 1972. Two years later in December of 1974, he was waived by the Lakers and not signed by any team until March of 1975, when the Golden State Warriors picked him up for the rest of the year. He retired at age 36 with over 11,000 NBA points and an average of 11.9 points and 11.9 rebounds per game. He worked as a scout for the Lakers for more than 20 years.

The Steers' second leading scorer was Larry Staverman, a 6' 7", 215 pound forward from Villa Madonna College (now Thomas More) in Covington, Kentucky, Staverman's hometown, just across the Ohio from Cincinnati. He was a big star at a small school, and that affected his draft placement; he went in the ninth round in 1958 to the Royals. In 57 games for them, he averaged 4.3 points per game in 1958–59, then 3.8 in 49 games in 1959-1960 and 4.6 in 66 games in 1960-1961. He then chose to leave the NBA and sign with the ABL. In 1961-1962 he averaged 17.5 points per game and 8.8 rebounds. He was a fabulous medium-range jump shooter and an 87 percent free throw shooter. In 1962-1963, his scoring jumped to 20.9 points per game, and after the ABL collapsed, he was back in the NBA with the Chicago Zephyrs (who had gotten his rights in a trade in June 1962) to complete the 1962-1963 season, averaging 7.2 points per game.

The next season Staverman began with Baltimore (which is where the Zephyrs had relocated) and was traded to Detroit in October for Kevin Loughery, which proved to be a great trade for the Bullets. Two months and 20 games later, Staverman was moved back to Cincinnati as part of a three-trade swap. He played in 34 games for the Royals, who failed to offer him a contract for 1964. He ended his NBA career with averages of 4.7 points and 3.8 rebounds.[8]

In 1965 he was hired as an assistant coach at Notre Dame by Johnny Dee, who had been his coach in 1962-1963 at Kansas City. He remained on Dee's staff for two years and was the initial coach for the Indiana Pacers when the ABA began in 1967. He led them to a 38–40 record and a first-round play-off loss to Pittsburgh. The next year he was fired after nine games and replaced by Bob Leonard. The following season (1969-1970) the Royals hired Staverman as their assistant general manager and promotions director, positions he held until 1978 when Phil Johnson

Five. The Coaches and the Starting Fives

The Steer, Kansas City's mascot, as depicted on one of their programs (Courtesy Dolph Briscoe Collection, University of Texas Archives).

was fired as coach of the Kansas City Kings (the Royals had moved in 1972) and Staverman finished the season as head coach. He had a record of 18 and 27 for the rest of the year, then returned to the front office as a vice president through 1981.

Staverman ended his professional career in baseball with the Cleveland Indians as stadium general manager. He had been a top pitcher in high school and college and was the batting practice pitcher for the Cincinnati Reds in 1961, then did the same for the Kansas City A's in 1962. With his baseball knowledge and front office experience, he was a natural hire and he served as stadium manager until 1996 when Municipal Stadium was demolished. He then worked as a consultant in Nashville, overseeing the construction of the stadium for the Tennessee Titans, which opened in 1999. He died in 2007 back home in Kentucky.

Gene "Bumper" Tormohlen came to the Steers after playing in the NIBL with the Cleveland Pipers from 1959 to 1961. He had been Syracuse's second-round pick in 1959 out of Tennessee, but opted to not sign with the NBA, initially. Originally from Holland, Indiana, Tormohlen was an aggressive and rugged rebounder at 6'9", 232 pounds, and was All Southeastern Conference both junior and senior years. In 1961-1962 he averaged 12.4 points and 10.6 rebounds per game. The next year, he averaged 14. 4 points and 13.4 rebounds in the 31 games played before the weakened league folded. The Steers were running away with the league when the season ended abruptly and the back line of the Steers was their greatest strength. Both Bridges and Staverman were First Team All League.

Tormohlen signed with the St. Louis Hawks for the remainder of 1962-1963 and averaged just under two points and two rebounds a game for the small amount that he played. He did play with the Hawks, however, for the next four years and averaged four points and four rebounds per game, playing about 12 minutes per game. In May of 1968 he was drafted by the Phoenix Suns in the expansion draft, chose to retire and coach, then was traded back to the Hawks in September 1969. He played just two games before returning to retirement at age 32. Tormohlen was an assistant coach for the Hawks until March of 1976. He was head coach for the last eight games of the 1975-1976 season for the Hawks, going 1–7.

From 1976 to 1982 Tormohlen was an assistant coach and head of scouting for the Chicago Bulls under a number of Bulls head coaches— Dick Motta, Ed Badger, Larry Costello, and Jerry Sloan. In 1982-1983 he was a scout, then took the same position for the Lakers, which he continues to do in a much reduced capacity, focusing on the Southeast.[9]

The starting guards for the Steers were Nick Mantis, a 1959 Northwestern graduate, and Maury King, a 1957 Kansas grad, who was the

Five. The Coaches and the Starting Fives

first African American starter for KU ever. King had served two years in the army following graduation from KU, where he had played one season with Wilt Chamberlain. In 1959 King played one game for the Boston Celtics, who had drafted him in 1957. He played in the Eastern League for two years (1959–1961). King averaged 7.8 points and 3.1 assists (tops on the club) in 1961-1962 for the Steers, then 14.7 points and 5.7 assists in 1962-1963. After the league ended, he immediately went to the Chicago Zephyrs (and coach McMahon) as a free agent to finish that season and averaged 5.8 points and 3.8 assists in 37 games.

King was through with pro basketball but returned to Kansas City, where he was born, raised and continued to live. He worked for Hallmark Cards until 1991, while also doing substitute teaching in the Kansas City schools. He died in 2007 at age 72.[10]

Mantis, from East Chicago, Indiana, was selected on the First Team High School All-American while at Washington High School. He was selected All–Big Ten at Northwestern in 1959. He was drafted by the Hawks, then traded to the Minneapolis Lakers and played in 10 games in 1959-1960, averaging 2.1 points per game. He was drafted by the U.S. Army and served two years before signing with the Steers for 1961-1962 at age 26. He scored 14.6 points per game that year (and was named to the Second Team of the All League team) and then jumped back to the NBA with the Chicago Zephyrs and Coach Jack McMahon for 1962-1963. The Zephyrs had acquired his rights from the Hawks in a September 1962 trade. In 33 games, Mantis averaged 5.9 points, playing just 19 minutes per game. He was not re-signed for the next year. In 1996 he was inducted into the Indiana High School Hall of Fame. He still lives in northwestern Indiana.

Win Wilfong, named team captain by Coach McMahon, also started about half the time and averaged 7.5 points per game in 1961-1962 and 7.3 points per game in 1962-1963. He was a native of Missouri and attended the University of Missouri before transferring for his last two years to Memphis State (now the University of Memphis). He was named MVP of the 1954 NIT tournament, then was drafted by the St. Louis Hawks and joined them after his military service. He averaged 7.8 points for the World Champion Hawks in 1957-1958, playing behind Jack McMahon. He averaged 4.1 in 1958-1959, then was traded to the Royals, where he averaged 10.1 points as a starter. The next year he lost his starting position to Oscar Robertson and averaged 4.6 points in 66 games, sharing a seat on the bench with former Steers teammate, Larry Staverman. Wilfong died in 1985 at age 52.

Los Angeles Jets

The Jets were the initial favorites in the Western Division because of their coach and personnel, but a lack of money, bad venues and poor play doomed the team that folded after 39 games with the second best percentage in the ABL (24–15, .615).

Bill Sharman was named player-coach which set off a legal battle for his services, one he and the ABL eventually won. Sharman had never coached before, but was an obvious student of the game and had been a Celtics star from 1951 (after spending most of 1950–51 with the Washington Capitols, who folded at mid-season) to 1961, helping the Celtics to win four championships.

Sharman went to Cleveland as coach in mid-season after Steinbrenner sacked John McLendon, then coached at Los Angeles State College (now Cal State–Los Angeles) for 1962-1963 and 1963-1964, compiling a 27–20 record. Then he agreed to become an announcer for the St. Louis Hawks and did that for two years. In 1966-1967 he became head coach of the San Francisco Warriors and took them to the NBA Finals where they lost to the 76ers in six games. The next year Rick Barry jumped from the Warriors to the ABA, and San Francisco finished at just 43–39, prompting Sharman to also jump to the ABA and the Los Angeles Stars. He coached them to the ABA Finals in 1969-1970, then moved with the team to Utah in 1970-1971, where Sharman and the Stars won the ABA championship.

Sharman resigned to become the head coach of the Los Angeles Lakers and in his first year (1971-1972) they won a then NBA record 69 games. They then crushed the opposition in the play-offs, dropping only three games in the three series and winning the NBA championship. Sharman is the only man to win championships in three major professional basketball leagues. (Alex Hannum won titles in the ABA and the NBA.) He remained coach of the Lakers through 1975-1976, when he became general manager. In 1982 he became Lakers president, and he retired from that in 1990. He was elected to the Basketball Hall of Fame as a player

Five. The Coaches and the Starting Fives

in 1975 and as a coach in 2004, only the third person to be enshrined in both categories, joining John Wooden and Lenny Wilkins.[11]

STARTING FIVE

Initially Sharman started alongside Hal Lear, who had been a unanimous All-American at Temple, graduating in 1956. Lear was from Philadelphia and the Warriors took him in the first round of the 1956 draft. He appeared in just three games before being dropped and ended up playing mostly in the Eastern League (where he averaged 35 points a game) and working in Philadelphia during the week. He went to Cleveland after the Jets folded, then was traded to Pittsburgh soon afterward. He averaged 13.1 points per game for the three teams in 1961-1962. He played in the Eastern League after that and later became an administrator in Philadelphia. After retirement he moved to Arizona.

The forwards were Yardley and Dan Swartz. Swartz was a rough rebounder and great shooter from Morehead State who had been selected in the fourth round of the 1956 draft by Boston, but was not retained because of being an undersized forward at 6' 4". After military service, Swartz played in the NIBL for the Wichita Vickers in 1959-1960 and was the NIBL MVP. When Wichita dropped from the league, he ended up with the Pipers for 1960-1961, helping them win the NIBL title, then went to the Jets when the ABL began. Swartz was First Team All League as he averaged 24.8 points for the Jets and the Tapers. In 1962-1963 he played in 39 games for the Celtics, averaging 4.5 points per game. He did not play in the play-offs but was a member of the 1963 NBA champions. He played in the Eastern League for a time, before returning to Kentucky, where he had a tobacco allotment and was eager to farm tobacco. Swartz died in 1997 at the age of 62.

Pittsburgh Rens

The Rens were coached by Neil Johnston, an All-Pro center for the Philadelphia Warriors. Johnston was an All-American player at Ohio State who left after sophomore year to pitch for the Philadelphia Phillies in their minor league chain, which he did for three seasons, before signing with the Warriors and basketball for the 1951-1952 season. He scored six points a game in a backup role to Ed Mikan at center, then took over

Abe Saperstein and the American Basketball League

Top Row: Neil Johnson, Jon Cincebox, Connie Hawkins, George Patterson, Jim Palmer, Danny Doyle. Bottom Row: Walt Mangham, Bucky Bolyard, Phil Rollins, Jim McCoy, Lee Patrone.

Pittsburgh Rens team photograph from the Rens program (Courtesy Dolph Briscoe Collection, University of Texas Archives).

at that spot the next year. In 1952-1953 Johnston led the league in scoring, minutes played and free throws made and attempted. The Warriors only won 12 games; they improved to 29 the next year, and Johnston did also, to 24.4 points per game, again leading the league. He led the league the next year before Paul Arizin took over the team scoring in 1955-1956 and Johnston dropped to 22.1 points per game, but the Warriors were NBA champions. He continued to score 20 points per game for two more years before being sidelined for more than half the 1958-1959 season with a knee injury, which ended his career at 29.

Johnston was made the coach of the Warriors for 1959-1960, winning 49 games, then 46 in 1960-1961, but resigned after the season, citing difficulties in getting along with Wilt Chamberlain, the team's star. During the 1961-1962 ABL season, he came back to play five games, averaging 9.8 before deciding that he should not be playing. After the league collapse in the middle of the next season, Johnston coached Wilmington in the Eastern League from 1964 to 1966. He served as an assistant at Wake Forest and as a scout for the Portland Trail Blazers from 1972–1974. He then became athletic director and basketball coach at North Lake Junior College in Irving, Texas, where he died of a heart attack in 1978 at age 49.[12]

Starting Five

The Rens were built around Connie Hawkins. The other starters were Bucky Bolyard, Phil Rollins, Walt Mangham and Jon Cincebox. Bolyard was a 5'11" guard from Aurora, West Virginia, and the University of West Virginia, where he starred in baseball and basketball. He averaged 10 points a game as the other WVU guard with Jerry West. He signed with the Rens for 1961 after going undrafted in 1959. He averaged 16.2 points in 1961-1962, then accepted an assistant coaching position at VMI for 1962-1963. For many years he coached and taught in the California (PA) School District while living in Belle Vernon, Pennsylvania. He was inducted into the WVU Hall of Fame, and a scholarship was later endowed in his name. Bolyard died in 2001 at age 73.

Phil Rollins was a 6'2" guard from Louisville (where he captained the 1956 NIT champions) who was drafted by the Warriors in the second round of the 1956 draft. He was in the service for two years, then played in 25 games for them in 1958-1959 before being traded to the Cincinnati

Royals for Vern Hatten. In 44 games, he averaged 5.2 points and returned to the Royals the next season, where he averaged 5.5 points playing in all 72 games. In November of 1960, shortly after the season began, Rollins was sold to the Hawks, who sold him to the Knicks a month later. In 65 games for the three teams, he averaged 4.5 points per game. Rather than return to the Knicks, Rollins signed with the Rens and averaged 13.8 points per game in 80 games in 1961-1962, as well as leading the team in assists. In 1962-1963 he averaged 13.0 points and 5.0 assists before the league shut down. He returned to the Louisville area and had his jersey retired by the university in 2000.

Jon Cincebox, a 6'7" forward from Syracuse, graduated in 1959 and was drafted in the third round by the Syracuse Nationals, but never played in the NBA. He was with the NIBL's Tuck Tapers for two years, before joining the Rens. He scored 8.9 points in 1961-1962, then left the league. Walt Mangham was not a consistent starter, despite the fact that he was the second best rebounder on the team, averaging 7.3, along with 10.8 points per game. Mangham was a 6'4" forward from Marquette, but hailed from New Castle, Pennsylvania, outside of Pittsburgh. At Marquette, he was also a high jumper, clearing 6'9¾". In 1962-1963 he scored at a 9.6 rate before the league ended. He later became a sales representative in the Pittsburgh region, retiring in 2004.

In 1962-1963 Jim McCoy, who had averaged 6.3 for the 1961-1962 Rens, became a starter and scored at a 15.9 pace, second on the club. He was a 6'1" guard, also from Marquette. Charley Curtis was a 1959 eighth-round pick of the Detroit Pistons and failed to make the team. He had graduated from Pacific Lutheran University and played in semi-pro leagues until signing with the ABL in 1961. He averaged 13.8 points and 7.1 rebounds in 1961-1962, then 13.6 points and 6.7 rebounds in 1962-1963.

San Francisco Saints

The Saints were coached by Phil Woolpert, initially. He had been a player at Loyola of Los Angeles (now Loyola Marymount) under legendary coach Jimmy Needles. A teammate on that squad was Pete Newell, who hired Woolpert as an assistant at the University of San Francisco during his tenure at USF from 1946 to 1950. When Newell

Five. The Coaches and the Starting Fives

moved on to Cal, Woolpert became the head coach at USF from 1950 to 1959. He was blessed to have an awkward, unrecruited player enroll at USF in 1952 named Bill Russell, and the Dons won two national championships under Woolpert. In 1958-1959, USF went 6-20 and Woolpert resigned. He agreed to be coach of the Saints, but resigned after 15 games with a record of 6-9. The next year he became coach of the University of San Diego and kept that position until 1969, when he stepped down, but remained as athletic director through 1972. In his later years he lived in rural Washington, where he drove a school bus, finding it a relaxing alternative to big-time coaching. He was posthumously elected to the Basketball Hall of Fame in 1992, having died in 1987 of lung cancer.

Woolpert was replaced by Kevin O'Shea, the general manager, who filled in for 12 games, going 8-4. O'Shea had graduated from Notre Dame in 1950 where he had been an All-American guard and then the first-round pick of the Lakers in 1950. He played three years with the Lakers, Bullets and Hawks, averaging 5.2 points per game. O'Shea was succeeded by Al Brightman, who finished the season but became the coach of the Long Beach Chiefs for 1962-1963.

Ermer Robinson was the Oakland Oaks coach for 1962-1963, coming from Saperstein's Chicago Majors organization. He had played many years for the Globetrotters. He died in 1982 of cancer.

STARTING FIVE

The Saints were led by Kenny Sears and Mike Farmer, two former NBA players for the Knicks. The other starters were Jim Francis, Whitey Bell and Gene Brown. Brown had played with Farmer at the University of San Francisco, graduating in 1958 as a Third Team All-American. A native of San Francisco, he averaged 9.9 points in 1961-1962, but just 5.0 for the Oakland Oaks in the abbreviated 1962-1963 season. After the league ended, Brown remained in the area, working with young people and law enforcement. He was named sheriff of San Francisco in 1978, but lost his reelection bid in 1979. Previously, he had served in the Department of Justice as civil rights director of the Western States Region of the Small Business Administration.[13]

Jim Francis was the leading scorer and rebounder for the Saints with 19.1 points and 10.4 rebounds per game. He was a rugged 6'8" center/forward who had played at the University of Akron, but never played in the NBA.

William (Whitey) Bell graduated from North Carolina State University in 1954, played in the Eastern League and was in the service before he signed with the New York Knicks in January of 1960 after being cut from the Royals. He had been originally signed by the Hawks, but never played for them, before being traded to Cincinnati in August of 1959. A 6' guard, he scored 5.4 points per game in 31 games, then returned to the Knicks for just five games the next season. In 1961-1962 he scored 12.4 points per game and 4.6 assists per game for the Saints. At the age of 28, he left the pro game.

John Beberich graduated from high school in 1956, then joined the marines and served until 1957. He enrolled at UCLA and played under John Wooden, then was drafted by the St. Louis Hawks in the fifth round of the 1961 NBA draft. He signed with the Saints and played for one year, averaging 10.1 points and 7.4 rebounds per game. Beberich returned to UCLA after the 1961-1962 season and entered a doctoral program in psychology; he received his Ph.D. in 1968 and became a professor of psychology at the University of Washington. He was a police consultant for the Seattle Police and was the first to profile the killer Ted Bundy, who had been a University of Washington student. Beberich died in 2002 at age 64.

The leading Oakland Oak scorer in 1962-1963 was Fred Lacour, who was California's Mr. Basketball in 1955 and 1956, a 1959 graduate of University of San Francisco and had played in the NIBL in 1959-1960. He played for the St. Louis Hawks for two years, averaging 5.6 and 7.8 points per game in 1960-1961 and 1961-1962, respectively. When he was cut by the Hawks, he returned to the Bay Area and played for the Oaks, averaging 19.7 points per game, as a 6'5" guard. After the league folded, Lacour crossed the Bay and played for the Warriors for 16 games, averaging 4.1 points per game. He died in 1972 at the age of 33.

John "Jack" Turner graduated from the University of Louisville in 1961 and was drafted in the second round by the Chicago Packers after averaging 16.1 and 10.6 rebounds per game for his college career. A 6'5", 200-pound forward, Turner played in 42 games for the Packers in 1961-1962 and averaged 4.8 points and 2.0 rebounds, but chose to play with the ABL the next year. With Oakland he averaged 14.9 points and 5.0 rebounds.

Five. The Coaches and the Starting Fives

Jim Hadnot, an All-American from Providence in 1962, was drafted by the Celtics, but failed to make the squad. He had gone to high school in Oakland so he returned to the Bay Area and signed with the Oaks, for whom he scored 14.4 points and gathered 13.4 rebounds per game. He opened a tavern and liquor store in 1963, which he maintained in Berkeley and Oakland until 1976. When the ABA began in 1967 he played for the Oakland franchise and scored 17.5 points and 12.2 rebounds per game. A 6'10" center, he surely could have stayed in the game, but decided to concentrate on his business enterprises. He was a scout for the NBA's Sacramento Kings and New Jersey Nets from 1987 to 1997 and died in 1998 at age 54.

Rolland Todd was from Visalia, California, and played at Fresno State, graduating in 1957. After graduating he played for AAU teams, the Peoria Cats and the Seattle Buchan Bakers, and was invited to the Olympic Trials for the Rome games. He signed with the Saints for 1961–1962 and averaged 8.2 points per game, then improved that the next year as a starter for the Oaks. He scored 14.1 points per game in 24 league games.

Todd moved into coaching, starting at Riverside College, then Cal State Los Angeles and then head coach at the University of Nevada–Las Vegas (then called Nevada Southern) from 1966 to 1970. He was named the first coach of the expansion Portland Trail Blazers of the NBA in 1970 and they went 29–53. He was fired in his second year with the team at 12–44. He coached in Sweden in 1975, then was coach at Santa Ana College from 1975–1982 and Taft Community College in Kern County, California, from 1982–1986.[14] He founded Todd Coaching LLC in 1986, which continues to operate as a coaching consultancy service.

Wayne Yates was the first-draft pick of the Los Angeles Lakers in 1961 out of Memphis State University. A rugged 6'8", 240 pounder, Yates played 37 games with the Lakers that year and averaged 1.9 points and 2.5 rebounds per game in 37 games. Traded to the St. Louis Hawks the next year, he instead played with the Oaks and averaged 10.1 points and 8.7 rebounds before he league ended. The next year he failed to make the Knicks after reporting to their pre-season camp. Instead, he returned to Memphis and in 1969 became an assistant to Head Coach Moe Iba, who was replaced the next year by Gene Bartow, who retained Yates. When Bartow left for UCLA, Yates became head coach and remained in that position until February of 1979. He had a record of 111–49. After a year out of coaching, he was hired at Northwestern Louisiana for the 1980-1981 season and remained there until the end of the 1985 season when he resigned; he was 48–67 in the five years.

Washington Tapers

The first coach of the Tapers was Stan Stutz (*né* Modzelewski), who had played college ball at Rhode Island State (now just URI) and was an All-American in his three last varsity years (1940–1942). He was College Player of the Year and led the nation in scoring. He played in the last years of the old ABL for the Baltimore Bullets in 1943-1944 and played there through 1946. He joined the Knicks of the newly formed BAA in 1946, played there two years, then one year for Baltimore of the BAA. He then refereed in the NBA from 1950-1959 before becoming the coach of the Tapers of the NIBL in 1959. He died of a heart attack in 1975.[15]

When the ABL began, Harry Lynn, owner of the Uline Arena and the Washington franchise, hired Elmer Ripley as coach, but when Paul Cohen bought 50 percent of the franchise, he installed Stutz before the season began. Stutz also served as a vice president and sales manager of Technical Tape Company, sponsor of the Tuck Tapers. The mid-season move to Long Island didn't help attendance, and the next year, Cohen, who had purchased Lynn's share of the team, started the season in Philadelphia with a new coach, Mario Perri. Perri was the athletic director for Technical Tape Company and led the Tapers to a 10–18 record in the shortened season.

STARTING FIVE

The Tapers started a variety of lineups because of the frequent trading in the league, but their core in 1961-1962 was Roger Kaiser, Sylvester Blye, Roger Taylor, Jack Adams, Ron Zagar and Dan Swartz, the latter four all obtained in trades or the reentry draft. Kaiser was the most heralded, initially, after being a First Team All-American at Georgia Tech in 1960-1961. Drafted by Chicago in the fourth round in 1961, he chose to sign with the Tapers for more money. A sharpshooting, 6'1" guard from Dale, Indiana, Kaiser averaged 19.4 points and led the Tapers in

Five. The Coaches and the Starting Fives

1961-1962 with 72 three-pointers. In 1962-1963 he scored 17.2 points and 25 three-pointers in 27 games.

Kaiser worked for Technical Tape in the Southeast for a number of years after the league ended. He had vowed not to become a coach, but then agreed to coach the University of West Georgia in 1970 and remained there for 20 years, winning the NAIA national championship in 1974. In 1990 he was recruited to start a new program at Life College (now Life University) in Marietta, Georgia. Kaiser led them to NAIA national titles in 1997, 1999 and 2000. In 2012 the NAIA celebrated 75 years of national championships by naming an All-Star team with 60 players and 15 coaches, of whom Kaiser was one of the latter. He retired from coaching in 2000 but remained as athletic director until 2010.

Taylor, an All-American at the University of Illinois, was drafted by Syracuse in the fifth round of the 1959 draft. Instead of going to the NBA, Taylor went with the NIBL and the San Francisco Investors, then played the next year with the Cleveland Pipers. He joined the Washington Tapers after being traded by Cleveland, along with Jack Adams, for Connie Dierking. Taylor fit in well, finishing the year with a 15.7 average, but the team leader in assists with 323. The next season, Taylor scored 12.6 points per game in 28 games. Adams, who had gone undrafted out of Eastern Kentucky, was a 6' 4" guard/forward, who played for the Peoria Cats in the NIBL before joining the Pipers, then the Tapers. He averaged 13.6 points for 1961-1962.

Ron Zagar was a 5'10" guard who went undrafted out of Iowa in 1960, played AAU ball for a year, then signed with Chicago for 1961-1962. He came to the Tapers in the deal for Tony Jackson. Zagar averaged 11.7 points and was second on the team with 52 three-pointers.

The biggest signee by the Tapers was Gene Conley, because of his fame as a pitcher for the Boston Red Sox as well as a 6' 8" backup center for the Boston Celtics. Conley only played in 45 games and averaged 8.2 points and 7.0 rebounds per game. After the ABL's first season, Conley, who had been drafted by the Packers in the NBA expansion draft, then traded to the Knicks by Chicago, played two years for New York, averaging 9.0 and 4.2 points per game for the two years. He also played just two more years for the Red Sox, going 15–14 in 1962, then 3–4 in 1963. Paul Cohen hired him for Technical Tape, and later Conley and his wife started a small paper products compay.[16]

Bruce Spraggins, a 6'6" guard/forward from Virginia Union, scored 8.5 points in 1961-1962 for the Tapers, then became a starter in 1962-1963 and averaged 13.1 in 27 games. He had been drafted in the fifth round of the NBA draft by the Philadelphia Warriors, but signed with Washington. Spraggins played in the Eastern League (and worked for Technical Tape) after the ABL collapsed, then joined the ABA in its first year (1967-1968), playing for the New Jersey Americans. He scored 12.2 points and had 4.7 rebounds per game in 70 games. He worked and bought a sporting goods store in Harlem (Appletown Sporting Goods), which he still co-owned as of 2012. That same year he was inducted into the Central Intercollegiate Athletic Association (CIAA) Hall of Fame.

Bill Chmielewski was the center of controversy when he signed with the ABL's Tapers before his class graduated. He had already left school because he needed money to support his wife and child, so the ABL allowed him to play in 1962-1963. Chmielewski was a 6'10" center from Dayton who had been the MVP of the NIT in 1962 when Dayton had won the tournament. After averaging 10.4 points and 7.4 rebounds for the Tapers, Chmeliewski taught school, worked for Ford (he was from Detroit) and tried out for both the Cincinnati Royals and Detroit Pistons before being the last player cut each time. He then turned to being an electrician, which he was for the next 40 years.

The ABL was a great training ground for many players and coaches, although very few ever saw big bucks in their basketball enterprises. They had a great love of the game and wanted to stay with it as long as they could. Many were successful in business, but almost all continued to play in some capacity until they physically were unable to do.

Six

Chicago, Battleground of the ABL and the NBA

Chicago, the nation's second largest city, had not been kind to pro basketball. In the tax court of 1970, in fact, Chicago was referred to as the "graveyard" of professional basketball.[1] The first national professional league was the American Basketball League of 1925–1931. One of the charter franchises was the Chicago Bruins, owned by George Halas, the owner of the Chicago Bears football team. The team did well enough for Halas to keep it in the league, but the Depression brought the entire league down.

Then in 1935, a new league was formed, mostly in the Midwest, called, eponymously, the Midwest Basketball Conference. The league was very loosely organized with no standardized number of games played and the play-offs created at the last moment of the league year. A late entrant was the Chicago Duffy Florals, named, as many of the teams were, after sponsors or the companies that the team owners also controlled. Most teams played a dozen league games; the Duffy Florals played five, going three and two. Despite not meeting the initial minimum number of games set for play-off qualification, the Duffy Florals did enter the play-offs where they defeated the Akron Firestones in round 1 (one game) and then the Indianapolis Kautskys in the championship game to claim the Midwest title.[2]

The next year, the league was only slightly more organized, and the Duffy Florals seemed to lose interest as the league season neared an end and stopped playing league teams. They did not get chosen for the play-offs. The next year (1937-1938), when the Midwest Conference reorganized and became the National Basketball League (NBL), no Chicago entry was part of the league. The NBL operated on the proverbial shoestring in its first years because of the difficult economic times. Almost all of the players had "real" jobs and used the NBL to supplement incomes and satisfy their need for competitive basketball. Most also were college graduates, a first for any professional basketball league, and for most professional sports leagues of the time.

In 1939 George Halas decided to try again with a team, retaining the name "Chicago Bruins" for his entry in the National Basketball League. Using the proven formula of signing players with local connections, the Bruins ended up with a roster dominated by Chicago-area high school stars, who had gone on to star for Chicago colleges. Of the Bruin starting five, two were products of DePaul University and two from Loyola University. The latter two were Wibs Kautz, a 6' guard, and Mike Novak, a 6'9" center with a good outside shooting touch. The two had led Loyola to second place in the 1939 NIT tournament, losing to undefeated Long Island University, as Loyola lost its only game of the year.

The Bruins played at the 132nd Armory, accessible from a number of bus lines and the Lake Street elevated stop at California and Lake. A number of games at the World Basketball Tournaments were played there from 1939 to 1948. The venue seated over 6,000, and the Bruins' games were well covered by the media. The team finished at 14–14, a game out of the play-offs, but had good attendance of 2,500 to 4,000 at each home game. In the World Tournament, played on their home floor, the Bruins ended up in the championship game in 1940 but lost 31–29 to the Harlem Globetrotters before a packed house.[3]

In 1940 the Bruins added more local talent in Ray Adams and Vince McGowan, both DePaul cagers in the 1930s, and Bill Hapac of Chicago Heights, who had played at the University of Illinois. Despite these additions, the Bruins finished 11–13 in the league and missed the play-offs by a half-game. Nevertheless, they continued to draw well.

The next season, 1941-1942, was instrumental in the Chicago reputation of being a graveyard for pro basketball teams. First, the Bruins lost many of their players to the war effort, then they lost their court to war training and had to play at another venue (the Chicago Coliseum) just south of downtown with fewer seats and transportation choices. On top of that the team record fell to 8–15, and the crowds stayed away in droves. Halas gave up the franchise after the season.

Six. Chicago, Battleground of the ABL and the NBA

In 1942-1943 the NBL shrank to four teams, and one, the Chicago Studebakers, was unique in being the first integrated pro basketball team in a recognized national league. The team was sponsored/owned by the United Auto Workers, and all of the players worked at the huge Studebaker defense plant on the south side of Chicago. The squad did not play well and finished, again, at 8–15 and played at four different home venues, making games hard to find, even for devoted fans. Not surprisingly the team did not draw well, and the franchise folded after the end of the season.[4]

In 1944, Maurice White decided to form another team and purchased an NBL franchise, as that league expanded to six teams in 1944-1945. The team was called the Chicago American Gears, after his company of the same name. The team was led by two rookies from Chicago schools, Stan Patrick from Illinois and Dick Triptow from DePaul. They played in the Chicago Coliseum, but drew better than the Bruin team had in that venue. The team finished 14–16, making the play-offs since four of the six teams qualified. The next year the Gears went 17–17, playing in Cicero Stadium, and missed the play-offs. They still were invited to the World Professional Tournament in Chicago Stadium, and Maurice White signed George Mikan, the top player in college basketball, immediately after his last college game at DePaul, so that he could join the Gears for the tournament. With Mikan, the Gears went to the semi-finals of the tournament, drawing more than 12,000 fans to the semi-final contests.[5]

Mikan had a contract dispute with White and missed much of the next season (1946-1947), but returned in time to lead Chicago to the play-offs, as the Gears went 26–18 in the 12-team league. They then swept through the play-offs, but were unable to play in the World Tournament because it overlapped the NBL play-offs. Still, the Gears drew well and looked to be powerful for years to come with Mikan, Triptow, Patrick, Bruce Hale and player-coach Bobby McDermott. Instead, Maurice White pulled his team from the league to try and start his own league, which failed in three weeks, taking down the Chicago Gears with it. The players were redistributed in the league, and Chicago lost its NBL team.[6]

That same season a new league, the Basketball Association of America, began, and Chicago had an entry in the league, the Stags, playing in Chicago Stadium, the best venue in the city. The Stags won the Western

Division with a 39–22 record, but lost in the league finals to the Philadelphia Warriors. The Stags did not draw well but survived for another year (1947-1948), as the league went from 11 to 8 teams. They managed to remain semi-solvent in 1948-1949, then to become one of the original 17 teams that became the National Basketball Association (NBA) in 1949-1950, when the BAA and NBL merged. The league lasted just a year as six teams dropped out, including Chicago, leaving the NBA with 11 teams for 1950-1951. Despite their success on the court (the Stags went 40–28 their last year under coach Phil Brownstein), they simply did not draw. Seymour Smith, the basketball reporter for the *Baltimore Morning Sun* at that time, recalled covering Baltimore Bullet–Chicago Stag games in Chicago Stadium where fewer than 2,000 fans showed up.[7] The losses were too much to sustain.

So from March 1950, when the Stags lost their play-off series to the Minneapolis Lakers, two games to zero, Chicago was bereft of a professional basketball team. Nevertheless, there was no dispute that Chicago was a great basketball town. Illinois high school basketball was one of the tops in the nation, although it took until 1958 when Marshall High School took the state title for a Chicago team to win the state championship.[8] Many Chicago high school players went on to college fame, and the colleges in the Chicago area had top teams and drew large crowds. These included DePaul, coached by Ray Meyer, and Loyola, coached by George Ireland. Bradley University, 100 miles south in Peoria, coached by Chuck Osborne, made frequent visits to Chicago Stadium for sold-out college doubleheaders.

It was apparent that Chicago fans would support basketball, but would they support *pro* basketball, particularly a team that was not an instant winner? Abe Saperstein was betting that with a better kind of play, that is, not as much scoring with little defense, as he saw in the NBA, his team and league could succeed in the Chicago market. The NBA hoped that their time had finally come in Chicago in 1961, and they selected a group headed by insurance executive Dave Trager as the ones to foster pro basketball excitement in the city.

The Packers

The NBA decided to expand in 1959, and the obvious place, it seemed, was the largest city in the country without an NBA franchise,

Six. Chicago, Battleground of the ABL and the NBA

Chicago. There were a number of Chicago groups that put forth bids for the new franchise. "Group after group was screened for the Selection committee and after thorough investigation and sifting of qualifications an organization headed by insurance company executive David Trager was awarded the franchise, but only after 15 months of negotiations."[9]

Dave Trager was a longtime Chicago sportsman and businessman who was president of Associated Life Insurance, a company no longer in existence, but known by some as the insurer of the Teamsters Union, then headed by Jimmy Hoffa. Trager had been involved with a number of businesses as well as promoting boxing and wrestling shows. A cigar almost always in his mouth (and not often lit), he was friendly to everyone and an inveterate talker.

Trager's syndicate involved six other Chicago businessmen. Club vice presidents were Sam Karlov, who owned a large roofing company, and Charlie Lubin, the president of Sara Lee Kitchens, a much smaller firm than today's conglomerate.[10] The secretary was Morrie Goldman, chairman of the board of Trager's Associated Life Insurance Company. The treasurer was Will Chulock, a certified public accountant (CPA) and partner in an independent accounting firm. The last two partners and board members were both prominent Chicago realtors, Henry Mann and Arthur Ludwig.

The NBA entry fee for the franchise was $250,000, and the partners put in another $250,000 in salaries, rental of the International Amphitheater and travel expenses, plus advertising. Initially, the Packers hoped to

Dave Trager, owner of the Chicago Packers (author collection).

Abe Saperstein and the American Basketball League

draw at least 5,000 per game, but the allure would be the rest of the NBA, rather than the Packers themselves. There was no question that the team would be weak; the unknown was how weak and whether that would repel fans rather than attract them to the struggling franchise.

The method of stocking the team was to give the new franchise the number one pick in the 1961 NBA draft, then have them draft in each subsequent round. At that time the NBA had as many as 15 rounds of drafting for the eight, soon to be nine, teams. Few teams had more than a scout or two, and lots of players were drafted that had never been seen by the teams. They were drafted on media reputation or the advice of college coaches. In addition to the college draft, there was a league pool from which the Chicago franchise could select players for their roster. Each of the eight teams was allowed to protect seven players from their roster, and the new franchise could select players from the unprotected players. No team could lose more than two players. There would be slim pickings.

The Packers and the Majors both ended up with Walter Bellamy as their number one college pick (the Majors in a trade with the Pipers), and both tried hard to sign him. Bellamy was a 6'11" All-American center from Indiana University who had been an integral member of the 1960 gold medal team at the Rome Olympics. Bellamy was a rebounding fiend at Indiana, garnering a record 649 his senior year at IU, a record that still stands. He had 33 in one game (a Big Ten record) and averaged 21 points and 16 rebounds per game for his three-year college career (freshmen were not eligible for varsity play at that time).

Bellamy's rookie status was the rule rather than the exception for the team. Of the 13 players on the roster in November, six were rookies, an extraordinary number. Of those six, only one, Horace Walker, averaged more than five points per game in his only NBA season. The Packers selected two players who became starters for them, Andy Johnson, who had averaged 9.5 points per game for the Philadelphia Warriors, averaged 14.3 points per game for the Packers. Bob Leonard had once been a starter for the Lakers, but at 31, his playing time had declined markedly. He had a resurgence with the Packers, averaging 16 points per game. Three of the Packers' three selections from the NBA restocking, Archie Dees, Vern Hatton and Barney Cable, were traded to the St. Louis Hawks 15 games into the season, setting off a league protest. In an agreement that the

Six. Chicago, Battleground of the ABL and the NBA

Packers made with the league in January of 1961, they agreed not to trade any of their players obtained in the special NBA draft without first securing the approval of four of the seven teams not involved in the proposed transaction. Subsequently, the deal was approved, both by the teams and league commissioner Maurice Podoloff, but it illustrated the continued difficulty that the expansion franchise would have.[11] In return for those players the Packers received Sihugo Green, Joe Graboski and Woody Sauldsberry. Graboski was later moved to Syracuse, but Sauldsberry and Green averaged 10.7 and 12.7 points per game. Lest one see the Packers as an offensive machine since all five of their starters, plus the sixth man, Ralph Davis, averaged in double figures, context must be considered. The Packers averaged 111 points per game, *last* in the league, a full five points behind the next lowest-

Chicago Packers at training camp, fall 1961. Standing, left to right, are: Dave Trager (president), Horace Walker, Bob McNeill, Dave Voss, Vern Hatton, Bob Leonard, Ralph Davis, Roger Kaiser, Howie Carl, Jim Pollard (coach); kneeling: Andy Johnson, Barney Cable, Walt Bellamy, George Bon Salle, Charlie Tyra, Archie Dees, John Turner. Roger Kaiser was drafted by the Packers, but starred for the Washington/New York/Philadelphia Tapers. Charlie Tyra played for the Pittsburgh Rens in 1962–1963. Archie Dees played for the Cleveland Pipers in 1961-1962. John Turner played for the Oakland Oaks in 1962-1963. (author collection).

scoring team, the Knicks. The Packers also gave up 119.4 points per game, which put them in the middle of the pack, but their point differential of -8.5 was five points worse than the next team, the Knicks with -4.9 points per game. The NBA was a run-and-gun league with defense an afterthought. Four teams averaged more than 120 points per game, and it was this lack of defense that Saperstein hoped to exploit with the ABL, offering a better game, so he felt.

The Packers selected Jim Pollard, former Minneapolis Lakers star (1947–1955) to coach the team. Pollard had coached LaSalle College for two years and the Lakers in 1960 for 39 games (he was 14–25), but he was working in sales in Minneapolis when the Packers hired him.

As discussed earlier, the best venue in the city was Chicago Stadium, but that was secured by the ABL franchise Chicago Majors, mostly because Saperstein and his Globetrotters brought in sellout crowds to the stadium as many as ten times a year. Immediately upon the awarding of the franchise and creation of the league in March 1961, Saperstein began negotiating for the use of Chicago Stadium.[12] So the Chicago NBA team contracted with the International Amphitheatre at 42nd and Halsted as their home venue. The facility was located next to the enormous Union Stockyards, and the site was the home of the National Stock Show and many other exhibitions like ice shows, circuses, horse shows and basketball games. One positive was parking, since the team claimed that "the Amphitheater has better parking facilities than any other indoor auditorium in the city."[13] The Packers also extolled the great visibility of the site and that it could seat 9,000 fans for basketball (not that they ever drew that many). As for the visibility, it was not impeded by pillars or overhangs, but the court was set up in the middle of the enormous arena and there were very few seats close to the court itself. All in all, it was a good place for a stock show, and the odor of the stockyards was often lingering before, during and after games.

The NBA had a poor record of obtaining and keeping national television contracts. Ratings and, subsequently, revenues were not good. Thus, it was a coup for the league to have a one-year contract with NBC to have 17 games shown on national television, all on Saturday afternoons. The Packers managed to secure an additional local contract with WGN-Channel 9 in Chicago to have 10 games shown on Saturday nights. It was minimal exposure, but it was hoped that seeing the Packers on

Six. Chicago, Battleground of the ABL and the NBA

television would draw more fans to live contests. It may have had the opposite effect, however.

The NBA schedule did no favors to the Packers either. In their first 40 games, the Packers went 9–31, but of the 40 games, only 12 were at home. The Packers lost $150,000 in the first half of the season. Part of that was the schedule since NBA home teams kept the entire gate. In addition the weather was poorer than usual, according to Dave Trager. Needing 54,000 fans to break even, the Packers only attracted 40,457, an average of 3,371 per game.[14]

The rest of the season was not much better, as the Packers duplicated their 9–31 record to end up 18–62 for the year. Attendance improved only slightly, and, like all NBA teams, there were "home" games played elsewhere, such as at DePaul's Alumni Hall where 2,981 fans saw the Syracuse Nationals play the Packers; Moline, Illinois, on March 4 where the Detroit Pistons met the Packers; and Green Bay, Wisconsin,, where the Pistons played the Packers on March 12. The Packers lost close to $300,000 in 1961-1962.

The Majors

As noted earlier, the Chicago franchise was not, initially, going to be run by Saperstein, but once he was in charge of it, he used his Globetrotters as a kind of farm team, and the league saw no problem with that. The Globetrotters were the only sure moneymaker that the ABL was able to use consistently, and all teams were able to have the Trotters as part of a doubleheader, at least two or three times during the season.

The Majors failed to sign Walt Bellamy, whom they had obtained in a trade with Cleveland for Henry Whitney of Iowa State, a territorial pick, and their roster was somewhat fluid throughout the season, due to trades, bringing up players from the Globetrotters' roster and the signing of free agents. In May the drafted list of the Majors had 23 players; 7 ended up playing at least a game for the Majors. One interesting draftee was Manny Jackson from the University of Illinois and the current Globetrotters owner.[15] As of June 1961, the Majors had signed contracts from seven players, five of whom were with them on opening day. There were 19 others on their "negotiating list."[16] A few did end up with the Majors—

John Wessels of Ilinois, Ron Zagar of Iowa and Sam Barnard of Iowa State. One ended up with the Packers, Howie Carl of DePaul.[17]

The season started with excitement for the team and the fans. The Majors lost to the Pittsburgh Rens in Pittsburgh on November 7, but 13,817 attended since the Globetrotters were the preliminary game of the doubleheader. The L.A. Jets then met the Majors in Chicago, defeating them 121–106. Herb Lee led Chicago with 20 points, and Kelly Coleman grabbed 12 rebounds. The Majors finally picked up a win on November 12, defeating Hawaii, 105 to 97. Ron Zagar had 26 and Bob Wilkinson 25 for the Majors. This was part of a doubleheader in Kansas City, with the Steers meeting the Jets in game two. Unfortunately, only 1,869 fans attended.[18]

The Majors played the Los Angeles Jets the next night in Muskegon, Michigan, one of their many "home" games not in Chicago Stadium. A good crowd of over 5,000 saw the Majors top the Jets, 97–87, led by Ron Zagar's 22 points. Lee, Coleman and Govoner Vaughn each had 13.[19]

Playing before over 12,000 in Chicago Stadium on November 17, 1961, the Majors rallied to top the San Francisco Saints, 94–91. The Harlem Globetrotters played game 1 of a doubleheader. Herb Lee led the Majors with 23 points, Jackie Fitzpatrick had 19 and Bob Wilkinson had 18.[20] Two weeks later Lee was traded to Hawaii for George Price.

The next week, the Majors' owner, in his role as ABL commissioner, announced that the All-Star Game would be in Pittsburgh in February and that he saw the ABL succeeding.[21]

The Majors went on their first Hawaiian trip in late November where they lost twice to Hawaii, dropped Joe Scott from their roster, picked up Tony Wilcox from the Globetrotters while giving them Mel Davis, and made the Lee-for-Price trade. They also drew less than 2,500 for each of their games in Hawaii, which turned out to be about average for that venue.

The Majors played another doubleheader in the Chicago Stadium in early December, but it was four ABL teams, rather than a game involving the Globetrotters, and the attendance was much different. The Jets, the Rens, the Pipers and the Majors only attracted 1,500 fans to the Stadium. Chicago was led by Herschell Turner (22 points), who had been discharged from the U.S. Army on November 23 and began play immediately for the Majors.[22]

Six. Chicago, Battleground of the ABL and the NBA

After a loss in Kansas City, 97 to 89, on December 10, the Majors were last in the Eastern Division of the ABL with a record of 8–14. Cleveland's Pipers led at 13–9.[23] The Majors stayed in town and were part of another ABL doubleheader three nights later. The Pipers topped the Majors, 117–95, in game 1 with Kansas City, running their win streak to eight with a victory over Pittsburgh. A crowd of 3,100 fans turned out for the games and saw some top offensive play by Connie Hawkins of the Rens (34 points), Nick Mantis of the Steers (34 points) and John Barnhill of the Pipers (39 points).[24] The same four teams all traveled to Pittsburgh for another doubleheader that saw Kansas City beat Cleveland and the Rens defeat Chicago, 119–106. The Majors were led by Ron Zagar (25) and Jack Fitzpatrick (17).[25] These games drew 3,692, not great, but as good as many NBA games of the period and enough to break even or show a modest profit.

Hawaii, in the midst of a long mainland road trip, rolled into Chicago and beat the Majors, 95–88, in mid–December. Attendance was 3,321, but the Majors were led by Nat "Sweetwater" Clifton, former Knick and Globetrotter, who was back shuttling between the Globies and the Majors at age 39. He had 20 points. This was part of an ABL doubleheader that featured Pittsburgh and Kansas City in the opener.[26] Following the games, the Chiefs and Majors teams then motored to Milwaukee where the Majors topped the Chiefs, 96–91, before just 1,500 paying customers. Hawaii was led in scoring by former Major, Herb Lee, with 20, and Chicago got 18 from Turner, 17 from Zagar and Clifton.

Two nights later the Majors played in Rockford, Illinois, before 900 and lost to the Pipers, 99–94.[27] The two squads met in Chicago the next night and played before 1,872, with the Majors beating the Pipers, 99–84. Then they boarded the train and went to Cleveland, where they met the next night, with Chicago winning again, 113–112. Kelly Coleman had 31 for the Majors, while Herschell Turner had 21. Continuing a tedious trip, the Majors moved on to Pittsburgh and defeated the Rens the next night, 102–89, before 3,813.[28]

The Majors spent an extra night in Pittsburgh, then played the Rens again on Christmas Eve, losing to the Rens, 100–86, before 2,986. Zagar (21) and Vaughn (15) were high for Chicago, with Hawkins leading Pittsburg with 30. Four nights later the two teams met in Pittsburgh again, with the Majors pounding the Rens, despite 32 from Hawkins and 20 from Bucky Bolyard. Coleman had 27 to lead the Majors. The next night the two squads met in Detroit's Olympia Stadium before 6,000. Hawkins scored 31 and Phil Rollins had 28, while Wessells had 23 for Chicago.[29]

The Majors traveled back to Chicago and hosted the Washington Tapers on December 30, a Saturday night, a game that drew 5,163, a good crowd for the Majors and the league. Two nights before, the Chicago Packers had played in Detroit and drawn 4,803 for the NBA contest.[30]

Chicago lost at Cleveland, then were edged in Kansas City a night later. They returned to Chicago and beat the Jets, 105–89. Fitzpatrick (20), Turner (18) and Leroy Gibson (18) were the high scorers for Chicago. There were 2,352 fans at the Chicago Stadium for the contest.[31]

Early in January, the Majors obtained Tony Jackson from the Tapers in return for Ron Zagar. The Majors also got Hank Whitney (an original draft pick) when the Los Angeles Jets folded, and the Majors went on to tie for the best record in the Eastern Division in the second half of the season. The crowds, however, failed to materialize, except when the Globetrotters were part of a doubleheader. The Majors lost around $150,000 for the season.

Between the two teams in Chicago, nearly $500,000 was lost in 1961-1962. The battle for Chicago continued the next season, but the ABL demise at the end of 1962 made it look like the Packers, now being called the Zephyrs, had won. The disappearance of the Majors seemed to do little to improve the fortunes of the Zephyrs, who were now playing at the Chicago Coliseum and continued their losing ways, going 25–55, after their initial 18–62. At the end of the year the team announced that it was moving to Baltimore for the 1963-1964 season. Both the Majors and the Packers/Zephyrs lost the battle. In three years the NBA would try Chicago once again, to better results in the long run.

Seven

The 1961-1962 Season (First Half)

The details of the 1961-62 season illustrate the excitement that most of the venues and franchises had as the season began, and the swift lack of interest that came about in a number of the cities, except for the occasional injection of tension or joy brought about by the inclusion of the Globetrotters in a doubleheader or the rarely successful efforts at hyping a big game between two top teams. The excitement of basketball should not obscure the tension present in the world at this time of the Cold War, especially in the divided city of Berlin. On the same day that the ABL season began, American and Russian tanks faced off across the Berlin dividing line, less than 300 yards apart. One slip and war might ensue.[1]

On November 6, the U.S. Post Office issued a new stamp honoring James Naismith, the inventor of basketball; it was hoped that this was an auspicious sign for the new basketball league. The rosters for the teams were set on opening day, but trades and roster changes occurred early on, altering the various rosters and lending an initial air of instability to the teams. Building a solid fan base would necessitate having a winning team, but also players that the fans could both identify and embrace. The changes in personnel made the latter requirement challenging for a number of franchises. The most volatile roster would be that of the Chicago Majors, which owner and league commissioner Abe Saperstein would use as a farm team for his Globetrotter teams (or it might have been vice versa; either way there was a lot of movement).

For most of the teams the season would start about November 1,

Abe Saperstein and the American Basketball League

but two teams would begin the season earlier, probably because of venue conflicts. Thus, the initial game of the American Basketball League was played on October 27, 1961, at the San Francisco Civic Auditorium, where the Saints entertained the Los Angeles Jets. The Jets roster, at least their starting five, looked quite formidable. The guards were former Temple All-American Hal Lear, who had been the Most Outstanding Player in the 1956 NCAA Tournament, where he scored 160 points in five games, and Bill Sharman, the Jets' player-coach, who had been an All-Pro with the Boston Celtics. Forwards were former NBA All-Pro George Yardley, the first to score 2,000 points in an NBA season, and Dan Swartz, former top-scorer of the National Industrial Basketball League. The center was 7'1" Bill Spivey, former All-American from Kentucky in the early 1950s, blacklisted by the NBA for supposedly shaving points.

The Saints were led by two former New York Knicks teammates, Kenny Sears from Santa Clara and Mike Farmer from the University of San Francisco. Gene Brown, Farmer's teammate at USF, was at one guard, with Whitey Bell at the other. The center was Jim Francis.

In a tight game, the Saints edged the Jets, 99–96, before 5,137.[2] In this game the first three-point shots in a regular-season professional basketball game were made. Three were by Farmer, two by Yardley and one by Larry Friend of the Jets, a former Boston Celtic. It appears that Farmer or Yardley made the first one.[3] The Jets had come into the contest having won four straight in pre-season, a reflection of Spivey joining the team for that run. The game was telecast live in Los Angeles on KTTV. Overall, the high scorers were Farmer with 26 for the Saints and Yardley with 23 for the Jets. The complete box score is below.

San Francisco (99)

	G	FT	P	TP
Bell	4	3–5	4	21
Brown	4	0–0	4	8
Farmer	10	3–3	3	26
Francis	5	2–3	5	12
Sears	1	2–2	0	4
Gunther	10	3–3	2	23
Beberich	2	1–1	4	5
Theus	0	0–0	0	0
Tolen	0	0–0	0	0
Totals	41	14–17	20	99

Seven. The 1961–1962 Season (First Half)

Los Angeles

	G	FT	P	TP
Swartz	5	2–4	3	12
Yardley	9	3–4	2	23
Spivey	8	4–6	2	20
Lear	7	3–5	4	17
Sharman	6	2–2	2	14
Whitney	2	3–4	1	7
Friend	1	0–0	0	3
Blue	0	0–0	0	0
Totals	38	17–25	14	96

Score by Quarters

San Francisco	26	29	27	17	–99
Los Angeles	22	25	34	15	–96

3 pt. FG-Yardley 2, Friend 1, Farmer 3.

For a number of teams, the ABL was the opportunity to show that they had a strong basketball heritage and could support a new pro franchise reflecting that heritage. A good example was the Pittsburgh Rens. First, their name was a paean to the great New York Renaissance team that had begun in the 1920s and passed from existence after finishing the 1948–49 season in the National Basketball League (NBL) season as the Dayton Rens.[4] Second, Pittsburgh had been a franchise in a number of prior leagues including the NBL; its forerunner, the Midwest Conference; the Basketball Association of America (BAA); and various western Pennsylvania pro leagues at the early part of the 20th century. In addition, the Pittsburgh Leondi club was one of the top African American squads in the 1920s. So Pittsburgh had a tradition and a strong interest in basketball history. They also had a new arena, the Civic Auditorium, constructed that year, in which to play, and this venue was seen as a real key to attracting and retaining fans. The owners, Lenny, Archie and Dane Litman and Edward O. (Sparky) Adams had been contacted by Saperstein at the suggestion of Al Abrams, the sports editor of the *Pittsburgh Post-Gazette*, and the new owners were excited about making Pittsburgh a respected, big-league basketball town.[5]

The *Pittsburgh Post-Gazette* ran a series profiling the players, starting in October and ending in November. The pieces were written by the paper's beat reporter for the ABL, Jimmy Miller. The one on Walt Mangham indicated some reasons why he was signed by the Rens: he was a local from New Castle, Pennsylvania; had starred at Marquette; and could really jump since he still held the national high school high jump record of 6' 9½".[6]

The opening exhibition for the team was held at Butler High School in Butler, about 35 miles north of Pittsburgh, because the Civic Auditorium was already booked, but there were 2,000 fans who made their way there and saw the Rens win an exhibition game, 97–92, over the Hawaii Chiefs on November 4, 1961. The game was also televised locally, and there was great anticipation of the opening of the season. Two nights later the Rens played their opener at the Auditorium (in later years called the Arena and the Igloo) and defeated the Chiefs before a crowd of 6,236 by a score of 87–82. That game featured the Four Freshmen, a popular, nationally known singing group as well as girl cheerleaders. Owners Litman, and others were pleased with the crowd, but sought even larger attendance by adding more entertainment at game 2 on November 7. There was a second game, pitting the Harlem Globetrotters against their usual foils, the Washington Generals, and the Cab Calloway Review at halftime of the Rens' game. A total of 13,817 fans were attracted to this doubleheader, and the Rens beat the Chicago Majors, 105–90, as part of the entertainment. The fans also could not help but notice that 19-year-old Connie Hawkins was a great player, perhaps the best in the league. He played 27 minutes in the game and scored 27 points.[7]

The Rens then took to the road, illustrating two patterns of the ABL, the playing of league games in non-league cities and the use of buses for travel, rather than planes. The Rens left at 11 a.m. for Washington, where they played the Majors as part of a doubleheader, with the Washington Tapers hosting the Hawaii Chiefs in the second game. Game 1 saw the Rens lose to the Majors by a score of 109–97, but Hawkins had 34 points for Pittsburgh. In Game 2 the Tapers beat Hawaii, 92–91, in their home opener, with Connie Dierking leading Washington with 17 and Dave Mills getting 21 for Hawaii. The next contest for the Rens was in Norfolk, Virginia, a home game for Washington within the region, designed to broaden the fan base. The result was not encouraging, as only 500 fans came out to see the Rens win 111–88; both teams, then, bused back to Washington. The Rens made it two in a row over the Tapers by a 95–84 score, but only 350 fans were there to watch the after-

Seven. The 1961-1962 Season (First Half)

noon game that was broadcast back to Pittsburgh on WIIC, the NBC affiliate in Pittsburgh (now WPXI).[8]

It was at this time that some of the coaches in the ABL questioned Hawkins' eligibility since he had only attended one year of college and his class was not scheduled to graduate until 1964. The ABL was adopting, more or less, the NBA rule so as to not raid colleges and cause animus between the league and universities. The owners had agreed that Hawkins should be eligible as a hardship case because he was the sole source of income (other than welfare) for his blind mother in Brooklyn, but the coaches wanted that to be reconsidered (obviously because he was so talented and would lead to Rens' victories, not because of ABL raiding, since Hawkins had been declared ineligible by the University of Iowa). The matter went to the commissioner, who met with Hawkins and Owner Litman, then reaffirmed the position that the owners initially had taken. (Certainly Saperstein considered the draw that Hawkins would be for basketball fans as he continued to score and rebound so impressively).[9] Following the ruling in Chicago, Hawkins returned to Pittsburgh to help the Rens beat Hawaii, 100–99 before a crowd of 3,003 in the Civic Auditorium. Hawkins had 20 and Bucky Bolyard had 23 for the Rens, with Frank Burgess getting 29 for the Chiefs. Two nights later the Rens topped Hawaii once again, with Jim Palmer, Bolyard and Hawkins leading the scoring with 23, 17 and 15, respectively, before an announced crowd of 2,743, the smallest of the season.[10]

In Kansas City, the new Kansas City Steers franchise met the Cleveland Pipers to open the regular season. The Pipers began with a victory, led by Roger Taylor, from the University of Illinois, who scored 35 points in the 110–106 win. Rookie Bill Bridges from the University of Kansas had 24 for the Steers. Ben Warley chipped in with 24 for Cleveland. Stan Musial threw out a ceremonial first ball. Musial was a minority owner of the Steers, having been asked to invest by Ken Krueger, the St. Louis businessman who was principal owner of the team.[11]

The other ABL teams also opened that week. Hawaii began in Washington, on November 8, topping the Tapers, 91–76. Frank Burgess and Bob Anderegg (who only played six games before leaving the league) topped the Chiefs with 20 and 16 points, respectively, while Chuck Curtis and Sy Blye had 14 a piece for the Tapers. In Los Angeles, the Jets hosted the San Francisco Saints in Olympic Auditorium, which was built for the 1932 L.A. Olympic Games as a boxing and wrestling venue. Despite its large seating capacity (about 15,000), it could not be configured for a regulation basketball floor. The large capacity was unnecessary, as only 1,788 were listed as attending the opening game in L.A., and things did not get much better as far as crowds were concerned. The Jets won, 110–98, led by Dan Swartz with 29 points and Bill Spivey with 28. Kenny Sears had 22 for the Saints.[12]

The Steers won their next game, edging Cleveland, 101–100, but only 1,035 fans came out for the contest, in which Jack Adams led the Pipers with 32 and Bill Bridges topped the Steers with 26. The rookie from Kansas was establishing himself as the top player on the Steers and one of the best in the league. He got 35 points and 17 rebounds in the next game, a victory over Hawaii, but only 2,248 fans attended that contest, despite this being an ABL doubleheader. In the other game, L.A. easily defeated Chicago, 121–106, as Swartz had 31, Henry Whitney 16 and 14 rebounds and Bill Spivey, 16 with 19 rebounds. The ABL owners assumed that they'd lose some money the first year, but hoped to establish a strong fan base, which would lead to profits in year 2. The hope was that the fans would come as the teams showed their winning ways, but the first few games across the league were not encouraging, except for doubleheaders involving the Globetrotters. That would be the pattern for the season.[13]

Two nights later the Steers hosted another doubleheader, but only 1,869 showed up to see the Steers defeat the Jets, 113–109, and the Majors beat Hawaii, 105–97. For Kansas City, Gene Tormohlen had 26 and Bill Bridges had 19 with 15 rebounds. L.A. was led by Dan Swartz with 29, Hal Lear with 28 and George Yardley, on one of his rare road trips, with 20. Yardley had retired from the NBA at age 32 to form the George Yardley Company, which sold mechanical engineering equipment. Yardley had a degree in engineering from Stanford and resumed playing in the ABL, as long as he could remain in California during road trips. Thus, the Kansas City excursion was quite unusual.[14]

The next night the Jets were back in L.A., taking on the Pipers, and Yardley had 27 to lead the scoring in the 108–99 victory for the Jets. Ben Warley had 24 for Cleveland.[15] That same evening the Majors defeated the Tapers in a Chicago home game played in Muskegon, Michigan, where attendance was 5,004 in the new Walker Arena, just completed in

Seven. The 1961-1962 Season (First Half)

1960. It would be one of the best-drawing games of the year for the Majors. Ron Zagar had 22 for the Majors with Govoner Vaughn, Herb Lee and Kelly Coleman each getting 13. For the Tapers, Roger Kaiser, the former Georgia Tech All-American had 18, and Tony Jackson, the St. John's All-American, had 17.[16]

Despite less-than-expected attendance at games, the overly optimistic ABL owners set an agenda for their league meetings in mid–November that would include expansion for 1962 and the All-Star game. Little was released after the meeting concerning expansion, but the decision to hold the All Star game in February in Pittsburgh was likely made on the basis of the large crowd that the Rens had played to when they combined with the Globetrotters for a doubleheader. Saperstein was his usual upbeat self in providing this information.[17]

Even at this early juncture, however, there were ominous signs from Los Angeles that the owner, Len Cobosiero, was severely undercapitalized. Regarding the low attendance there, Cobosiero was quoted as saying, "We'll last until Christmas, at least," which proved sadly prophetic.[18] What was even more disturbing was that the Jets had drawn relatively well in the limited dates, posting attendances of 3,178 and 2630 for their last two games at that point. There were 2,016 at the next game after the comment, and 3,227 in the game after that. The Jets' problem was that they were simply undercapitalized for the player salaries that they were paying. Lear was getting $20,000, and both Spivey and Yardley would have been getting similar salaries, although Yardley's might have been prorated because of his refusal to play away from the West Coast.

The Majors, playing in Lansing, Michigan, in another "home" game drew 6,000 in a victory over the Tapers, 96–91. Two nights later, November 14, they had 12,073 in the Chicago Stadium for a Globetrotter doubleheader, with the Majors topping San Francisco in game 2 in overtime, 94–91. Jim Francis of the Saints had 30 for game scoring honors. A more ominous event, that went largely unrecognized as such, was the decision by President Kennedy on November 18 to send 18,000 military advisers to South Vietnam. This was the beginning of the escalation that would spread unrest to college campuses and big cities over the next eight years, as the military draft increased quotas each year.

In late November the Globetrotters infused Cleveland's attendance as part of a doubleheader that had the Rens meeting the Pipers. Cleveland won easily, 137–94, and the games drew over 10,000 fans. In Kansas City, the Jets defeated the Steers as Bill Sharman, player-coach, had 10 points in the second half of the 81–72 win before 2,225.[19] Two nights later, attendance was 2,215 in Cleveland for a victory over the Steers.[20]

By the end of the month, there were four ABL players averaging more than 20 points per game, Bridges with 24.5, Lear at 22.7, Hawkins at 21.5 and Swartz at 20.8. Yardley, Spivey and Warley all topped 19. Hawkins set a new game record for the young league by getting 40 points in a victory at Cleveland on November 25. The Rens also made news when their coach, Neil Johnston, decided that he would return to the floor as a player-coach beginning December 1. Johnston had retired from the NBA's Philadelphia Warriors in 1959, at the age of 29, because of a knee injury. He had been an All-Pro previously, averaging more than 20 points per game in five different seasons, and in 1990, he was enshrined in the Basketball Hall of Fame. His comeback lasted five games, during which he scored 49 points, just under 10 per game. That same day, Saperstein traded Herb Lee to Hawaii for George Price and shifted players back and forth between the Majors and the Globetrotters; Joe Scott was dropped and Tony Wilcox went from the Globies to the Majors, while Mel Davis did the opposite.[21]

In early December, disturbing patterns continued for the league. Phil Woolpert was fired as San Francisco's coach, Cleveland played a home game in Columbus and drew less than 4,000, and the Rens' attendance began to slide as they drew only 1,093 for a game against the Steers. Even these numbers may be suspect because Pittsburgh owner Len Litman is quoted by David Wolf as saying he often made up attendance numbers. "In the second quarter, I'd look at the scoreboard, and if the score was 34–26, I'd tell the sports writers the attendance was 3,426."[22]

Later in the month, Roger Kaiser scored 51 points for the Tapers, including 5 3-pointers, and Gene Conley (the former Celtic and major league pitcher) had 20 in a 123–117 victory over Hawaii in a game played at the Schofield Army barracks in Honolulu, also the principal setting for the novel *From Here to Eternity*.[23]

Early December saw Kansas City with the best record in the league at 16–5. Cleveland led the East with a 13–9 record. The standings reflect relative competiveness in the ABL with the worst record 8–14. Standings are below.

Seven. The 1961-1962 Season (First Half)

Kansas City	16–5	Cleveland	13–9
Los Angeles	12–11	Pittsburgh	12–11
San Francisco	10–11	Chicago	10–15
Hawaii	9–14	Washington	8–14

The league scoring leaders were led by Swartz, Lear, Hawkins and Bridges, all over 20 points per game. The top seven scorers are listed below.

Swartz, L.A.	22.2
Lear, L.A.	21.5
Hawkins, Pittsburgh	21.3
Bridges, Kansas City	20.6
Burgess, Hawaii	19.6
Spivey, L.A.	19.1
Kaiser, Washington	17.6

An ABL doubleheader in the Chicago Stadium drew only 1,500 to see the Jets top the Rens, 104–93, and the Majors defeat Cleveland, 101–93. Leading scorers for the four teams were Swartz of L.A. with 29, Bucky Bolyard for Pittsburgh with 20, Roger Taylor for Cleveland with 26 and Herschell Turner with 22 for Chicago.[24]

The Pipers were heavily dependent upon their Tennessee A&I connection, Coach John McLendon, and three of his former players, John Barnhill, Rossie Johnson and Ben Warley, but they were hoping to obtain a fourth former Tiger, Dick Barnett. He had played two years for Syracuse, averaging about 22 and 27 minutes per game and 12 and 17 points per game, but he was not a starter, despite being the third leading scorer on the team. Syracuse had one African American starter, Hal Greer, the second leading scorer, and Barnett felt, rightly, that Syracuse would not have two African American starting guards in the backcourt. So he jumped to the ABL, and his case ended up in the courts. It came to trial, finally, in December, and he testified that he was unhappy not starting.[25] He hoped that the ABL would not be as bound by the unspoken NBA quota system of having no more than two African American starters and never more than three on the floor at the same time. This was true for all NBA teams in 1960-1961, although Red Auerbach in Boston began to push the envelope, having Russell, Sam Jones, K.C. Jones and Satch Sanders on the floor together a few times. The ABL, it was hoped by some African American players, would break that "tradition." For Cleveland, there were two African American starters, but gaining Barnett would surely lead to three. Chicago had two, but their roster was so fluid that three often were on the floor together. Pittsburgh had only three rostered African Americans for most of the year, and Connie Hawkins did not initially understand why he was the only consistent starter, despite the other two, Jim McCoy and Walt Mangham, seeming to him to be superior to their white counterparts.[26]

At about this time (December 11) the war in Vietnam began, although few thought the U.S. would be engaged in it for long. In mid–December the Steers went on a roll and won nine games in a row and the hope was that this would excite the fans of Kansas City. On December 10th they met the Majors in a Ladies' Day game, whereby every woman was free, if accompanied by a man, but the attendance was still only 1,276 as the Steers won their seventh game in a row. Then, three nights later, they prepared to meet the Rens and the league's most exciting player in Connie Hawkins. Surely this would be the formula for a big crowd. At that point the Steers had played 12 home games and drawn 20,576 fans, an average of 1,715 per game. The break-even point was supposedly 3,000, but the biggest crowd of the year, 3,347, was barely above that.[27] The doubleheader on Wednesday, December 13, drew 3,100 fans, and they saw the Steers extend their streak to eight with a 109–102 victory. In game 1, Cleveland defeated Chicago, 117–95, with John Barnhill getting 39 points while Govoner Vaughn and Jackie Fitzpatrick each had 20 for the Majors. In game 2, Hawkins excited the crowd with his 33 points, punctuated by his incomparable dunks and ball handling, while Nick Mantis had 34 for the winning Steers.[28]

It should be noted that the NBA was not drawing enormous crowds, either; they were simply more than the ABL drew. On December 13, there were 1,977 fans in Syracuse to see the Cincinnati Royals. In a doubleheader in Boston, 6879 saw the Warriors play the Celtics and the Chicago Packers play the New York Knicks. Two nights later a doubleheader in Philadelphia had 2,891 fans, and Detroit at Cincinnati drew 3,067. There were games that topped 10,000 at times, but not many. Pro basketball was not a sport in high demand and would not be until the NBA secured a television contract for regular weekly telecasts. It would not be until the mid to late 1970s that the NBA began to become more popular and then exploded in growth and interest in the 1980s. Thus,

Seven. The 1961-1962 Season (First Half)

what the ABL was doing was not that far off from the NBA. The question was whether the ABL owners had deep enough pockets to survive for a couple years until they began to turn a modest profit. The answer, ultimately, was no.

On December 16, the Steers' win streak was snapped at nine, in Chicago, by the Rens, 114–105. Connie Hawkins had 29 and Allen Seiden 23 for the Rens. Larry Staverman had 25 and Larry Comley had 24 for Kansas City. Game 2 saw the Chiefs beat Chicago, 95–88, with Frank Burgess getting 32 for Hawaii and Nat "Sweetwater" Clifton, 20, for Chicago. The attendance was 3,321.[29]

Reported that same day was the Jets–Saints game of two nights before when the Jets extended their win streak to four with a victory. The game drew a reported attendance of 266, making owner Corbosiero's earlier comments very prescient. The Rens drew over 6,000 to a Sunday game versus the Steers the night after the Steers' streak was snapped, and the Rens won again, 100–96, as Hawkins got 29 and 22 rebounds to lead all scorers and rebounders.[30] Both the Rens and the Steers needed to rent cars that morning and drive from Chicago to Pittsburgh when Chicago's Midway Airport was socked in by fog after mechanical problems had initially delayed the flight. They arrived 12 hours later at 8 p.m., then played at 8:30.[31] That same night the Jets drew 256 to another win over San Francisco, while the Los Angeles Lakers returned to their former home in Minneapolis to play the Pistons before 6,213 fans.

Snow hampered the Rens again on December 22 as they didn't arrive in Kansas City for their game until 30 minutes before the tip-off, because of snow delays in Chicago, where they initially flew. The night before, the Jets were in Washington where L.A. completed a sweep of their three-game series, 102–96, as Swartz (33) and Spivey (25) topped the scoring.[32] More ominous numbers were the attendance figures, which the *Washington Post* said were 300. The Tapers and the Jets were hardly drawing anyone. Cobosiero had few places to turn, but Washington owner Harry Lynn was rumored to be moving the team to Camden.[33] In a statement a few days later, he said he was "not interested in the team's going anywhere else," and said any announcement would come after the ABL meetings in Chicago, December 30.

The league was looking for good news of any kind and received some on December 22 when it was announced that Dick Barnett would

Abe Saperstein and the American Basketball League

be able to play for the Pipers. Syracuse had agreed to let him go, but the terms for such an agreement had not been announced. In addition, Kenny Sears would no longer be enjoined by the Knicks from playing with the San Francisco Saints.[34]

Connie Hawkins scored 49 points in Cleveland on December 23, but the Rens lost, 132–117. High for Cleveland was Larry Siegfried, the rookie guard from Ohio State. Dick Barnett had seven in limited action in his first game of the season. The Rens returned home to top Chicago, before 2,986, their second consecutive game with at least that number (they drew 3,813 earlier), as Hawkins led with 26 in the 100–86 win.[35]

The next day, Archie Dees agreed to join the Rens, having been released by the St. Louis Hawks. Despite him being "rejected" by the NBA, Dees did have the cachet of having led the Big Ten in scoring in 1959 while at Indiana. He never played for the Rens, instead going to Cleveland for Lowery Kirk. Dees played 34 games for the Pipers and scored just under ten points a game.[36]

On December 26 and 28, the Tapers played Cleveland at what would be the last two ABL games in Washington's Uline Arena. The Tapers maintained their strange mastery over the Pipers, winning 109–98 before 1,110 fans, then 123–106 before 1,187. Dick Barnett was rounding into form, getting 20 in the former game and 25 in the latter, while Roger Kaiser had 26 for Washington, then 23.[37]

The end-of-calendar-year stats released by the league had some interesting figures. Dan Swartz led in free throw percentage with 252–265 for 91.3 percent. Larry Staverman of the Steers (who Monte Moore, their radio announcer, said was the best shooter he ever saw[38]) had 105–116 for 90.5 percent. Connie Hawkins led in field goal percentage with 48.6 percent with Staverman second at 48.4 percent. Gene Tormohlen was fourth with 48 percent. Moore said that Tormohlen was one of the worst shooters he ever saw; Tormohlen restricted himself to putbacks and layups, however. Bill Bridges was number one in rebound average and second to Hawkins in total rebounds.

Chicago played its game December 29th in Detroit's Olympia Stadium and drew 6,000, more than the Pistons usually drew, as Pittsburgh won over the Majors, 96–92. Hawkins, the likely source of the increased fan interest, had 31 points for the Rens. Cleveland drew 3,158 that same night to see the Pipers top the Tapers, 124–98. Barnett had 27 for Cleve-

Seven. The 1961–1962 Season (First Half)

land and Kaiser 22 for Washington. Ben Warley had 22 points and 22 rebounds for the Pipers.[39]

The year-end ABL owner meetings opened with suggestions of expansion, despite the fact that both L.A. and Washington were clearly in trouble. They also announced that they would be discussing play-off sites and plans for mid–January for the First Half Championship. The play-off announcements were deferred and there were no announced plans of expansion. What did happen was that the Washington Tapers left for Long Island. In a statement, Owner Lynn said he thought that they'd lose $50K in year 1, but they had already lost $105K and he felt that moving to Commack, Long Island, where they'd play in the Commack Armory, would be an improvement. General manager Paul Cohen of the Technical Tape Company was from New Rochelle so he would be closer to all team events.[40]

The team transfer was a non-event in most other places, even ABL cities, getting no mention in either Pittsburgh or Kansas City until days later. To help contextualize the public impact of the ABL, consider this. On December 30, the *Kansas City Times* had a display ad for the upcoming Harlem Globetrotters' visit on January 4. There was an additional line in the ad that said, "Added Attraction 1st Place K.C. Steers vs. Chicago Majors." Tickets were $1.50, $2, $2.50, $3 and $3.50.[41]

At this time the Steers were in Hawaii on their only Pacific adventure, splitting two games there. League coaching issues arose at this time. The Saints replaced the fired Phil Woolpert (and interim coach Kevin O'Shea, who was general manager) with Al Brightman, a former coach at Seattle University, and the team responded with a win over Los Angeles that drew 3,045 to San Francisco's auditorium. Meanwhile, John McLendon was being pressured by his owner, George Steinbrenner, to win no matter what. This was a precursor to later problems that Steinbrenner caused McLendon.[42]

The move of the Tapers and the shakiness of the Jets made the new year appear a bit unsure for the ABL, but the end of the first-half play-offs would begin in mid-month and be played at the Eastern Division champions' court. The leaders were Kansas City in the West and Cleveland in the East. In a New Year's Eve doubleheader in Los Angeles, the Steers edged the Saints, 91–90, and the Jets defeated the Rens, 119–108, in the second game. Hawkins had 39 for the Rens, increasing his league-leading scoring, then at just over 25 per game. Dan Swartz had 25 and George Yardley 24 for the victorious Jets. The Steers were still a bit jet-lagged from playing the previous night in Hawaii, where they had beaten the Chiefs, 91–81. The Steers won two games, 3,000 miles apart, in less than 18 hours. Despite the attractive games, only 1,798 fans found their way to the Olympic Auditorium in Los Angeles.[43] In Chicago, 5,163 fans celebrated the end of 1961 with the Majors and the Tapers and saw Washington win its last game as a representative of D.C. by a 108–95 score. Roger Kaiser had 30 points for the Tapers.

The NBA was not packing them in, either, at this time of year. Syracuse at Cincinnati drew 2,596, and St. Louis at Detroit, 2,563, on New Year's Day. A doubleheader with Boston, St. Louis, Detroit and the Knicks attracted 8,264 to Madison Square Garden the next night, but that was offset by the crowd of 1,861 in Chicago to see the Packers entertain the Syracuse Nationals.[44]

The Steers continued their West Coast swing on January 3 with a loss to San Francisco, a game lowlighted by a young man snatching the game ball when it went out of bounds with five seconds left in the contest, then fleeing the auditorium with the ball, delaying the game for almost ten minutes until a new ball could be found to end the contest, 102–99. The 2,534 fans in attendance were probably dumbstruck by the audacity of the lad since no one pursued him.[45]

The Steers returned home the next night to benefit from the Globetrotter presence and win 94–93 over Chicago before 9,172, a standing room only crowd. Monte Moore said that the arena seated about 8,000 for basketball. The Steers, it was noted, arrived home so late that they didn't have their home uniforms and had to play in their away garb. Game highlights included Tormohlen grabbing 19 rebounds and Bill Bridges, 17.[46]

In a game postponed a day because the Tapers could not land due to a snowstorm, the Steers beat the Tapers, 118–88, before 1,168, to secure the first-half Western Division title. Maury King and Bryce Vann led the Steers with 21 and 20 points, respectively, while Roger Kaiser had 26 for the New York Tapers. The next day, it was announced that all three playoff games would be in the Eastern Division champion city (either Pittsburgh or Cleveland).[47]

The Steers topped the Tapers again, but only 908 fans bothered to

Seven. The 1961-1962 Season (First Half)

attend the Sunday-afternoon contest. The Pipers played that day in Columbus, Ohio, and scored 140 points in pounding the Saints by 33 points. Johnny Cox had 39 and Dick Barnett 37 for the Pipers. In Honolulu, the Rens kept the lead in the East as they beat Hawaii, despite Hawkins being held out with an ankle injury.[48]

The play-off picture was still in flux regarding both the Eastern Division representative and the location/date of the play-offs, just a week before their scheduled beginning. Owner Ken Krueger of the Steers had received approval for the first game to be in Kansas City with the other two in the East. The Steers were not drawing impressively at that time, however, having only 828 at a win, in overtime, over Chicago, 122–120. Tony Jackson, recently acquired by the Majors from the Tapers, scored 30, three of which were three-point shots. Roger Kaiser led the league in three-pointers made, but Jackson would have a great second half, playing more for the Majors.[49]

The Rens lost to San Francisco in Los Angeles, and the Pipers defeated New York in Lorain, Ohio, resulting in the Pipers winning the East by a game with a record of 24–18 to the Rens' 23–19. The first-half play-offs would open on January 12 in Kansas City, then go to Cleveland for games 2 and 3 (if necessary) on January 13 and 14. The stated arrangements were that the winning players would get 35 percent of the net receipts and the losers 25 percent. Tickets in Kansas City would be $1 for upper balcony, $2 for lower balcony and $3 for boxes and loge seats.[50]

The play-offs opened before 5,286 fans in Kansas City's Municipal Auditorium, and the Steers sent the fans home happy with a 106–93 victory. Larry Staverman had 25, Maurice King and Nick Mantis, 17 each, and the team shot 47 percent from the field. For the Pipers, Jack Adams had 23 and Larry Siegfried, 18.[51]

Game 2, played in Cleveland, saw the Pipers win 98–87 before 4,276 patrons. Roger Taylor with 17 and Ben Warley with 15 led a well-balanced Piper attack. Bridges had 22, Staverman and Tormohlen, 19 each, as the Steers relied on their frontcourt for almost all their scoring and outrebounded the Pipers, 56–35.[52]

The final contest was played the next night, again in Cleveland, and the Steers overcame the small crowd of 2,313 to topple the Pipers and win the first-half title. This meant that they would play for the overall championship against the second-half title winner in a manner yet to be determined. Nick Mantis had 25 and Larry Staverman 24 for the Steers, while Jack Adams had 30 and Larry Siegfried 26 for the Pipers. Each team shot well, the Steers 55 percent and the Pipers 54 percent in the 120–104 game.[53]

With this game, the season was half over. There was a champion, a team was rumored to be in trouble and another had shifted the franchise. Attendance was much lower than expected, let alone hoped for. Coaches had been replaced and many players traded. Monte Moore, the Steers' radio announcer, said that so many players were traded or rosters adding and dropping players that one needed to study the rosters carefully at the beginning of each new series. One thing the ABL would not demonstrate was stability.[54]

Eight

The 1961-1962 Season (Second Half)

Immediately following the first-half championship, the Steers and Pipers traveled to Pittsburgh to participate in an ABL doubleheader that had the Steers facing the Tapers and the Pipers meeting the Rens. The Steers crushed the Tapers, 122–96, as Bridges (24) and Staverman (19) led a hot-shooting squad (52 percent shooting to New York's 38 percent). In game 2, Cleveland edged the Rens, 110–108, although Connie Hawkins set an ABL record with 54 points. Dick Barnett had 40 to lead the Pipers.[1] San Francisco 49er wide receiver, R.C. Owens (who had played a year of AAU basketball with the Seattle Buchan Bakers) played for the Saints in the game. He scored two points; he played in three other games and scored a total of four points before ceasing to play.[2]

Rumors were rampant that the Jets were going to move, but where was not clear. Various rumors had them moving to a suburban L.A. site, specifically Long Beach or Pasadena, as well as out of state, with Fort Worth, Houston and Portland, Oregon, being mentioned most prominently. None had them ceasing to exist.[3]

On January 16, a new league crisis emerged; the payroll in Cleveland was late and the players were sore about it and said so. According to Coach John McLendon, who spoke up for the players, they were not paid on January 15 and were unhappy about it. Apparently, George Steinbrenner didn't have the cash, but the situation would be ironed out, according to McLendon. Steinbrenner, as it turned out, took umbrage at his coach taking up the issue for the players rather than covering for him. Steinbrenner was said to be angry over the play-off loss to Kansas City and withheld the paychecks for that reason. Either way, the players were mad, the press was informed and Steinbrenner was angry about that.[4]

That same day, expansion/franchise movement stories in both the NBA and the ABL were on the sports pages. The NBA, which had initially intended to accept two franchises for 1961-1962, but would not allow Baltimore to enter without an acceptable arena, now said that the league would not expand in the near future. An exception, however, would be Baltimore, if their arena was ready. Were there to be expansion, a plan for stocking the franchise and paying the entry fee would be used. Chicago had paid $200K and selected one player from each team (they could each protect seven) and also got the number one pick in the NBA draft when they had entered the NBA. There would be a new plan.[5]

The ABL's Jets were the object of a possible purchase by a wealthy Texan, Charles Weisenberg. Were he to actually purchase the Jets, he would have been the fourth or fifth Jewish owner in the league. Some were confused and thought Steinbrenner was Jewish; Saperstein may have initially thought so, too, but it was not the case. Weisenberg would probably move the team, which had drawn 33,957 in 16 home dates, an average of 2,123 per game. The Lakers, by contrast, had drawn 106,000 in 17 dates in their new L.A. home, an average of just over 6,000 per game.[6] Los Angelenos were not exactly coming out in droves to support pro basketball.

The Pipers and their owner, George Steinbrenner, were not happy to have lost the first half title to the Steers and knew that they needed to improve their rebounding to compete and win. They would have to give up outside shooting to get a good rebounder. Ultimately they would trade Jack Adams and Roger Taylor to the Tapers for 6'9" Connie Dierking, who had played in the NBA for two years before jumping to the ABL. Roger Kaiser remembers that Dierking was a good, big player, but suddenly he was gone one day. He had been traded for Taylor and Adams. Kaiser noted that "players were always coming and going in the league."[7]

A more amazing rumor had the Pipers merging with the Syracuse Nationals and making a stronger NBA franchise. The source for this was not identified, but it very well could have been George Steinbrenner, from what we see transpired the next off-season and based on his career as a Yankee owner.[8]

Meanwhile the ABL second half of the season continued, and the crowds were getting smaller rather than larger. A doubleheader in Cleveland drew only 2,221 fans. In L.A. the Jets' games were postponed as so-

Eight. The 1961-1962 Season (Second Half)

called revisions were being made. The next day (January 17) the Jets withdrew from the league. The team was to "reorganize" the next year in Long Beach and the players would go out "on option." An unnamed ABL spokesperson said that three factors contributed to this situation: (1) financial difficulties, (2) competitive pressure from the Lakers, and (3) the illness of Len Corbosiero, team president. An *L.A. Times* story said that the Jets had 1,762 stockholders, with the principal owner being Vi Guarino. The story just said the team didn't have enough funds. A story the next day said that the Jets had reportedly lost $189K. Two days later, Saperstein put on a slightly different spin and said that the league was healthy and that the Jets' withdrawal was because of the illness (not specified) of owner Len Corbosiero. According to Saperstein, Corbosiero had $85K in the bank and said that they'd be ready for readmission next year, after they "get their house straightened out." With no one able to carry on, Corbosiero had to withdraw for a time.[9] If anyone believed that story, he or she was still waiting for the tooth fairy. There were even stories at the time that Len Corbosiero did not even exist, that the name was a front for someone else. Hal Lear denied that; he had met him once or twice and said that he did, indeed, exist![10]

Additional problems continued to plague the league at times. Snow caused the Chicago Majors to arrive at 9 p.m. for an 8 p.m. contest in Kansas City, which was then delayed starting until 9:55. Amazingly, most of the crowd of 3,840 stayed around and waited for the late tip-off. The Steers won 114–96 behind Bridges (28) and Staverman (24), but it was not all good times for the team as their locker room was robbed during the game. A statement from the club said "no major losses were suffered."[11]

In a rematch of the play-offs, Cleveland came to Kansas City on January 20 and the result was a play-off type game in which the Steers won 115–114. Siegfried and Barnett each had 26 for the Pipers. Bridges (44) and Staverman (26) led the Steers as both teams shot better than 43 percent for the game.[12] In Chicago another tight contest ensued as the Majors defeated the Rens in overtime, 114–111. A highlight was Tony Jackson's six three-pointers in the contest.[13]

Cleveland returned home to face the Steers, once again, and the result was another high-scoring, good-shooting contest (both teams bested 44 percent from the field), which the Pipers won, 132–120. Newly signed Archie Dees (he had started the season with the Chicago Packers, but had recently been cut) led Cleveland with 23, and John Barnhill had 21. Bill Bridges had 30 points and 16 rebounds for the Steers. Only 2,296 viewed the game on a Sunday evening. The Saints drew 3,814 to witness their game against the New York Tapers, and the Saints rewarded those fans with a 108–105 overtime win. Kenny Sears had 36 for the home team, and Sy Blye had 33 for the Tapers. The biggest crowd that night was in Pittsburgh where the Rens defeated the Majors, 97–82, before 6,843. Hawkins had 29 and Phil Rollins 28 for Pittsburgh, while Bob Wilkinson had 20 for Chicago. In Moline, Illinois, the Chicago Packers drew only 2,531 for their NBA game against the New York Knicks.[14]

Although the teams were playing for a first-and second-half championship, the individual records were compiled for the entire season. Connie Hawkins was leading in scoring with 28.2, Dan Swartz was at 23.6, Roger Kaiser at 21.6, Bill Bridges at 20.8, Frank Burgess at 19.0 and Bill Spivey, now playing for Hawaii, at 18.8

Other Jets signing besides Spivey were Jim Palmer with the Rens, Hank Whitney with Chicago, Dan Swartz with the Tapers, and Hal Lear with Cleveland. George Yardley chose to retire, once again, and Larry Friend retired to go into investment banking.[15] Bill Sharman was out of a job, at least for a while.

The next week, Tony Jackson broke his three-point record when he made seven in one game in a 100–99 loss to the Rens in Pittsburgh. There were just over 3,000 in attendance to see him score a total of 30 in the game. The night before (January 25), Pittsburgh had drawn 3,862 to witness the Rens' loss to the new, improved Tapers, 110–101, despite Hawkins' 33 points.[16]

Outside the basketball court, the Organization of American States had suspended Cuba on January 22. In December, Fidel Castro had declared Cuba a Marxist socialist nation, and in early January he had signed a trade pact with the Soviet Union. In early February the U.S. imposed a trade embargo on Cuba, one still in effect as of 2012, but modified by the Obama administration.

Fritz Kreisler, the Steers' beat reporter, wrote a reflective piece on the league that appeared in late January, in which he noted that the ABL was a great league, but for the lack of superstars. On that same page there was an ad in the paper for the upcoming doubleheader with the

Eight. The 1961-1962 Season (Second Half)

Globetrotters in game 1 and the Steers versus the Tapers in game 2. Cab Calloway and his orchestra would play, and tickets were $1.50–$3.50.[17] Kreisler seemed to not recognize Hawkins as a superstar, but he continued to act like one on the court, getting 39 in a win over the Majors, in a game played at New Castle High School, outside of Pittsburgh.[18] Attendance was not given, but the next night the Rens were back in the Auditorium in Pittsburgh, where they drew 4,096 to see them beat Chicago again, despite Hawkins sitting out with a sore elbow. The night before, Cleveland had lost to the Chiefs in Honolulu before 3,531, as Spivey had 41 to lead all scorers in the 106–94 game.[19] The Rens continued their home victory skein, topping the Tapers, 124–107, before 3,351. Hawkins was back and scored 30, but Dan Swartz led the game with 38 for the Tapers.[20]

At this time stories arose that John McLendon was in trouble in Cleveland because of his defense of the players over their late pay. George Steinbrenner didn't appreciate McLendon standing up for them and not him, and he particularly didn't like being seen as cheap in the press (even if it were true). The Pipers also made the trade for Connie Dierking, sending their captain, Jack Adams, to New York in return.[21]

McLendon resigned before Steinbrenner could fire him. Steinbrenner had demanded that his players issue a retraction for a statement that they would not play for Steinbrenner without their paychecks clearing. McLendon convinced the players to sign such a statement, then felt that he couldn't continue to coach for Steinbrenner without further emotional situations such as these that would undermine his authority as a coach and the players' ability to win. McLendon declared, "As much as I sincerely love my team and Cleveland fans and friends and wanted so much to make my home here, I cannot see any course open to me other than the one I am following at this time." Steinbrenner said that the players didn't hate him and that McLendon could not resign because he didn't give 60 days notice . The two then met and tried to find a mutually satisfying result. Ultimately, McLendon did resign, and Steinbrenner offered the position to Jack Adams as player-coach. Adams declined out of loyalty to McLendon and was immediately traded to New York. Steinbrenner then signed Bill Sharman as coach, in an effort to sign a big-name coach and win over the public. Then, to add to the bizarre events, Steinbrenner announced that McLendon had agreed to return to the team as the vice president of the Pipers in order to help the transition to the new coach. It was the first of many Steinbrenner firings and rehirings that would characterize his later career as the owner of the New York Yankees.[22]

In December 2011, a *New York Times* article revisited these incidents and recounted them in an article filled with errors. Based on a newly published book by a Cleveland sportswriter, Dan Coughlin, the article misrepresented the formation of the ABL, the location of teams in the league, the resignation of McLendon and the second-half performance of the Pipers. Providing some publicity for the league in the 21st Century was a plus, however.[23]

Despite Steinbrenner's denial, the Pipers (and George) were in need of cash, and he decided to sell most of the team to Ralph Wilson, the owner of the Buffalo Bills of the AFL, for a rumored $175K, which would be amazing, considering the losses throughout the league. In addition Steinbrenner remained as president of the club.[24]

The move to New York was not helping the Tapers in drawing fans. In a big win over the Rens on a Tuesday night, there were an estimated 300 fans in attendance, which likely meant they might have been 300 if all players and various employees in the building were counted. Dan Swartz scored 40 in the 114–93 Tapers' victory.[25]

Hawkins was scoring against everyone. He had 45 against the Majors in a loss in Milwaukee before 2,450 fans. He had 26 in another loss to Chicago, this time at Waukegan (Illinois) High School, where only 427 viewed the game. He had 24 in a victory over the Majors in Chicago Stadium, part of a doubleheader, with the Globetrotters playing the Green Bay Packers in game two. The games drew 20,482.[26]

With the Jets' demise in Los Angeles, the Hawaii Chiefs played some home games there and on February 4 lost to Kansas City, 105–92 with 7,817 in attendance, more than the Jets ever drew. Spivey got 30 for Hawaii, Burgess 25, and Bridges led the Steers with 26. The previous night, both teams had played in Honolulu before the Chiefs' biggest crowd of the year, 3,848, as they defeated the Steers, 100–91. Spivey had 27 for Hawaii and Staverman 19 for the Steers, while Tormohlen had 15 to go with 20 rebounds. That same night NBA attendance was about the same—Knicks at Boston had 4,319, L.A. at Chicago had 3,750, Hawks at Detroit had 3,883 and Syracuse at Philadelphia drew 4,958.[27]

Eight. The 1961–1962 Season (Second Half)

Another result of the Jets' demise was the constant reworking of the ABL schedule. Two Steers games with Chicago were canceled; they were to have been played in Moline, Illinois, and Milwaukee. Most of the schedule remained the same, as the league tried to keep the number of games played comparable and minimize unnecessary travel. With seven teams, this was a bit more challenging, especially as teams played home games away from their own city. Cleveland lost to San Francisco in Sandusky, Ohio (85 miles from Cleveland). Jim Francis had 36 for the Saints; Dick Barnett had 32, Connie Dierking, 28, for the Pipers.[28]

League scoring leaders looked as follows:

Hawkins, Pittsburgh	28.0
Swartz, New York	24.3
Spivey, Hawaii	22.4
Kaiser, New York	21.5
Bridges, Kansas City	20.9

Standings as of February 8, 1962

Eastern Division		Western Division	
Pittsburgh	8–9	San Francisco	10–2
Chicago	4–7	Kansas City	8–4
New York	5–8	Hawaii	5–6
Cleveland	3–9		

On February 7, the Pipers hosted an ABL doubleheader that drew only 1,738 on a Wednesday night. Swartz had 28 as the Tapers beat Pittsburgh, 130–111. Hawkins led the Rens with 21. Cleveland ran away from San Francisco, 144–115, as Warley had 30 and Johnny Cox 26. Jim Francis had 27, Kenny Sears 24, for the Saints.[29]

A doubleheader with the same teams, this time in Pittsburgh the next night, drew 3,917 fans to the Civic Auditorium to see Pittsburgh defeat the Tapers, 129–115, as Hawkins went for 42 and Sy Blye led New York with 27. In game 1, Cleveland defeated the Saints, 129–118, as Barnett got 43. Francis had 24, Mike Farmer 22, for San Francisco.[30]

The next night, Kansas City and Hawaii returned to action once again, with the Steers winning, 113–94, before 3,584 fans in Kansas City's Municipal Auditorium. Staverman had 35 to lead all scorers, while Spivey had 20 for Hawaii.[31]

Hawaii had a couple days off in Kansas City, and Fritz Kreisler used that to do a feature on Bill Spivey, who claimed he was no longer very bitter over his exclusion from the NBA. Spivey said that he used to believe in the Bill of Rights, but didn't anymore, at least in his case. He had successfully fought in court, but was tainted by game-fixing stories anyway. His trial in New York in 1952 had been declared a mistrial when jurors deadlocked, reportedly, 9–3 for acquittal. Charges were later dropped, but the NBA banned him anyway. In 1959 he tried out for the Royals, but NBA commissioner Maurice Podoloff blocked the move, with no stated reason. Spivey later sued for $820,000 but settled out of court for $10,000. In 1961, he had signed with Cleveland but was traded to L.A. with Hank Whitney for Nick Romanoff (who ended up averaging 3.0 per game for Cleveland). Spivey went to Hawaii after L.A. folded.[32]

In an amazing turnaround (which may not have been true), 3,166 fans were said to have come to Commack and saw the Tapers top the Saints, 123–119, as Dan Swartz had 40 and Jim Francis 27, to lead their teams' scoring. In Pittsburgh, the Pipers defeated the Rens, 125- 114, despite Hawkins' 36 markers.[33] In Kansas City, Bill Spivey had 22 for Hawaii, which was matched by Maurice King and George Pruitt for the Steers, as K.C. won, 91–88, before 2,163.[34]

The next game, Kansas City drew 6,463 fans, who saw the Steers rally late to top the Majors, 97–91. George Pruitt had 18 for the Steers and Bill Bridges 17, along with 15 rebounds. Hank Whitney had 18 for Chicago. Both teams shot poorly, 39 percent for the Majors and 34 percent for the Steers. That same evening, the San Francisco Saints came back and beat the Tapers, before a more likely crowd of 764 in Commack.[35]

The Steers had won seven in a row when they met the Rens in Kansas City on February 18 before 3,576, and the Pittsburghers ended the skein with a 95–88 victory. Hawkins had 27 and Bridges led K.C. with 28. The Steers turned the tables the next night, 121–93, with 3,603 in attendance. Bridges led again with 33.[36]

Then another ABL crisis arose as the Pipers were censured for a series of unspecified league Constitution infractions, announced at league meetings in Chicago. A Cleveland spokesperson thought it would all work out. The league also said that it planned to add two franchises (probably Portland, Oregon, and Dallas). The next day the ABL took action against Cleveland, initiated by the San Francisco club. The violations, which Cleveland had called clerical errors, were more than that,

Eight. The 1961-1962 Season (Second Half)

said the other league members. The violations included the sale of the club without notifying the league office. They had failed to submit financial reports for the first two play-off games and they had not paid the 5 percent of gate receipts of all games since December 1. Saperstein met with Steinbrenner for five hours on February 19, and a vote was scheduled on the complaints for the 20th. The league decided to keep the Pipers in the ABL by a vote of 5–1.[37]

Meanwhile league action was occurring in a variety of venues. In Tulsa, Hawaii defeated New York before 5,100. The two teams had played in Oklahoma City the night before.[38] The Steers played a home game in St. Louis and drew 10,064 to Kiel Auditorium to see them stop the Tapers by a 114–106 score. Nick Mantis led with 34, Bridges had 31 for the Steers, while Dan Swartz had 34 for New York.[39]

Besides Hawkins, Swartz and Spivey as the top scorers, Bridges and Hawkins were tied as top rebounders with 12.9 each. Spivey was the leader in field goal percentage at .523, Swartz topped in free throw percentage at .912 and Kenny Sears led in assists with 4.7 per game.[40]

The Steers had their attendance pumped up as a result of a doubleheader with the Globetrotters on February 21. The Steers beat New York, 130–104, but many of the 9562 spectators had left after game one. Bridges set a new team record with 28 rebounds.[41]

The next ABL rumor had Wilt Chamberlain *not* jumping leagues to play in the ABL, according to Abe Saperstein (who said he had considered it?). He also noted that 10 teams were possible for 1962-1963, presumably Portland, Dallas and Long Beach. The ABL draft was set for March 25th, the day after the NCAA Finals.[42]

Chicago claimed first place in the East over the Rens and Pipers with a win over Hawaii on Saturday, February 24th, 106–99, in Honolulu. There were 2,307 fans who saw Herschell Turner get 27 and Tony Jackson 19 to lead the Majors. The Pipers were not helping themselves by losing two in a row to the New York Tapers in Commack.[43]

The Pipers and Majors met on March 3, and the Majors won 115–111 before 5,228 in Chicago Stadium. Barnett had 24, Cox and Bob Keller had 16 each for Cleveland, while Turner had 26 and Jackson 25 for the victorious Majors. That same day an article appeared that placed some of the salaries and attendance in a different perspective. It was noted that in the prior season (1960-1961) the NBA set a new attendance record

Abe Saperstein and the American Basketball League

by drawing just over 700,000 to their games. In 2010, that would have put the league in the middle of TEAM attendance figures. Admittedly there were only eight teams, but these numbers are quite low and they led to mediocre salaries.[44]

Attendance was picking up in Pittsburgh, Chicago, Kansas City and Cleveland, but not in San Francisco or New York. Hawaii's attendance was never high and capacity was less than 4,000, but it was usually between 2,000 and 3,000, not enough to sustain a team with such high league expenses for travel. It was, however, a great gig for the players, as they looked forward to the road trips there. John Barnhill said that he and some of his teammates rented a car and drove all over Oahu, then spent time on the beach and by the pool. They all loved it.[45] Sy Blye remembered that the trips were great, but long. "Sitting in airline seats for so long, especially when you're tall, you paid for the pleasure of Hawaii."[46]

Roger Kaiser said that they were in Hawaii for a week and mostly played at the Scofield Barracks. "It had a sunken floor and a half roof and maybe 3,000 seats. I had my best game there, getting 51 points."[47]

The Steers hit a "bump in the road" in early March losing in Pittsburgh (before 4,182), 114–93; in Canton, Ohio (before 1396) to the Pipers, 104–92; and in Commack, 108–107, before winning in Pittsburgh (before 5,182) to clinch the Western Division. In the East, Chicago and Cleveland were battling evenly. On March 5 the Majors beat New York to take the lead, with Tony Jackson scoring 26 for the Majors and Dan Swartz leading New York with 38. Then, both Chicago and Cleveland lost, to maintain Chicago's slim lead. On March 8 the Pipers beat the Saints to take a half-game lead. John Barnhill had 33 for the Pipers in the win.[48]

The Majors tied the Pipers the next night in a victory over Hawaii, in a game played in Miami Beach as a Hawaii home game before 7,322. Turner had 23 for Chicago, Jackson 20 with two three-pointers.[49] With three weeks left in the season, the individual stats still had Hawkins (27.6), Swartz (24.5), Spivey (22.7) and Bridges (21.8) as the leading scorers. Tony Jackson had come on to rank second in 3-pointers made (96) to Bucky Bolyard (97).

In the ever-changing schedule, the Rens and Pipers agreed to play two more games in order to match the number that New York and

Eight. The 1961–1962 Season (Second Half)

Chicago would have in the second half of the season (39). The play-offs were still not decided as to when, where and how. The league standings showed only three teams playing better than .500 in the second half.

Eastern Division		Western Division	
Pittsburgh	16–14	Kansas City	21–10
Chicago	16–15	Hawaii	15–18
Cleveland	13–16	San Francisco	15–19
New York	14–18		

In another of his league assessments, Fritz Kreisler saw the ABL at a critical juncture regarding its future and the search for top talent. With the expressed willingness to expand to ten teams, Kreisler saw a need to sign impact players for the next year. From a player's point of view, he felt that the ABL could more greatly assure a rookie starting or playing a lot and pointed to Tony Jackson, Roger Kaiser, Bill Bridges and Larry Siegfried as examples. He now saw the ABL needing to worry about the NBA raiding the ABL for talent.[50]

From Miami, the Chiefs and Majors moved up the coast to play in Jacksonville, where 5,500 came out to see the Majors win, 111–95, as Turner had 23 and Jackson 22 for Chicago. For Hawaii, Spivey and Burgess had 19 each. The two teams played the next night as part of a Globetrotters doubleheader, and the Majors won again, to extend their lead over Cleveland to a full game. Turner (24) and Jackson (23) again led Chicago's scoring.[51]

The next night Chicago met the Pipers in Ashtabula, Ohio, 53 miles northwest of Cleveland, and the Pipers tied for the lead by winning, 110–101. Played before 1,300 in the high school gym, Barnett had 35 and Cox 25 for the Pipers, while Kelly Coleman had 25 and Jackson 18 for Chicago. The next night the Pipers won again, 124–122, despite Tony Jackson scoring 53 points and setting an ABL record with 12 three-pointers. Barnett had 41 for Cleveland.[52]

In Commack, the two cellar dwellers met and Hawaii lost to the Tapers, 102–98, before an announced "crowd" of 658. The next night Hawaii won, 110–95, but the crowd was even smaller, 463.[53]

On March 17, the Pipers took the divisional lead by topping Hawaii in Cleveland, 107–100. Dick Barnett had 35, Johnny Cox 30, for the Pipers. Bill Spivey (21) and Herb Lee (19) led the Chiefs. The next night, the Pipers solidified their lead by beating Chicago in Cleveland, 111–102.

Cox had 24, Barnhill 23, while Jackson had 31 for the Majors. Jackson followed that with 34 (7 three-pointers) the next night in Chicago, to lead the Majors to a 112–108 win over Hawaii in Chicago Stadium, before 3,128. He now had 133 for the year and the league lead in three-pointers.[54]

On March 21, the ABL office said that the play-offs would begin with a six-team tournament and the winner would play the Steers in a best-of-five series, starting March 31 or April 1. Details would follow. Locations would probably depend on availability of venues, since the ABL had little leverage on most arenas.[55]

The Majors fought back for the Eastern lead and defeated Pittsburgh before 8,885 in Pittsburgh, by a score of 121–120. Turner (27) led Chicago, and Curtis and Mangham topped Pittsburgh with 25 each.[56] The Pipers retained their lead the next night by beating Pittsburgh in Cleveland, 124–102. Then, the Majors made the race closer by defeating the Rens, as the Pipers lost to New York in a Pittsburgh doubleheader. Tony Jackson was the top scorer in the game with 35 (with 5 three-pointers). Then the Rens beat Cleveland the next night to make the race even closer. Connie Hawkins had 38 to lead the Rens, and he was also named league MVP that day. Dick Barnett had 35 for Cleveland. The All-League teams had been announced the day before, and both had been on the first team.[57]

The two teams moved back to Cleveland where the Pipers won, 136–126, but the crowd was a disappointing 1,000. Hawkins had 42 for Pittsburgh, Cox 41 for Cleveland. That same night the Steers defeated San Francisco, before 2,805, ending the Steers' regular season with a total of 93,250 for 34 home dates (2743 per game), plus 5,286 at the one play-off game. This was an encouraging beginning for the team's first year.[58]

The next night the Pipers tied for the Eastern Division lead by winning 114–106 over Pittsburgh, before 3,441 fans, in Rochester, New York. Dierking had 28 and Barnett 26 for Cleveland, and Hawkins had 29 for the Rens. The ABL also held its college draft that day, and a franchise for Long Beach was awarded to Art Edwards, a paint manufacturer. Long Beach selected Zelmo Beatty in the first round, but he later signed with the NBA's St. Louis Hawks. The team would play in the newly completed Long Beach Arena with a seating capacity of 13,500.[59]

The league finally announced the play-off plans on March 26. On March 29, the New York Tapers would meet Hawaii and the San Francisco

Eight. The 1961–1962 Season (Second Half)

Saints would meet the Rens in a doubleheader in Pittsburgh with byes to Cleveland and Chicago. The second round would be in Cleveland with the winner playing Kansas City for the title in five games after that.[60]

The Tapers defeated the Chiefs and the Saints beat the Rens with both games going into overtime. In the Taper victory, Swartz had 42, Kaiser 30 for New York, while Herb Lee had 33 and Spivey 28 for Hawaii in the 125–116 game. Kenny Sears led San Francisco with 24 and Connie Hawkins had 41, but that wasn't enough, as the Saints won, 107–103. The doubleheader drew 3,450.[61]

The two winning squads traveled to Cleveland to play two nights later, before a Saturday-evening crowd of just 1,600. New York upset Chicago, 115–108, led by Swartz (35) and Kaiser (25). Chicago countered with 27 from Tony Jackson and 20 from Leroy Gibson. In game 2, Cleveland defeated the Saints, 117–112. Dierking had 23, Cox 22, for Cleveland, while John Beberich had 19 and Ken Sears 18 for San Francisco.[62]

The Pipers and Tapers flew to Kansas City and met the next night for the right to face the Steers for the ABL championship. Cleveland won 107–84 in a rugged game that saw Dan Swartz ejected with 8:35 to go in the third quarter after knocking out Jimmy Darrow with a punch. Barnett led the Pipers with 24 and Dierking had 20. Syl Blye had 26 and Roger Kaiser 16 for the Tapers. Sixty-nine free throws were shot in the contest.[63]

The championship series opened in Kansas City on April 1. The Steers were rested. The Pipers had played the night before and had played three games in four days in three different cities. These differences showed on the court, where the Steers won 126–115 before 3,246 spectators. Bill Bridges had 36, Larry Staverman 25, and the Steers shot 58 percent from the field. The Pipers shot 40 percent, with Barnett and Dierking each scoring 31 points.[64]

Two nights later, the Steers won again, 118–82, led in scoring once again by Bridges (26) and Staverman (18). Cox had 21 and Archie Dees 12 for the sluggish Pipers. It looked like the Steers would be the first ABL champion.[65]

The Pipers found enough to win game three, when the series shifted to Cleveland the next night. Before 7,624, many of whom came to see the Globetrotters in the first game, the Pipers won 116 to 114 as Barnett scored 36, Dierking 30 (and 22 rebounds), to lead the team. Bill Bridges had 34 points and 22 rebounds and Larry Comley 25, but the Steers fell short. The fourth game, played three nights later, was just as close, as the Pipers edged the Steers, 100–98. Barnett had 21 and Bridges 28 to lead their teams.[66]

The championship came down to the final game, to be played in Kansas City on April 9. Unfortunately, the Municipal Auditorium was unavailable for the contest at such short notice and an alternative venue had to be found quickly. George Steinbrenner, the Pipers' president said that he wouldn't play in Kansas City, but rather a neutral site, like St. Louis. His view was not shared by Saperstein, who finally secured the field house at Rockhurst College (now Rockhurst University), about three miles south of downtown Kansas City, for the game.

An estimated 3,000 (a good crowd, according to Monte Moore, Steers radio announcer) found their way to the campus on Monday night, April 9, hoping to see the first Kansas City championship in a major professional sport. They left disappointed as the Pipers defeated the Steers, 106–102, to win the ABL title. Each team went to its top play-off scorers for leadership and all four responded. Barnet (26) and Dierking (20) led Cleveland, while Bridges (31) and Staverman (26) topped the Steers.[67]

It was an exciting ending to a difficult, but potentially rewarding, season. All teams had lost money, but larger crowds in Kansas City, Pittsburgh and sometimes Cleveland seemed to be laying the foundation for later success. A team had left the league and one had transferred, but seven teams had finished the season. A continued presence in Hawaii was unlikely; expenses were simply too high and scheduling was crazy. The Saints were likely to be impacted in the Bay Area, as the NBA announced the move of the Warriors to San Francisco for 1962-1963. Nevertheless, Saperstein said that new franchises wanted to join the league, and the next season seemed promising.

A week later the U.S. and a ragtag group of Cuban "freedom fighters" mounted a series of attacks on Cuba at the Bay of Pigs, which resulted in an ignominious defeat for the U.S.-backed forces. It would take until late December of 1962 before Cuba would release the last 1,113 prisoners from the invasion. The world was becoming more treacherous with Cuba, Vietnam, and the Cold War with the Soviets. The basketball wars seemed mild compared to the direction the world was taking.

Nine

The ABL Begins a Second Year, 1962-1963

The ABL ended 1961-1962 with seven teams, but Saperstein promised at least eight, once again, for the ensuing year, and possibly ten. It would appear that all of the ABL teams lost money. Kansas City and Cleveland, the top two teams, would have been the closest to breaking even, depending on the kind of additional income they garnered to go along with the attendance at their home venues. Pittsburgh had some big gates, as did Chicago, but the latter team was often not in Chicago, as the Majors played all around the region. The Rens' attendance decreased steadily as the season continued.

In the off-season, Saperstein traveled a lot with the Globetrotters or was at his home in London. Much of the league's work and information came from Allan Bloch, the lead league counsel in Chicago. The financial troubles that George Steinbrenner seemed to have may have been real or it may have been that Steinbrenner was overextended and wanted to delay "unnecessary" payments like league dues as long as he could. The problem might have been a "cash flow" problem, rather than a lack of funds. Either way, it should have raised red flags with any entity or individual with whom he dealt.

Thus, it was quite a surprise when Steinbrenner and Jerry Lucas announced in mid–May of 1962 that Lucas had signed a two-year contract with the Cleveland Pipers. According to media reports, the Cincinnati Royals had chosen Lucas as their territorial pick in the NBA draft and had offered a three-year contract of $100K to $105K. The Pipers had offered $60K for two years, but Steinbrenner had convinced Lucas that he could finish his degree more easily by playing fewer games in the ABL and they'd allow him to begin after he finished his degree in December 1962. Steinbrenner had implied (or said) that the league would not open until December, rather than November, so that Lucas would hardly miss any games.[1]

With the signing of Lucas, Steinbrenner then began a campaign to get his Cleveland squad into the NBA as the tenth team to balance the divisions. The NBA had previously announced that it planned to expand for the 1962-1963 season, most likely to Baltimore, but negotiations seemed to have gone awry in that process. Thus Steinbrenner's pursuit of the NBA was timely. Apparently he carried on his discussions only with Maurice Podoloff, NBA president, who chose to keep the talks to himself.

During this time, the ABL was having its own internal problems, and some of the teams were considering not continuing. The Rens' owner, Lenny Litman, was in a dispute with the Pittsburgh Civic Auditorium regarding financial payments. Each said that the other owed money to the other party for the 1961-1962 ABL season.[2]

In early July it was announced that Cleveland was likely to get the tenth NBA franchise. According to the newspaper article, the NBA Board of Governors would vote on Monday (the 9th) on this issue at a meeting that was to include ABL officials. George Steinbrenner claimed that at an ABL owners' meeting the previous week, he had been given a free hand to negotiate with Podoloff and that he (Steinbrenner) "wouldn't let the rest of the ABL down, should the rest of the owners want to continue (as a separate ABL league) and that he won't force Jerry (Lucas) into anything."[3]

Clearly, there were some loose ends, however. The Cincinnati Royals (who owned Lucas' draft rights) were not happy and opposed the Cleveland entry to the league, especially with the potential loss of Lucas, and they released a statement to that effect the next day.[4] Lucas weighed in a couple days later, saying that he was not required to play for the Pipers were they to join the NBA. The NBA meeting was reportedly "stormy" and ended with no decision being made on the Cleveland application.[5]

Despite this pessimistic appraisal of the meeting, the NBA admitted the Pipers the next day with agreement from all NBA owners and Abe Saperstein, according to Podoloff. It was also noted that George McKeon, the owner of the San Francisco Saints and Ken Krueger, the owner of

Nine. The ABL Begins a Second Year, 1962-1963

the Kansas City Steers (and other unidentified ABL owners) were to be principal stockholders of the Pipers. The entrance fee for the Cleveland club was rumored to be $360,000 (most of which was to go to the Royals for territorial infringement) as well as a $100,000 performance bond. The new NBA alignment would have Cleveland playing in the Eastern Division and would now leave the ABL with just six teams—Kansas City, Chicago, Hawaii, San Francisco, New York and Pittsburgh.[6]

That same day, however, it was reported that the ABL would be folding, according to Lenny Litman, who had been informed of such by Allan Bloch, league counsel. George McKeon had told the *San Francisco Call-Bulletin* that the ABL had folded.[7] If this all sounds like a mass of contradicting and conflicting statements, it is only because that was the case. Communication was not good within or between the leagues, and the result was the seeming chaos, which continued. George Steinbrenner said that he would be stepping down as president of the Pipers, but would remain as principal stockholder while Krueger and McKeon would join him as co-owners of the club. Under consideration for coach would be Jack McMahon, the coach of the Steers the previous year; Neil Johnston, the coach of the Pittsburgh Rens the previous year; and current coach, Bill Sharman.[8] Sharman, meanwhile, removed himself from the running by declaring that, "other commitments would not permit him to coach the Cleveland Pipers, recently switched from the American Basketball League to the National Basketball Association."[9] Shortly afterward, he accepted the position of head coach of Los Angeles State College. Sharman had gone to high school in California and had attended the University of Southern California before joining the NBA in 1950. He would be head coach and an instructor in physical education.

A few days later Sharman wrote to Abe supporting the announcement that the ABL would head into a second season, noting that he had "a very enthusiastic opinion and desire to see the A.B.L. succeed." He went on to note that he had been receiving letters and calls from former Jets players inquiring about still not receiving their money for finishing in second place in the first half of the 1961-1962 season and asking what could be done in this matter.[10]

Two days later Marie Linehan replied to Sharman's letter, explaining that Saperstein was still in South America, but would return within the next two weeks. She went on to say that they agreed that the play-off money situation must be taken care of. It has not been forgotten, but the mechanics of solving some of the problems of the A.B.L. have become somewhat involved, and all things will be done. With the decision to continue ... and the revision of the franchise set-up.... Abe has to do things one at a time ... and I don't have to tell you how much of a burden for everything falls on his shoulders. However, I think the reconstruction of the league will be stronger, more compact, and very workable. Please tell any of the men involved to be patient just a bit longer.[11]

Meanwhile the NBA was signing away stars and coaches from the ABL, just as the ABL had done the previous year with Barnett, Sears and others. The St. Louis Hawks signed seven ABL players—Bill Bridges, Nick Mantis and Gene Tormohlen of the Steers; Mike Farmer of the Saints; Bucky Bolyard and Chuck Curtis of the Rens; and Hal Lear of the Tapers. The Chicago Zephyrs, formerly the Packers, signed Larry Staverman of the Steers, after obtaining him in a trade with the Royals for Dave Piontek. Staverman had formerly played for the Royals before jumping to the ABL.[12]

But there were hints that the enmity between the leagues was to end, as an NBA announcement had the ABL owners sharing in the new NBA club, the Pipers, and were supposedly going to "ratify" this at a meeting on the 15th of July. The NBA wanted all the ABL owners to own a piece of the Pipers, according to this report. Eugene Litman of the Rens said that the Pipers would play some home games in Pittsburgh's new Civic Auditorium and that the Rens would fold. Connie Hawkins, he said, was not eligible for the NBA until his class graduated in 1964 (although he ultimately had to sue to enter the league and did not do so successfully until 1969), but he was under a personal services contract with Lenny Litman.[13]

If all one knew was what one read in the papers, as Will Rogers said was true of him, there would have been a lot of confusion at this point. The ABL owners' meeting did little to untangle the contradictory information. Meeting in Chicago, with Saperstein participating by phone from London, the owners declared that the ABL would not, in fact, fold. George McKeon did say that he would not operate his club in 1962-1963, but Krueger (Kansas City), Kim (Honolulu), John Crossan (NY Tapers) and the Litman brothers (Pittsburgh), as well as Allan Bloch (representing Chicago and the ABL as counsel) announced that the league would continue with their squads. In a great statement of seeming obliviousness

Nine. The ABL Begins a Second Year, 1962-1963

(today we'd call it "spin"), Bloch said, "I don't know where these rumors started, but there is no foundation to what's been said about the league's folding."[14]

The next day Saperstein sent a wire/letter to Marie Linehan instructing her to send it on to Allan Bloch, Phil Brownstein, Ken Krueger, Art Kim, Paul Cohen, Ben Katuray, Red Klotz, Lenny Litman, Bill Margolis and Walter Kennedy—his owners, administrators and counsel with the ABL and the Globetrotters. In the letter he noted the dramatic and mammoth step of continuing the ABL for its second season, seeing it as "an obligation to American basketball itself!" He noted the 100-to-1 chance of success, necessitating that they would work twice as hard as before and cooperate fully with each other for the league and their team's success. He went on to provide a list of things to do to improve the likelihood of success. These included the following:

1. Gaily decorate your home office with team and league pictures.
2. Furnish the league office with the most up-to-date information on your office data.
3. Give me a list of open dates at your venue that you plan to use so that I can make a schedule that will save transportation monies.
4. Re-sign old men whom you want to keep and sign new men who are available to you. I recommend paying on a monthly basis since it looks better to have $1,000 per month (for five months) than $5,000 for a season (or a year)
5. We'll need to stock the Denver club so give me suggestions on players that you can spare
6. If you have worked out any radio or television deals, let me know and also contact us to get ideas for grocery deals, auto agency tie-ins, etc. One drew over 20,000 to the stadium last February.
7. Need a league meeting between August 18 and 27; suggest preferences. Potential agenda items include scheduling, play-offs, refereeing, Denver club stocking, review visiting team percentages and other suggested innovations.[15]

Despite this "whistling in the dark," indications were that the ABL would field a slate of teams for 1962, though how many, where they'd play and who would play for them was not readily apparent. Cleveland might still play in the ABL, according to Saperstein, noting that they were not yet in the NBA (referring to unconfirmed reports that they were having trouble raising the necessary money to join that league) and might consider jumping back to the ABL.[16]

Some ABL efforts at continued life were now playing out. The league announced that the New York Tapers had moved to Philadelphia, replacing the lost NBA franchise Warriors, which had been moved to San Francisco for the 1962-1963 season. The ownership group for the team would include Albert Greenbaum, William Banks, Red Klotz and Ben Katuray. The Philadelphia Tapers would be joined by Chicago, Denver, Pittsburgh, Kansas City and Long Beach in the league. Long Beach had acquired the personnel of the Hawaii Chiefs, and Denver was to field a new team. Abe Saperstein also said that the NBA and the Pipers would be sued if they left the ABL for the NBA.[17]

The next day, there were clear indications that Maurice Podoloff had not received a unanimous vote supporting the Pipers' entrance into the NBA. Tom Grace, the executive vice president of the Cincinnati Royals called Podoloff's actions regarding the Pipers, "stupidity," saying that the Pipers had made no payments to the league on the scheduled dates of July 10, 17 or 24.[18] Two days later Steinbrenner denied that the Pipers would be unable to enter the NBA, but two days after that, the NBA rejected the application of the Cleveland Pipers to enter the league for two major reasons. One was that no money had been paid by Steinbrenner, as agreed upon by the parties involved, and second was the threat of a lawsuit by the ABL.[19]

John Barnhill of the Pipers recalled, "In the summer of 1962, we were supposed to join the NBA with Jerry Lucas, but the league said he'd have to play for the Cincinnati Royals. One day we were in, the next we were out."[20]

Thus, the "entrance" and exit of the Cleveland Pipers from the NBA all played out in July of 1962. It would not be until the fall of 1970, eight years later, that Cleveland would have a franchise in the NBA with the Cavaliers (who were joined by Portland and Buffalo as new entrants that fall).

The ABL, meanwhile, continued to lose quality personnel. The Chicago Zephyrs named Jack McMahon their coach on July 24 in one of Frank Lane's first hires as the new general manager of the team. Lane,

Nine. The ABL Begins a Second Year, 1962-1963

a longtime baseball general manager, known as "Trader" because of his propensity to deal, had been hired by Dave Trager to provide some "action" for his Chicago team, which he hoped would lead to a significant improvement over their record-setting season of futility that resulted in a mark of 18 wins and 62 losses.[21]

A couple weeks later, the Steers named Johnny Dee, former Alabama coach, as their coach and general manager, indicating that they did appear to be ready for a second season in the ABL. Shortly after that, they signed their first player to a 1962-1963 contract when Maurice King inked a contract.[22]

And it still wasn't clear how many teams would be in the ABL and who they'd be. With the rejection of Cleveland by the NBA, would the Pipers be back in the ABL? Jerry Lucas' adviser, Joe Hardy, seemed to think so, based on his discussion with Allan Bloch. And Hardy said that Lucas was then likely to play with the Pipers in the ABL. That was on August 1, but within a month, a *Cleveland Plain-Dealer* article said that the Pipers were finished for 1962 because of financial problems. The ABL, it was stated, would go with five teams for the upcoming season, and Lucas was unlikely to play at all in 1962-1963.[23]

In August Saperstein was still trying to finalize a Pittsburgh franchise's ownership and appealed to Lou Jacobs, a friend and head of a sports service business in Buffalo, for help. He also summarized his view of the problems for the upcoming season. Saperstein said that he, Ken Krueger and Art Kim would co-sign any loan needed for a prospective franchisee in Pittsburgh and that the three would cover nominal back debts. Long Beach, Kansas City and Chicago franchises he termed "good and sound." Saperstein emphasized that time was of the essence in getting a Pittsburgh franchise owner and the league rolling.[24]

Saperstein contacted a former reporter for the *Pittsburgh Post-Gazette*, Harry Kodinsky, then the president of a Pittsburgh public relations firm, regarding finding someone to take over the ABL franchise there. In mid-September, Kodinsky wrote to Saperstein that he had talked to a number of local folks about the franchise, but had no takers. He did note that the Auditorium (which he visited) was "magnificent" and that Al Abrams, sports editor of the *Post-Gazette*, was in Saperstein's corner. He also said he'd call Saperstein at home and follow up with another note.[25]

Two days later Kodinsky wrote another note to Saperstein saying that he thought Pittsburgh was a good franchise, but would need "3–5 years to jell (if the franchise money can hold up) to establish star player names that will draw fans!!" He also reiterated his very positive impressions of the Auditorium and said that "if it existed in Chicago, it would be at least five times more valuable to establish pro basketball!!" He also declined any involvement with running a franchise, but said that he'd be a good "trouble shooter" for Saperstein and help set up a foundation, do promotions, season ticket sales and scheduling preliminary games. He pushed Sparky Adams as a potential franchise leader and said that both Adams and Al Abrams felt Pittsburgh only lacked promotion to be successful.[26]

In September the ABL announced that there would be a 72-game schedule with six teams. Denver had disappeared as a franchise, but Oakland was now the sixth franchise. Play was to begin November 14 and end March 17, although an official schedule had not yet been released. Also that month the Steers announced the signing of their second-round draft pick, John Windsor, a 6'8" forward from Stanford. He would back up the returning front line of Bridges, Tormohlen and Staverman. The latter had apparently not signed with the Chicago Zephyrs after his trade from Cincinnati, despite the announcement of mid–July attesting to the signing.[27]

In late September, Saperstein sent a note to all clubs requesting the list of 20 ball players under contract as well as those players unsigned and/or under negotiations. On October 31, the list would need to be pared to 15, 9 active and 6 in reserve. An additional note regarding the schedule said that cramming 72 dates into 125 days would necessitate using more than one building for some franchises. These included Philadelphia (Convention Hall, Arena, Camden, Baltimore's "new" Auditorium), Kansas City (Auditorium and American Royal Building) and Chicago (Chicago Stadium and 20 other dates in a dozen spots). The schedule would include a number of 30-minute doubleheaders.[28]

In October the teams headed to training camps, and there was a rash of alterations and cuts to rosters. Most notably, the Long Beach Chiefs, formerly of Hawaii and owned by Art Kim, cut two former NBA players, Ray Felix, 31, and Bob Hopkins, 28. Felix had played the previous year with the Lakers, but was not re-signed. Ultimately, he retired after

Nine. The ABL Begins a Second Year, 1962-1963

not making the Chiefs. So, too, with Hopkins, although he had been out of the NBA for two years, last appearing with Syracuse in 1960. Since both were big men, the Chiefs seemed to feel that their inside game was adequate, and that proved correct. In addition, the same article said that Johnny Green had been in training camp, but that would appear coincidental, at best, since he was only in his fourth year in the NBA (of a 14-year career).[29]

Despite the opening of the training camps, rumors continued to float that the ABL would not be able to begin the season. Some of the poor communication was due to Saperstein's absence, either at his home in London or traveling and not being in the league office in Chicago. Paul Cohen, the president of the Tapers said that Saperstein would resign as commissioner as soon as a successor could be named (which was never). He also noted that the Tapers would be naming a new coach to replace Stan Stutz, who was handling training camp in New Rochelle, New York. Paul Arizin, who had retired from the NBA, rather than follow the Warriors to San Francisco, had been offered the position (supposedly for $20,000), but turned it down. Instead, he would maintain his former off-season position at IBM and play basketball weekends in the Eastern League.[30]

The official schedule was released on the 21st, prompting Dave Condon of the *Chicago Tribune* to say that two leagues were not needed and that the NBA and ABL should merge, adding three teams to the NBA — Philadelphia, Kansas City and Cleveland — dumping Pittsburgh, Chicago, Oakland and Long Beach in the process. To increase the gate, the NBA should use the Globetrotters (Saperstein and the ABL's cash cow) on NBA cards.[31]

A few days later it was announced that the Litmans would be giving up the Pittsburgh franchise because of financial difficulties, and Nick Triolo of Philadelphia said that he was interested in the franchise. A week later, Saperstein announced at a luncheon in Pittsburgh that the new Rens owner would be Bill Rosenhohn, a fight promoter from Philadelphia, with Sydney Berkenfield of New York as vice president and Joe Gordon of Pittsburgh continuing as the general manager. Saperstein also said that the ABL play-offs would follow the model of the six-team National Hockey League.[32]

The ABL schedule would have the Globetrotters at 29 games, 17 of which would involve the Chicago Majors and 12 with other teams. The Long Beach franchise would play in the 13,500-seat arena in Long Beach, the Rens would play in the new City Auditorium, Oakland would have the Municipal Auditorium as a home court, Chicago would play in cavernous Chicago Stadium, the Tapers would be at either the Philadelphia Arena or Convention Hall and the Steers would play in the Municipal Auditorium in Missouri (mostly for the rest of 1962) or the Memorial Hall in Kansas (for most of the 1963 part of the schedule).[33]

In addition to the schedule, the ABL announced that it would continue seeking innovations that would interest and draw fans to ABL games. One experiment would be to have two teams play a doubleheader, consisting of two games of 30 minutes each with halves of 15 minutes. Both games would count in the regular standings.[34] The league owners had previously agreed to this; it was apparently the first formal public announcement.

The Pittsburgh franchise was still unsettled just two weeks before the opening of the season, judging by a letter to Al Abrams, the *Post-Gazette* sports editor, from Saperstein. He denied saying that he or the league would pick up the Litmans' franchise indebtedness, despite apparent claims to the contrary the previous month. Saperstein clarified that the league was offering to underwrite back debt to the Auditorium (that would be repaid) and that the league would supply some cash to the Litmans to get started with practice sessions and front office efforts. These would also be loans.[35]

The season finally got under way on November 15 with similar but different rosters. Kansas City had lost guard Nick Mantis to the Chicago Zephyrs, but George Pruitt and Maurice King were back to be the backcourt regulars with Bridges, Tormohlen and

Ermer Robinson, the coach of the Oakland Oaks (author collection).

Nine. The ABL Begins a Second Year, 1962-1963

Staverman. They would be favored to win the league championship with Cleveland and its stars, Dick Barnett (Lakers), John Barnhill (Hawks) and Johnny Cox (Zephyrs) in the NBA. Oakland would be led by Jim Hadnot (released by the Celtics) and Fred LaCour (two-year backup with the Hawks). Roland Todd from the Saints would join the Oaks, as would Govonor Vaughn from the Hawaii Chiefs, Nick Romanoff from the Pipers, Gene Brown from the Saints, John Turner who had played for the Chicago Packers the year before, and Wayne Yates, who had played for the Lakers the previous year. The coach would be Ermer Robinson, former Globetrotter star, who would be the second African American basketball coach in a major professional league.

The Oakland game programs indicated a degree of excitement regarding the franchise. There it was declared that Oakland was to be considered the next season, but with the withdrawal of Cleveland, Oakland would join "professional major basketball right now!"[36]

On the opening day, Bill Sharman sent a letter to Saperstein in which he praised the doubleheader idea, noting that he thought it would make the "game more appealing to the crowd." He also said that he planned to experiment with both the 30-second clock and the three-point basket in some of his college games during the season and hoped that "someday we will get the N.C.A.A. to adopt the rules for all schools," which did happen, although it took another 20 years for both to be implemented fully.[37]

Even on opening day there were still loose ends to the league's finances. Marie Linehan sent a memo to Saperstein asking him to clarify if the league was implementing the motions passed at the league meeting in March regarding the distribution of gate receipts. These were that in a single game, the home team paid the visitors either $600 or 10 percent of the gate. In a doubleheader the home team paid $400 or 10 percent to each of the clubs, whichever was greater. The league would receive $200 or 10 percent from a single game and $300 or 10 percent, whichever was greater, in a doubleheader. The memo was written on stationery that still had the Los Angeles, Honolulu, San Francisco, Washington and Cleveland clubs and Pittsburgh still had Lenny Litman as team president. In tough economic situations, even stationery was not to be wasted.[38]

The Steers edged Oakland in the home opener for the Oaks, 105–103, before 2,438 fans at the Municipal Auditorium. LaCour with 24 and

Romanoff with 22 led Oakland, while Bridges and King, former KU stars, had 27 and 21, respectively, for the Steers.[39] That same night the Tapers defeated the Majors, 116–98, in Philadelphia before an estimated crowd of 1,700. Later revelations would show that almost all ABL printed estimates were made when crowds were below 200 or so, and the newspapers went along with it, since coverage was so poor that stringers, rather than beat writers, covered many of the games. The Tapers were led by "Warren" (i.e., Bruce) Spraggins (25), Sylvester Blye (22) and Roger Kaiser (20), while Chicago got 21 from Kelly Coleman and 16 from Herschell Turner.[40] The Oaks and Steers played again the next night, but the attendance (1,372) was half of the previous night as the Steers won again (123–111) behind Bridges' 30 points.

That same night the first of the new doubleheader formats was tried in Philadelphia before 1,262 fans. The Majors and the Tapers split the two games of 30 minutes each, with the Tapers winning 51–46 and the Majors by a 65–63 score. Fans were polled and overwhelmingly disliked the contest; this was the first and last of these doubleheaders.[41]

The next night the Rens had their home opener and drew 8,233 fans to watch them lose to the Chicago Majors, 97–89. The Globetrotters also played in this doubleheader, the likely source of the large crowd. Connie Hawkins (24) and Jim McCoy (19) led the Rens while Jeff Cohen, the former Hawaii Chief (24), and Bucky Bolyard, the former Ren (20), topped the scoring for Chicago.[42]

The Steers went south in California to play Long Beach and proceeded to lose to the Chiefs three games in a row. Bill Bridges kept up his hot scoring with 61 points in the three games. Bill Spivey and Ben Warley (former Piper) were high scorers for the Chiefs in the three games that drew 2,294 and 1,000 in reported attendance for two of the three games. Even more impressive than the wins was the fact that Kansas City suffered its worst defeat in two years in the 103–74 loss on November 18.[43] Long Beach's roster, besides the 33-year-old Spivey and Ben Warley, had Ron Horn (who had played for the Saints, the St. Louis Hawks and attended Iowa); Jerry Grote; Grady McCollum; Charlie Hadden (a former L.A. Jet); Garner and Sells. The roster had only two Chiefs from the previous season.

Oakland picked up its first victory, over Chicago in overtime, on the 18th, and the Rens topped the Tapers that same night. The Majors lost to Oakland the next night, also.

Nine. The ABL Begins a Second Year, 1962–1963

As the Steers returned home to face Chicago, they made a trade with the Rens of Jack Audon for John Ritter, who had played at little St. Benedict in Atchison, Kansas, and might have hometown value in attracting a few more fans. Audon was later released by the Rens, but Ritter contributed for the rest of the year.[44]

The Steers topped the Majors in their home opener at Municipal Auditorium, 111–85, with Maurice King (29) and Gene Tormohlen (18) leading the scoring. Coleman (20) and Cohen (15) led the Majors. An encouraging sign was the 4,180 fans who turned out for the contest.[45] That same night Syracuse played the Boston Celtics in Philadelphia and drew 4,490. The next night the Steers drew their biggest crowd ever for a game where the Globetrotters were not part of a twin bill, with 8,721 fans crowding into the Municipal Auditorium, but the Steers lost at the buzzer to Chicago, 91–90. The team's top scorer was John Windsor, the rookie from Stanford.[46]

The Steers seemed to be establishing a solid fan base, as did Pittsburgh, at least initially, but Oakland and Long Beach were still tenuous. The Rens played a home game in McKeesport (PA) at the end of the month and still drew 1,913 fans, not great, but acceptable.[47] Saperstein had Chicago playing "home" contests all over the region, perhaps sensing that the Chicago fans had not demonstrated a deep involvement with the team. Perhaps the lack of home games was a factor, but, more likely was the overall lack of interest in pro basketball with all the top college teams in Chicago at that time—Loyola, DePaul, and Northwestern, as well as Bradley, which came up from Peoria frequently for games in the Chicago Stadium. The Tapers continued their inability to draw in Philadelphia, as had been the case in Washington and Long Island.

Chicago managed to draw 6,829 to a "home" game in Toronto (which probably also had the Globetrotters in a second game) with the Chiefs, who won their seventh game in a row, 96–87. Long Beach would win number 8 in Rochester the next night against the Majors where an estimated 5,000 showed up to see Ron Horn (22) and Bill Spivey (21) lead the 103–74 rout of the Majors.[48]

At this point the league faced its first issue not involving attendance; this was an ethical issue. On November 29, the Philadelphia Tapers signed Bill Chmelewski to a contract. Chmelewski was a 6'10" center for Dayton who had quit school earlier in the fall to support his wife and expected child. With few actual job opportunities, he chose to sign with the Tapers, but the league had a rule that prohibited players from playing until their class had graduated, which was 1964 for Chmelewski. Only the Steers, specifically Coach Johnny Dee and vice president Mike Cleary, protested the signing, and both said that they would quit over the issue, since they felt it damaged the ABL's reputation, as well as their own. The fear was that colleges would prohibit ABL representatives from campuses, were this to be allowed, although the Tapers then said that it was a hardship signing, just as that of Connie Hawkins had been.

The Steers were in the midst of a winning streak, but Dee refused to coach. He did watch from the stands for a couple games before returning home to Denver briefly. The Tapers refused to back down, and Dee was absent for a week. He returned to coach on December 5, saying that he would protest every game the ABL played. Cleary's resignation was permanent, but the hardship contention seemed to be accepted and the season continued with Chmelewski a member of the Tapers.[49]

The Chiefs continued their season-opening winning streak, but the Steers were also winning consistently, after their uneven start. The first week of December found the Chiefs at 10–1, after dropping a game to the Rens in Pittsburgh before 4,774 fans. The rest of the standings were as follows:

Long Beach	10–1
Pittsburgh	5–2
Kansas City	8–6
Philadelphia	4–6
Chicago	5–10
Oakland	2–9

Bill Bridges led the league with the most points, although Connie Hawkins had the highest average. The leaders by average were

Hawkins	28.5
Bridges	25.8
Spivey	21.1
Horn	20.0
Staverman	18.6
Warley	17.7

Nine. The ABL Begins a Second Year, 1962-1963

Attendance was beginning to settle at lower levels, with occasional bursts of higher totals. The Chiefs attracted 3,847 to Chicago on November 30, probably as a result of their impressive winning streak. It continued as Spivey, McCollum and Warley all topped 20 points in a 118–99 win over the Majors.[50]

In a cost-saving measure, all ABL teams were required to have their rosters at 9 players by December 3. This would lead to some problems in the next few weeks due to illnesses and injuries. The Rens traded for Charlie Tyra and dropped Jack Ardon, whom they had obtained from the Steers. The Tapers received a draft pick in 1963 for Tyra.

After losing to the Rens to end their streak at 10, the Chiefs came back to top the Rens, before just 1,679 fans in Pittsburgh. That looked great, compared to the "crowd" in Philadelphia where only 394 paid to see the Tapers defeat Chicago, 113–87. At their next home game the Tapers drew 874. In Kansas City, the Steers began the first of their games on the Kansas side, playing in Memorial Hall with a capacity of 2,800. The Steers nearly filled the building (2,587) in their win over the Chiefs, 112–91, as Bill Bridges got 44 points and 26 rebounds and Larry Staverman got 34 points. Spivey was ejected in the third quarter with 17 points for his rough play and fighting. This was a pattern that the Chiefs had established and practiced from the start of the season.[51]

Pittsburgh began to have triple-digit attendance as 942 watched the Rens top Chicago. The Steers, however, continued to draw adequately. Nearly 2,600 squeezed into Memorial Hall for a pounding of Long Beach, 113–90. Bridges and Tormohlen dominated the big front line of the Chiefs with 36 points, 24 rebounds, and 27 points, 21 rebounds, respectively. Connie Hawkins drew a few fans (1,872) into Chicago Stadium to see him score 34 points in a Rens' victory. Still, attendance was perilously low for the league.[52]

Not that the NBA was doing so well, with crowds that were often at around 4,000 to 5000, but they also did have a few crowds of more than 10,000, particularly at Madison Square Garden doubleheaders. About a quarter to a third of NBA games were doubleheaders, so that meant fewer home games overall, plus the visiting teams got none of the gate. So the NBA was not bringing in big bucks, either, but they were staying afloat, and their owners usually owned the arenas (and often the

NHL teams, too) and didn't have to pay rent and had more opportunities to sell out their stadia.

The Chiefs began to "come back" to the league and were 12–4 by December 10, while the Steers were 12–6, Pittsburgh 8–4 and the Tapers 7–4. In a game on the 9th, the Chiefs slipped by the Rens, 109–107, before only 682 fans. The biggest loss, however, was Hawkins, who scored 33 points, but near the end of the game was hammered by Spivey and had to leave the contest. Spivey was ejected. Hawkins then missed two weeks as one eye was not able to focus properly. He was hospitalized, treated and returned to the lineup on December 26.[53]

On the same night that Hawkins was injured, Bill Bridges started his own hot streak. He had 55 points (a new ABL record, breaking Hawkins' mark of 54) in a 125–123 win over Oakland, then followed that with 49 in an overtime win over Chicago before 3,166 at the Municipal Auditorium for "Youngsters Night." The attendance was deceptive because of the reduced rates for youngsters.[54] Bridges followed with totals of 34, 32, and 17 in the Steers' wins over Chicago and Pittsburgh twice.[55]

The declining attendance, the rough play of the Chiefs and the loss of Hawkins from the lineup, which exacerbated the drop in attendance, forced the league to institute a formal fine for excessive fighting. Any technical for starting a fight would result in a $50 fine and the potential for suspension. This may seem mild, but most players were not making more than about $10,000 so it was more onerous than it appears today, though it was still a mild reprimand.[56]

The Steers and Bill Bridges continued their hot play as the team ultimately won ten games in a row. Following his five games of averaging 37 points per game, Bridges scored 27, 35, 35, 28, 19 and 32 in the next six games for an average in those 11 games of 32.8 points per game. The Steers extended their win streak to ten, but still weren't drawing more than 2000 fans except for two doubleheaders involving the Globetrotters. First, the Steers beat the Tapers in Kiel Auditorium in St. Louis before more than 7,500 fans. Then, they returned home and topped the Tapers before 10,228 in a 108–97 victory.[57]

The rumors of the league collapsing were becoming more widespread. Ken Kruger, the Steers' team president, denied that the season would come to a halt, although he admitted that "the financial situation was not the best, but we certainly don't want to stop now." For

Nine. The ABL Begins a Second Year, 1962-1963

the season the Steers had drawn 49,802 in 22 games, but things had picked up over the past 11 games, Kruger noted. The previous year had been slightly ahead of the 1962-1963 pace, but had improved significantly over the last 11 games as the team ended 1961-1962 at 92,586. In this new season, however, replicating that would be difficult in the smaller confines of the Memorial Arena in Kansas, where most of the game would be played.[58]

That week, attendance in Pittsburgh (6,914), Philadelphia (4,007) and Oakland (3,448) reached levels that would have been more than sufficient to sustain the league. Oakland's crowd was their largest of the season as they won their ninth in a row on their home floor.[59] But it may have been too late.

On December 29, league president Saperstein issued a denial that the ABL was folding. He noted improvements at the box office on the West Coast and Kansas City, but conceded that attendance was down in Chicago, Philadelphia and Pittsburgh. The next day, in what would be the last game of the season and the league, the Tapers defeated the Majors in Cleveland where 7,000 fans came to show their continued support for pro basketball in that city. The Tapers won, despite having only six players in uniform.[60]

One not in uniform was Roger Kaiser. He had severe abdominal pains, and the doctors in Cleveland wanted to do surgery. He quickly vetoed that, saying "My car was in New York, my wife was in New Jersey and my home was in Georgia. I took a plane back to New York, where I was diagnosed with an ulcer. While in the hospital, my family visited and my little cousin said that I didn't have a job anymore since the ABL had folded. And that's how I heard that I was finished as a pro basketball player."[61]

And on the last day of 1962, the American Basketball League ended its existence. Paul Cohen, the Tapers' president and owner of Technical Tape Corporation, revealed that he had been the owner of two teams in the league, the Tapers and the Rens. Bill Rosenhohn had been "bearding" for Cohen in order to keep the league at a necessary minimum of six teams. In addition, Cohen went on to reveal that Saperstein was the owner of both the Majors and the Oakland Oaks. He said that not a single team was operating in the black and that if the league had carried on, "each team would have lost a quarter of a million dollars." This was a significant amount, even for wealthy men with other sources of income like Cohen.

For Cohen, most of the losses were in Philadelphia; in Pittsburgh the team had drawn about 4,000 per game, he said. The Tapers had drawn only 4,500 paid admission for their last ten games, despite what had been publicized, and this with a half-price ticket giveaway as part of a food chain promotion. The last three games, paid admissions were 96, 56 and 52 (all at the Arena), with only 181 for the last game played at Convention Hall.[62] Cohen noted, though, "If you think our crowds were bad, you should have seen Chicago. They had 31 paid one night."[63]

Reactions ranged from shock on the part of owner Kruger, who called the news "horrible," to opportunistic on the part of Chicago Zephyrs' general manager Frank Lane, who said that he would try to sign players such as Roger Kaiser. Krueger, in a statement, said that he wanted to keep the league alive with Pittsburgh, Oakland, Long Beach and Kansas City, but that was not able to be done.

Final standings for the attenuated year were as follows:

Team	Record
Kansas City Steers	22–9
Long Beach Chiefs	16–8
Pittsburgh Rens	12–10
Oakland Oaks	11–14
Philadelphia Tapers	10–18
Chicago Majors	8–20

Kansas City was declared the champion. An interesting aside, Chicago and Long Beach never met during the season.

A number of players went on to or continued NBA careers following their time in the ABL. This included Bill Bridges, Larry Staverman, Nick Mantis, Larry Siegfried, Ben Warley, Dick Barnett, Johnny Cox, Connie Dierking, John Barnhill, Mike Farmer and Kenny Sears. A few players were able to extend their careers in the ABL another year or so after finishing in the NBA. These included Bill Sharman, George Yardley, Hal Lear, Archie Dees and Nat (Sweetwater) Clifton. A few star players in the ABL were never given a chance in the NBA because they had done most of their "damage" as three-point shooters, an adoption that the NBA didn't make until 1979. Thus, Bucky Bolyard, Roger Kaiser and Tony Jackson never played in the NBA. Jackson was implicated in the 1960 point-shaving scandals for not reporting a bribe, as was Hawkins,

Nine. The ABL Begins a Second Year, 1962-1963

and Spivey in the early 1950s. Spivey was also given no chance by the NBA, but Connie Hawkins successfully sued the NBA, after a short career with the Globetrotters and in the ABA, before entering the league with the Phoenix Suns in 1969 at the age of 27.

Coaches in the ABL were all capable and had either played or coached previously in the NBA. Former NBA players Jack McMahon, Neil Johnston, Bill Sharman and Stan Stutz (actually only a BAA player) illustrate that point. John McLendon and Ermer Robinson became the first two African American coaches in professional basketball in 1961 and 1962, respectively, years before Bill Russell became the first African American coach in the NBA in 1966.

As for the league, the three-point shot was adopted by the ABA in 1967 when the league began and remained in effect until that league was dissolved in 1976. The wider lane, in a slightly different form, was also adopted and adapted by the NBA and into international rules. The unusual series scheduling was never adopted by the NBA, nor was the idea of smaller rosters, but the NBA Players Association, once it gained recognition, would never have allowed such a notion.

Saperstein continued with the Globetrotters, but never fully mended his relationship with the NBA, a league he had helped nurture through the 1950s. The NBA dropped their doubleheaders within two years, as well as their franchises in the smaller cities of the old NBL. The Syracuse Nationals moved to Philadelphia in 1963 and became the 76ers, abandoning the last small NBL city still operating in the league. The Zephyrs left Chicago for Baltimore in 1963, voiding Chicago of a franchise until 1966 when the Bulls began play.

There are few films existent of the ABL, and the myth of an inept league is popular, if anything is remembered at all. But the quality of play compared to the NBA was nearly equivalent, though the depth of talent was much shallower.[64]

Shooting in the ABL was excellent and defense was as good or better than the NBA, which had little emphasis on it at that time, other than the Celtics with Bill Russell. The ABL is gone and largely forgotten — unfortunate considering its large impact on professional basketball during its play and following its demise.

Ten
The ABL, and Then What?

The ABL died about four years into its original conception and one and a half seasons into real play. It was a short but meaningful life. What can be learned and observed from the American Basketball League's existence and demise?

Most significantly, it was clear that there was more than sufficient basketball talent to sustain more professional teams than the nine that the NBA had in 1961–1963. The NBA responded, although slowly, by expanding to ten teams in 1966-1967. The Warriors moved to San Francisco in 1962, partly as a result of the sale of the team to Bay Area basketball enthusiasts, but the NBA was not averse to the move in order to try and "claim" the Bay Area from the upstart ABL San Francisco Saints/Oakland Oaks. It is most likely that the NBA would have been in the Bay Area soon, but the presence of the ABL there certainly accelerated that plan. The move to San Francisco by the Warriors left Philadelphia without a team and the next year the Syracuse franchise relocated to Philadelphia as the 76ers in order to reclaim one of the original BAA cities with its rich basketball tradition.

In 1966 the NBA decided to try Chicago once again, and the Chicago Bulls were formed. They were almost as unsuccessful as the Packer/Zephyrs had been, but they did play in a better venue (Chicago Stadium) and had better financial backing, in addition to better shared television revenue from the league. The Bulls finally improved enough to make the play-offs in 1969-1970, and attendance began to slowly increase as a result. The franchise began regularly selling out games in the early 1970s when Chet Walker, Bob Love and Jerry Sloan (later joined by Norm Van Lier) led the franchise to regular 50-win seasons.

The ABL led other, more deep-pocketed individuals to believe that

Ten. The ABL, and Then What?

a second league could thrive, and the American Basketball Association began in 1967-1968 with 11 teams. Responding to that, and seeking to establish their league in new locations, the NBA expanded that same year to Seattle and San Diego. Both franchises ultimately departed their original locations (San Diego to Houston in 1971 and Seattle to Oklahoma City, after 41 years, in 2008). The next season (1968-1969) the NBA expanded again, adding Milwaukee and Phoenix to the league, while the ABA continued to scuffle without a major television contract and relocating teams. In 1970 the NBA expanded again, adding teams in Cleveland, Portland and Buffalo. In four years the league had gone from 9 to 17 teams, and the ABA continued with 11 teams in those cities almost totally devoid of an NBA team.

Clearly the ABL notion had been correct; there were many more cities where the professional basketball game could exist and possibly thrive. Would the NBA have expanded as swiftly and the ABA even have existed if not for the forays of the ABL? That is highly unlikely. The NBA club of owners had a nice deal with the ten clubs, limiting revenue sharing and giving players few choices if they decided to turn professional. The ABL changed the thinking, and that carried over into the ABA and the player wars of the late 1960s and early 1970s that led to the ABA agreement to fold four teams (Denver, Indiana, New York/New Jersey and San Antonio) into the NBA in 1975. Clearly, the ABL was the catalyst for what was wholesale change in professional basketball in the 1960s and 1970s.

Of the eight initial ABL teams, six were in cities with no pro team. Today, only three do not have a team, but one, Kansas City, shared the Kings from 1972 to 1985, before the team moved to Sacramento. Los Angeles now has two franchises, again, with the Kings, ironically, possibly moving in 2013. Hawaii has never had another major franchise, and Pittsburgh had an ABA franchise, but has never been awarded one in the NBA. Washington and Cleveland are established franchises, and San Francisco/Oakland/Golden State got an NBA franchise in the ABL's second year.

On the court, many players and coaches were the product of ABL success and carried that success into the NBA. Coach Jack McMahon went from the Steers to the Zephyrs, then the Royals and Rockets. Bill Sharman, who parted from the Celtics, and Walter Brown, under less

Abe Saperstein and the American Basketball League

than ideal circumstances, returned to the NBA as coach of the Warriors in 1967, then later coached the Lakers, after a three-year stint in the ABA. Sharman remains a Lakers vice president.

Although John McLendon never coached in the NBA, his singular achievement as the first African American head coach of a major professional franchise cannot be dismissed. His "run and gun" offense was highly influential in college and pro ball, and he was enshrined in the Naismith Memorial Basketball Hall of Fame in 1979 as a contributor.

Ermer Robinson was the second African American coach in pro ball, leading the Oakland Oaks for the 1962-1963 season. He had been a star with the Harlem Globetrotters, most notably the 1948-1949 team that upset the Minneapolis Lakers, led by George Mikan. Robinson died in 1983 at the age of 59 or 60. His obituaries neglected any mention of his ABL coaching or his role as business manager of the 1961-1962 Chicago Majors.

Left to right: George Steinbrenner, Pipers owner, and John McLendon, Pipers coach, flank rookie Larry Siegfried at Siegfried's contract signing (The Cleveland Press Collection, Michael Schwartz Library, Cleveland State University).

Ten. The ABL, and Then What?

The unspoken quota on black players in the NBA forced a number of African Americans to look for alternative venues to play pro basketball and the ABL provided that. Of the 1961-1962 rosters, African Americans comprised the following numbers of each team: Chicago (6 of 11); Cleveland (6 of 13); Hawaii (2 of 11); Kansas City (4 of 10); Los Angeles (3 of 11); Pittsburgh (3 of 9); San Francisco (2 of 12); and Washington (4 of 12). Comparable data on the NBA had two to four African Americans on the rosters of the nine teams with almost all starters, leaving only nine blacks as non-starters.

The most well-known former NBA players returned to the NBA, either following the 1961-1962 season, or after the ABL folded on December 31, 1962. These included Dick Barnett, who returned to the NBA with the Lakers for three seasons, then had nine with the Knicks that included two NBA championships. Gene Conley, the Red Sox pitcher, returned to the Knicks for two years. Archie Dees, cut by the Pistons, returned to the league and played 21 games with Chicago and St. Louis in 1962-1963. Connie Dierking returned to the NBA in 1963 and played ten more years, mostly with Cincinnati. Larry Staverman played in 1963-1964 with Chicago/Baltimore, Detroit and Cincinnati. He later coached in the ABA for three years. Nick Mantis played with Chicago and St. Louis in 1962-1963 in his return to the NBA. Kenny Sears returned to the Knicks in 1962-1963, but they traded him to the Warriors during that season, and he played there in 1963-1964 before retiring. Mike Farmer played four more years with the St. Louis Hawks from 1962 to 1966. Ron Horn played for the Lakers in 1962-1963, after the ABL folded, then played in the ABA in 1967-1968 with Denver. Maury King played with the Chicago Zephyrs in 1963 after the ABL folded.

A number of other players went from their debuts in the ABL to playing in the NBA and/or the ABA. These included Hank Whitney, Herschell Turner, Johnny Cox, Ben Warley, John Barnhill, Larry Siegfried, Dan Swartz, Bill Bridges, Gene Tormohlen and Larry Comley. Tony Jackson and Connie Hawkins played in the ABA, before Hawkins managed to win his court battle and play in the NBA. Jackson remained barred from the NBA, played two years in the ABA where he averaged 15.9 points per game, then worked as a recreation director in Brooklyn. He died in 2005 at age 65 of cancer.

Off the court, the league had an influence, also. There were referees that either went on to the NBA or had some prominence as a result of other positions they held. Among the latter was Doug Harvey who began as an ABL referee doing Oakland and Long Beach games the year that he began as a rookie umpire in the National League. He umpired until 1992 and was inducted into the Baseball Hall of Fame in 2010. That same season (1962-1963), a journeyman baseball player named Whitey Herzog began refereeing in the ABL, mostly Kansas City home games. Herzog, of course, began a long managerial career in 1972 with the Texas Rangers, but found his greatest success in Kansas City and St. Louis with the Royals and Cardinals, respectively. He ended up with 2,409 career managerial victories and was also inducted into the Baseball Hall of Fame in 2010.

John Vanak began his pro referee career with the ABL in 1961-1962, doing mostly Pittsburgh home games, and was hired by the NBA in 1962 for that season, remaining there until 1969 when he led a number of NBA referees to jump to the American Basketball Association. He returned to the NBA in 1976 and remained until the late 1980s.

Monte Moore, the voice of the Kansas City Steers, was heard on air by Charlie Finley, who had just bought the Kansas City A's. He hired Moore to be the voice of the A's, and he moved with the club to Oakland where he continued as their announcer until 1977 on radio and until 1980 on television.

Another person involved with broadcasting, in this case, San Francisco Saints games, was Franklin Mieuli, whose Franklin Mieuli Radio and Television Consulting produced games for a number of major sports and teams. In 1962 he became the principal owner of the Golden State Warriors and remained in that position until 1986 when he sold the team.

The most famous owner was, of course, George Steinbrenner, who, at the age of 31, was the youngest owner in the ABL and certainly the most "hands on," as he later reiterated with the Yankees. Steinbrenner brought in Ralph Wilson as a financial partner. Wilson was one of the founders of the Buffalo Bills AFL franchise and remains its president at age 93 (as of 2012).

And then there was Abe Saperstein, who bankrolled most of the league in its second year and lost a bundle. He did pursue his dream of a second league, but it did not succeed. He continued to lead the Globetrotters, the most famous professional basketball team in the world, as they toured more than 100 countries and popularized basketball inter-

Ten. The ABL, and Then What?

nationally, long before the NBA and before Michael Jordan made the NBA even more popular. Saperstein, unfortunately, died a sudden death in 1966 at the age of 63. He was inducted into the Naismith Memorial Basketball Hall of Fame in 1971 as a contributor.

The ABL was the first pro league to use the 30-second shot clock, adopted by FIBA in 1956. In 1971 the NCCA adopted the use of the 30-second clock for women, but didn't adopt a clock for men until 1985, and it was 45 seconds. That was changed to 35 seconds in 1993, and there is continued pressure to reduce it to 30 seconds.

The NBA soon adopted the wider foul lane, and that has been altered to wider lengths since. The trapezoidal lane, which was favored by FIBA for international play, has still not been adopted, by the NCAA or the NBA. That still may happen. What won't happen will be the doubleheaders with the same teams playing reduced game lengths. The split schedule with winners in the first half meeting second half winners never was adopted either, except for the 1981 baseball season, when the league adopted the format because of the strike that year.

The most widely adopted ABL rule has been the three-point shot, derided as a gimmick by NBA owners in 1961 and also looked askance by the NCAA. FIBA, however, adopted the three-point shot in 1984, at a shorter distance, 20.5 feet. The ABA had taken the three-point shot as their own from the beginning of that league in 1967, but the acceptance of ABA teams into the NBA in 1985 essentially ended the use of the shot until it was adopted by the league, at a distance of 23'9", in 1979. The distance has been modified but is back at the original adopted distance, still shorter than that of the ABL. The NCAA allowed leagues to use the shot in the 1980s, but the distances varied. In 1986 it became a standard 19'9" for all NCAA games. It was moved a foot back for men in 2008-2009. The shot has truly changed the game.

During the two brief ABL seasons, the Topps Gum Company failed to print any regular sets of basketball cards of the ABL or the NBA. The only cards made in a regular, national set were from the Fleer Gum Company who produced a 66-card set with 44 players pictured, less than half the NBA players. Topps had no basketball sets from their inaugural set, in 1957, until 1969.

The only former ABL players depicted on Topps cards (the only company producing national sets from 1969 to 1981 are Bill Bridges,

Dick Barnett, Connie Dierking, Connie Hawkins and Larry Siegfried. It is instructive to note the way that Topps, a partner with the NBA, explained (or did not explain) the careers of these NBA players during 1961-1962.

In Bill Bridges' 1970-1971 card, there are no statistical data for his years in the ABL; rather it appears that his career started with the Atlanta Hawks in 1962-1963 when he played in just 27 games. This was the statistical information on his prior card (69–70) and would remain the same throughout his career, which ended in 1975. Only in the text of the 1970-1971 card is there any mention of the fact that Bridges started in the ABL, with the one-sentence history: "Bill joined the Hawks following the collapse of the American Basketball League in January, 1963, after a season and a half with Kansas City." As noted, later cards omitted this, and the ABL's existence was not acknowledged.

Connie Hawkins' "card career" also did not begin until 1969-1970, after his successful suit against the NBA and his rookie NBA season in 1969-1970. Topps acknowledged Hawkins' earlier years with the ABA and provided those data, as Topps would for all of Hawkins' cards until his retirement in 1976. Again, as with Bridges, the second Hawkins card provided acknowledgment of his ABL career in a sentence. "After attending Iowa, he joined the Pittsburgh Rens of American Basketball League where he was loop's MVP at age 19." No further recognition of Hawkins in the ABL came after this in any of Hawkins' five cards.

Dick Barnett's cards tell a different story. His 1969-1970 and 1970-1971 cards say nothing about the ABL, and his career statistical data omit the 1961-1962 season totally. Barnett played five games in the 1973-1974 season before retiring at age 36. Barnett's last cards in 1971-1972, 1972-1973 and 1973-1974 all took a different approach to his ABL year of 1961-1962. Rather than simply skipping that year with no explanation, these cards now had a notation for 1961-1962, "DID NOT PLAY."

Connie Dierking had cards in 1969-1970 and 1970-1971. None mentioned the ABL or the NIBL, and the gap of two years in the statistical record was not noted. So, too, with Larry Siegfried; his three cards (1969-1970, 1970-1971, 1971-1972) all start his career as a pro with 1963-1964, when he joined the Celtics. His year in the ABL with Cleveland went unmentioned.

In its own way, Topps provided a revisionist view of pro basketball

Ten. The ABL, and Then What?

history. In that they helped a new generation of youngsters in not knowing that the ABL ever existed.

Clearly the ABL gave rise to the ABA, which speeded up the expansion of the NBA and the pro game overall. But the ABL not only goes without credit or acknowledgment; it is totally forgotten by most basketball followers, and when mentioned is usually associated with or identified as the ABA. Thus this volume and its efforts to rectify a slight that has lasted 50 years. Thanks, Abe.

Appendix 1
Team Standings, 1961-1962

EASTERN DIVISION

	First Half			Second Half			Season		
	W.	L.	PCT.	W.	L.	PCT.	W.	L.	PCT.
Cleveland	24	18	.571	21	18	.538	45	36	.556
Pittsburgh	23	19	.548	18	21	.462	41	40	.506
Chicago	18	26	.409	21	18	.538	39	44	.470
New York	14	28	.333	17	22	.436	31	50	.383

WESTERN DIVISION

	First Half			Second Half			Season		
	W.	L.	PCT.	W.	L.	PCT.	W.	L.	PCT.
Kansas City	28	12	.700	26	13	.667	54	25	.684
Los Angeles	24	15	.615						
San Francisco	19	17	.528	19	21	.475	38	38	.500
Hawaii	13	28	.317	16	25	.390	29	53	.354

Appendix 2
ABL Scoring, 1961-1962

Tables on following pages.

ABL Scoring, 1961-1962

INDIVIDUAL STATISTICS
EASTERN DIVISION

Chicago	G	2P GA	2P GM	3P GA	3P GM	PCT	FTA	FTM	PCT	PF	Tot REB	A	TP	Per AVG.	Game Min.
Tony Jackson, NY	72	663	259	383	141	382	398	319	802	163	346	110	1,260	17.5	2,232
Herschell Turner	72	901	427	78	19	456	379	283	747	220	359	190	1,194	16.5	2,652
Kelly Coleman	77	1,058	391	189	56	358	229	147	642	220	551	85	1,097	14.2	2,313
Bob Wilkinson	75	602	240	97	32	389	296	245	828	211	209	129	821	10.9	1,569
Henry Whitney, LA	74	656	278	0	0	424	189	123	651	273	662	47	679	9.1	1,791
John Wessels	64	527	236	1	0	447	208	167	803	205	319	45	639	9.9	1,605
Jack Fitzpatrick	65	462	205	0	0	444	290	196	676	267	476	74	606	9.3	1,662
Leroy Gibson	78	492	209	3	0	422	166	128	771	205	278	80	546	7.0	1,647
Nat Clifton	61	459	186	17	3	397	184	143	777	258	425	138	524	8.5	1,716
George Price, Haw	25	191	87	1	1	458	75	50	667	71	140	32	227	9.0	666
Ron Sobie	8	64	29	10	5	459	41	35	854	36	34	17	108	13.5	239
Tony Wilcox	18	42	20	0	0	476	19	13	684	32	55	6	53	2.9	243
Joe Scott	10	63	17	9	3	278	13	9	692	14	11	9	52	5.2	141
Mel Davis	17	42	14	0	0	333	5	4	800	14	26	2	32	1.8	123
Sam Barnard	4	8	4	0	0	500	3	2	667	5	4	0	10	2.5	34
Frank Burks	3	3	0	0	0	000	3	2	667	5	3	1	2	0.6	20
Ken Peterson	1	1	0	0	0	000	0	0	000	0	0	0	0	0.0	5

Appendix 2

Cleveland	G	2P GA	2P GM	3P GA	3P GM	PCT	FTA	FTM	PCT	PF	Tot REB	A	TP	Per AVG.	Game Min.
John Cox	80	1,026	470	152	50	441	483	392	812	232	685	122	1,482	18.5	2,844
Dick Barnett	50	1,018	506	15	2	492	371	296	798	110	352	147	1,314	26.2	2,041
Ben Warley	72	820	328	26	10	400	293	216	737	224	717	84	902	12.5	2,109
John Barnhill	75	623	295	133	40	443	194	142	732	87	229	153	852	11.3	1,861
Connie Dierking, NY	69	757	311	14	3	407	278	190	683	209	515	94	821	11.8	1,726
Larry Siegfried	71	496	209	23	3	408	247	212	858	133	158	148	639	9.0	1,659
Jim Darrow	55	448	194	5	1	430	121	91	752	160	66	114	482	8.7	1,219
Bob Keller, NY	54	359	162	1	0	450	179	122	682	162	361	34	446	8.2	1,222
Archie Dees	34	218	114	4	1	518	108	87	806	93	175	34	318	9.3	606
Lowery Kirk, Haw-Pit	53	233	95	10	3	403	105	80	762	119	128	39	279	5.2	997
Nick Romanoff	70	187	80	1	0	426	80	53	663	187	240	44	213	3.0	1,008
Rossie Johnson	27	164	62	20	9	386	35	23	657	33	77	10	174	6.4	313
Gus Guydon	8	10	3	4	1	286	1	1	000	3	2	5	10	1.2	61
Bevo Francis	2	5	2	0	0	400	0	0	000	4	6	0	4	2.0	21
Max Jameson	1	0	0	0	0	000	0	0	000	2	0	0	0	0.0	3

ABL Scoring, 1961-1962

New York	G	2P GA	2P GM	3P GA	3P GM	PCT	FTA	FTM	PCT	PF	Tot REB	A	TP	Per AVG.	Game Min.
Dan Swartz, LA	70	1,245	503	81	34	405	697	631	905	327	630	171	1,739	24.8	2,792
Roger Kaiser	80	1,020	456	238	72	420	481	428	890	220	261	232	1,556	19.4	2,947
Sy Blye	81	1,057	487	5	1	460	485	324	668	266	625	106	1,301	16.0	2,696
Roger Taylor, Clev	79	1,074	462	21	8	429	339	293	864	259	192	323	1,241	15.7	2,815
Jack Adams, Clev	82	713	309	34	12	430	562	469	835	260	456	160	1,123	13.6	2,316
Ron Zagar, Chi	79	830	297	165	52	351	263	177	673	185	198	207	927	11.7	2,150
Bruce Spraggins	78	585	252	7	1	427	241	160	664	232	354	34	667	8.5	1,612
Leroy Wright	77	408	148	9	1	357	193	74	383	171	506	58	373	4.8	1,732
Gene Conley	45	291	111	26	10	382	162	118	728	186	320	38	370	8.2	932
Ed Willis	47	352	116	14	3	325	127	74	583	97	140	106	315	6.7	1,098
Dick Brott-Cle-Haw	63	292	117	0	0	401	107	60	561	188	435	58	294	4.6	1,289
Jack Sullivan	41	253	93	24	6	357	97	71	732	95	68	59	275	6.7	729
Bob Hopkins	15	80	30	0	0	375	17	12	706	18	62	2	72	4.8	204
Jim Daniels	17	58	14	5	2	254	42	27	643	31	23	11	61	3.5	338
Bob Clarke	8	35	9	0	0	257	3	2	667	5	17	11	22	2.7	72
Willie Jones	5	9	3	2	0	273	7	4	571	6	2	4	10	2.0	24

Appendix 2

Pittsburgh	G	2P GA	2P GM	3P GA	3P GM	PCT	FTA	FTM	PCT	PF	Tot REB	A	TP	Per AVG.	Game Min.
Connie Hawkins	78	1,490	760	6	1	509	787	622	790	260	1,038	183	2,145	27.5	3,349
Bucky Bolyard	79	809	335	309	104	393	401	304	753	238	171	240	1,286	16.2	2,813
Phil Rollins	80	561	266	299	89	413	368	312	848	280	184	296	1,111	13.8	2,660
Walt Mangham	79	747	330	24	11	442	219	161	735	232	594	65	854	10.8	2,251
Hal Lear, LA-Clev	60	670	290	6	3	433	251	199	793	127	137	160	788	13.1	1,631
Charlie Curtis, NY	58	703	289	3	1	411	182	137	753	202	422	60	718	12.3	1,746
Jon Cincebox	65	494	229	10	2	458	154	119	773	209	401	54	583	8.9	1,659
Jim McCoy	76	462	182	18	8	396	42	93	655	157	260	60	481	6.3	1,608
Skeeter Sullins	41	274	115	1	0	418	82	62	756	113	172	17	292	7.1	801
Allan Seiden	21	142	62	9	0	411	98	71	724	35	24	26	195	9.2	385
Ed Washington	16	85	30	1	0	349	51	30	588	43	70	13	90	5.6	356
Niel Johnston	5	37	15	1	1	421	24	16	667	17	18	10	49	9.8	106
Lee Patrone	12	49	21	3	0	404	7	3	429	16	15	6	45	3.7	106
Danny Doyle	8	35	12	1	0	333	16	9	563	15	31	0	33	4.1	131
Bob Smith	3	14	5	1	0	333	9	3	333	0	4	3	13	4.3	38
Bob Pawlak	1	3	1	1	1	500	0	0	000	1	0	1	5	5.0	10

ABL Scoring, 1961-1962

INDIVIDUAL STATISTICS
WESTERN DIVISION

	G	2P GA	2P GM	3P GA	3P GM	PCT	FTA	FTM	PCT	PF	Tot REB	A	TP	Per AVG.	Game Min.
Hawaii															
Bill Spivey, LA	78	1,234	640	5	0	5,165	612	493	806	228	875	126	1,773	22.7	2,874
Frank Burgess	80	1,015	424	39	6	408	426	363	852	201	262	120	1,229	15.3	2,645
Herb Lee, Chi	84	897	359	287	98	383	229	187	817	287	168	208	1,193	14.2	2,499
Dave Mills	74	847	348	15	3	407	340	258	759	176	559	72	963	13.0	2,238
Govenor Vaughn, Chi	79	828	339	9	2	407	175	150	857	218	340	77	834	10.5	2,049
Jeff Cohen	76	796	315	9	0	391	252	196	778	223	500	46	826	10.8	1,935
Grady McCollum, Clev	73	687	273	33	11	394	198	140	707	183	341	70	719	9.8	1,991
Dick Wise	74	582	241	17	4	409	153	109	712	216	531	51	603	8.1	1,724
Lee Harman	72	477	161	147	34	313	281	175	623	277	294	226	599	8.3	2,179
Fred Sawyer	72	319	121	7	0	371	127	82	646	184	281	20	324	4.5	1,051
Max Perry	18	112	50	28	2	371	33	26	788	40	30	26	132	7.3	369
Dave Denton	18	59	23	13	4	375	22	18	818	38	31	6	76	4.2	171
Bob Anderegg	6	41	10	2	0	233	24	16	667	7	16	5	36	6.0	96
Bob Young	8	23	6	0	0	261	7	6	857	12	3	3	18	2.2	80
Rick Herrscher	5	26	5	0	0	192	6	3	500	10	6	3	13	2.6	68

Appendix 2

Kansas City	G	2P GA	2P GM	3P GA	3P GM	PCT	FTA	FTM	PCT	PF	Tot REB	A	TP	Per AVG.	Game Min.
Bill Bridges	79	1,400	638	12	3	454	587	412	702	302	1,059	181	1,697	21.4	3,259
Larry Staverman	79	1,015	521	8	1	510	394	342	868	347	697	207	1,387	17.5	2,777
Nick Mantis	77	803	340	240	89	411	242	182	752	216	220	214	1,129	14.6	2,432
Gene Tormohlen	76	780	347	55	17	436	297	202	680	302	808	145	947	12.4	2,301
Maury King	78	506	195	88	34	386	145	118	814	196	205	246	610	7.8	2,105
George Pruitt	79	484	197	23	7	402	291	191	656	124	202	139	606	7.6	1,506
George Patterson, Pitt	75	502	226	1	0	449	161	106	658	162	330	49	558	7.4	1,462
Bryce Vann	76	445	171	136	36	356	121	87	719	148	262	90	537	7.0	1,304
Win Wilfong	69	389	153	111	25	356	179	140	782	204	219	210	521	7.5	1,669
Larry Comley	36	416	159	30	8	374	117	89	761	68	217	36	431	11.9	821
Charlie Henke	36	161	88	2	0	540	58	41	707	63	88	15	217	6.0	371
Bob McDonald	6	15	5	1	0	313	6	2	333	9	12	5	12	2.0	55

ABL Scoring, 1961-1962

	G	2P GA	2P GM	3P GA	3P GM	PCT	FTA	FTM	PCT	PF	Tot REB	A	TP	Per AVG.	Game Min.
San Francisco															
Jim Francis	73	1,029	532	0	0	5,170	421	331	786	269	760	109	1,395	19.1	2,372
Ken Sears	75	821	390	72	24	464	559	478	855	228	471	347	1,330	17.7	2,676
Mike Farmer	67	695	279	194	60	381	253	224	885	179	480	165	962	14.3	2,071
Whitey Bell	71	823	312	54	13	381	277	224	809	250	273	322	887	12.4	2,405
Gene Brown	75	689	286	16	3	410	229	165	721	221	437	314	746	9.9	2,528
John Beberich	73	571	257	28	4	436	287	213	742	203	541	59	739	10.1	1,416
Jim Palmer, Pitt-LA	72	463	222	44	9	456	184	134	728	196	350	76	605	8.4	1,504
Ron Horn	53	417	183	10	2	433	119	80	672	122	275	72	452	8.5	994
Roland Todd	53	398	156	39	10	380	125	94	752	176	215	197	436	8.2	1,328
Larry Beck, LA-Pitt	51	207	82	57	14	364	71	40	563	113	110	49	246	4.8	720
Carroll Williams	12	59	27	1	1	467	31	28	903	33	25	24	85	7.0	228
Bill McClintock	17	73	27	3	0	355	46	22	478	29	57	14	76	4.4	265
Joe Gardere	15	50	22	13	2	381	23	21	913	27	31	11	71	4.7	177
Al Tolen	22	71	23	22	3	280	22	14	636	31	17	17	69	3.1	261
Dave Gunther	7	61	26	3	0	406	17	15	882	15	41	7	67	9.5	151
Hal Theus	12	40	13	1	0	317	17	10	588	13	36	4	36	3.0	139
Jack Allain	17	23	10	0	0	435	11	5	455	39	38	5	25	1.4	101
R.C. Owens	4	3	0	0	0	000	8	4	500	4	9	1	4	1.0	23

Appendix 2

Los Angeles	G	2P GA	2P GM	3P GA	3P GM	3P PCT	FTA	FTM	PCT	PF	Tot REB	A	TP	Per AVG.	Game Min.
George Yardley	25	378	159	37	14	417	148	122	824	95	172	65	482	19.2	948
Larry Friend	39	270	98	163	58	360	88	62	705	93	146	137	432	11.0	1,254
Bob Blue	37	190	77	21	7	398	86	67	779	76	99	60	242	6.5	821
Bill Sharman	19	80	35	8	1	409	37	34	919	30	43	37	107	5.6	346
George Finley	17	22	7	0	0	318	20	12	600	15	21	4	26	1.5	124
Jim Powell	10	18	7	0	0	389	13	6	462	11	22	4	20	2.0	89
Charlie Hadden	6	9	6	3	1	583	0	0	000	9	6	5	15	2.5	51

Appendix 3
Team Standings, 1962-1963

	Won	Lost	PCT.		Won	Lost	PCT.
Kansas City	22	9	.710	Oakland	11	14	.444
Long Beach	16	8	.667	Philadelphia	10	18	.357
Pittsburgh	12	10	.545	Chicago	8	20	.286

Appendix 4
ABL Scoring, 1962-1963

Tables on following pages.

INDIVIDUAL STATISTICS

ABL Scoring, 1962-1963

Chicago Majors	G	2P GA	2P GM	PCT	3P GA	3P GM	PCT	FTA	FTM	PCT	PF	Tot REB	A	TP	Per AVG.	Game Min.
Kelly Coleman	26	493	168	341	135	39	289	67	41	612	75	198	42	494	19.0	1,055
Tony Jackson	27	266	103	387	144	41	285	164	135	823	57	104	26	464	17.1	769
Ron Sobie	28	177	62	350	87	30	345	166	141	849	83	173	94	355	12.6	880
Jeff Cohen	26	328	133	405	1	0	000	77	60	779	95	201	29	326	12.5	794
Mel Davis	27	262	113	431	0	0	000	55	30	545	91	216	34	256	9.4	875
Herschell Turner	27	230	92	400	17	3	176	83	52	627	57	64	40	245	9.0	619
Bucky Bolyard	24	166	54	325	70	25	357	69	46	667	49	51	46	229	9.5	609
Dave Gunther	26	171	74	433	2	0	000	68	46	676	57	117	33	194	7.4	538
George Patterson	18	38	15	395	1	0	000	30	18	600	18	62	7	48	2.6	208

Kansas City Steers	G	2P GA	2P GM	PCT	3P GA	3P GM	PCT	FTA	FTM	PCT	PF	Tot REB	A	TP	Per AVG.	Game Min.
Bill Bridges	29	606	312	515	2	0	000	289	225	779	97	437	87	849	29.2	1,185
Larry Staverman	31	438	240	548	4	3	750	189	160	847	112	259	97	649	20.9	1,134
Maury King	31	330	142	430	98	30	306	105	82	781	94	140	178	456	14.7	1,213
Gene Tormohlen	30	394	176	447	32	6	188	107	63	589	116	402	62	433	14.4	1,112
George Pruitt	31	278	117	421	26	5	192	115	71	617	69	113	88	320	10.3	807
John Windsor	28	246	94	382	0	0	000	90	59	656	74	147	12	247	8.8	548
Win Wilfong	28	133	57	429	70	16	229	55	43	782	70	75	102	205	7.3	752
Bryce Vann	31	145	56	386	44	10	227	41	26	634	49	99	32	168	5.4	471
John Ritter	23	79	24	304	9	2	222	13	7	538	38	43	23	61	2.6	290

Appendix 4

		2P	2P		3P	3P						Tot			Per	Game
Long Beach Chiefs	G	GA	GM	PCT	GA	GM	PCT	FTA	FTM	PCT	PF	REB	A	TP	AVG.	Min.
Bill Spivey	24	433	199	460	1	0	000	180	144	800	79	217	38	542	22.5	838
Ron Horn	24	367	175	477	3	0	000	134	100	746	74	172	31	450	18.7	871
Ben Warley	24	241	89	369	82	23	280	147	106	721	71	226	23	353	14.7	765
Grady McCollum	24	235	101	430	20	5	250	78	54	692	54	108	30	271	11.2	692
Charlie Hadden	24	181	69	381	66	25	379	49	37	755	72	64	58	250	10.4	707
Jerry Grote	24	124	54	435	35	12	343	46	36	783	52	99	56	180	7.5	588
Charlie Sells	24	131	59	450	7	2	286	25	14	560	79	115	17	138	5.7	517
Bill Garner	24	107	40	374	0	0	000	39	25	641	64	103	4	105	4.3	312
Lee Harman	9	41	12	293	5	2	400	22	9	409	35	29	31	39	4.3	163
Jim Hanna	12	32	13	406	2	0	222	6	3	500	19	30	7	29	2.4	128

		2P	2P		3P	3P						Tot			Per	Game
Oakland Oaks	G	GA	GM	PCT	GA	GM	PCT	FTA	FTM	PCT	PF	REB	A	TP	AVG.	Min.
Fred LaCour	25	397	179	451	6	1	167	169	133	787	91	211	92	494	19.7	901
John Turner	25	378	165	437	15	5	333	42	28	667	65	127	72	373	14.9	930
Jim Hadnot	25	309	147	476	0	0	000	106	66	623	107	332	25	360	14.4	960
Roland Todd	24	294	123	418	24	7	292	86	72	837	76	135	75	339	14.1	733
Wayne Yates	25	256	94	367	10	4	400	117	68	581	87	217	30	268	10.7	624
Nick Romanoff	25	196	76	388	26	8	308	67	49	731	108	157	42	225	9.0	755
Dave Mills	21	128	52	406	1	0	000	75	51	680	22	98	17	155	7.3	359
Bob Wilkinson	23	71	28	394	50	11	220	51	39	765	42	52	32	128	5.5	339
Govoner Vaughn	22	122	49	402	10	5	500	11	9	818	38	50	31	122	5.5	350
Gene Brown	19	97	37	381	4	0	000	28	21	750	36	61	46	95	5.0	326

ABL Scoring, 1962-1963

	G	2P GA	2P GM	2P PCT	3P GA	3P GM	3P PCT	FTA	FTM	PCT	PF	Tot REB	A	TP	Per AVG.	Game Min.
Philadelphia Tapers																
Sy Blye	28	452	191	423	3	0	000	172	114	663	113	280	27	496	17.7	975
Roger Kaiser	27	329	134	407	56	25	446	145	124	855	53	140	75	467	17.2	978
Bruce Spraggins	27	311	146	469	7	1	143	96	61	635	77	216	21	356	13.1	746
Roger Taylor	28	335	129	385	26	5	192	95	82	863	78	107	134	355	12.6	1,007
Andy Johnson	28	242	106	438	40	12	300	122	66	541	96	132	44	314	11.2	732
Bill Chmielewski	20	242	94	388	1	0	000	31	20	645	71	148	17	208	10.4	528
Leroy Wright	28	191	74	387	3	1	333	103	44	427	78	257	32	195	6.9	813
Cleo Hill	22	121	48	397	11	2	182	62	43	694	34	78	22	145	6.5	422
Bob Clarke	16	69	23	333	0	0	000	21	13	619	46	64	5	59	3.6	21
Pittsburgh Rens																
Connie Hawkins	16	326	160	491	0	0	000	165	127	770	50	205	42	447	27.9	668
Jim McCoy	22	288	127	441	24	5	208	102	81	794	68	95	55	350	15.9	847
Charley Curtis	22	266	112	421	1	0	000	91	77	846	77	148	16	301	13.6	666
Henry Curtis	20	273	116	425	0	0	000	60	43	717	67	241	25	275	13.7	596
Phil Rollins	17	91	41	451	70	22	314	90	73	811	53	43	85	221	13.0	611
Walt Mangham	22	207	82	396	8	3	375	61	40	656	53	138	21	213	9.6	529
Charles Tyra	23	203	91	448	1	0	000	48	30	625	49	121	16	212	9.2	518
Bob Weisnhahn	15	106	42	396	0	0	000	22	17	773	35	77	6	101	6.7	252
John McCarthy	18	83	29	349	13	6	462	36	19	528	49	36	26	95	5.2	420
Whitey Bell	7	62	26	419	1	1	1,000	15	14	933	18	24	33	69	9.8	223
Walt Kennedy	5	46	18	391	0	0	000	20	14	700	14	37	5	50	10.0	91

Appendix 5

ABL Most Valuable Player and All-League Teams, 1961-1962

MOST VALUABLE PLAYER

Connie Hawkins, Pittsburgh Rens, received 41 of a possible 54 votes.

PLAYERS' ALL-LEAGUE TEAMS

To determine the Players' All League Teams, every general manager and coach would list their choice of players for the first and second teams. For every voth for the first team, a player would receive two points, and for every vote for the second team a player would receive one point. The accumulated points, tallied by the league office, decided whether players were on the first or second team.

Table on following page.

MVP and All-League Teams, 1961-1962

Players' All League Teams

First Team

Player	Team	Hgt.	Wgt.	School	Home Town	Points
Connie Hawkins	Pittsburgh	6'8"	210	Iowa	Brooklyn, NY	108
Bill Bridges	Kansas City	6'5"	225	Kansas	Hobbs, NM	89
Dan Swartz	New York	6'4"	215	Morehead State	Morehead, KY	82
Dick Barnett	Cleveland	6'4"	185	Tennessee State	Gary, IN	81
Larry Staverman	Kansas City	6'7"	215	Villa Madonna	Covington, KY	66

Second Team

Player	Team	Hgt.	Wgt.	School	Home Town	Points
Johnny Cox	Cleveland	6'4"	190	Kentucky	Hazard, KY	61
Herschell Turner	Chicago	6'3"	195	Nebraska	Indianapolis, IN	52
Ken Sears	San Francisco	6'10"	215	Santa Clara	Watsonville, CA	52
Bill Spivey	Hawaii	7'1"	250	Kentucky	Los Angeles, CA	49
(Tony Jackson)	Chicago	6'4"	187	St. John's	Brooklyn, NY	46
(Nick Mantis)	Kansas City	6'2"	195	Northwestern	East Chicago, IN	46

Chapter Notes

INTRODUCTION

1. James P. Banks, "N.I.B.L. Makes Some Changes for This Season," *Sports Review*, Basketball Issue, 21 (1), January 1961, p.90.
2. "ABL Bulletin," June 24, 1961. Abe Saperstein Papers, Box 166/2.
3. "Saperstein Gets Chicago Pro Entry," *Chicago Tribune*, 3/19/1961, Pt.2, page 6.
4. Robert Sturman to all member clubs of the ABL, April 4, 1961. Abe Saperstein Papers, Box 166/2.
5. Fritz Kreisler, "Celt Owner Fails to Faze A.B.L.," *Kansas City Times*, 11/1/61, p.7C.
6. "The Chicago Packers Organization," in *Chicago Packers Official Program*, 1961–62, p.8.
7. "Podoloff Bars Cage Deal," *Kansas City Times*, 11/21/61, p.26.
8. "New Chicago Basket Team Gets Bellamy," *Chicago Tribune*, 3/20/61, Pt.4, p.2.
9. "Rumors Grow Jets Will Shift L.A. Franchise," *Kansas City Times*, 1/16/61, p.11.
10. "Leader Claims A.B.L. Healthy," *Kansas City Star*, 1/21/61, p.4B.
11. Maury Fitzgerald, "Tapers Quit Washington; Transfer to Long Island," *Washington Post*, 1/1/62, p.A20.
12. Jimmy Miller, "Rens to Fight to Keep Hawkins," *Pittsburgh Post-Gazette*, 11/11/61, p.11.
13. "A.B.L. Owners Will Discuss Expansion, All-Star Game," *Kansas City Times*, 11/16/61, p.48.
14. "Phil Woolpert Fired," *Kansas City Times*, 12/2/61, p.26.
15. Fritz Kreisler, "Steers Nail Down Title," *Kansas City Times*, 1/15/62, p.24.
16. "Sale of Pipers Now Complete," *Kansas City Times*, 2/1/62, p.38.
17. "A.B.L. Set to Boot Pipers," *Kansas City Times*, 2/19/62, p.23.
18. Fritz Kreisler, "A.B.L. at Critical Point in Battle for Talent," *Kansas City Star*, 3/11/62, p.3B.

CHAPTER ONE

1. Michael Shapiro in *Bottom of the Ninth* (New York: Henry Holt, 2009), pp.2 and 275, quotes this poll at least twice.
2. See Neil Sullivan, *The Dodgers Move West* (New York, Oxford University Press, 1989) for details on the political machinations that led to the franchise relocation.
3. Shapiro, p.89.
4. Shapiro, p.274.
5. See Ed Gruver, *The American Football League: A Year-by-Year History, 1960–1969* (Jefferson, NC: McFarland, 1997), for example, for more details on these franchise developments and shifts.
6. Harry Glickman to Abe Saperstein, April 21, 1959. Abe Saperstein to Harry Glickman, April 23, 1959. Abe Saperstein Papers, Box 166/2.
7. Abe Saperstein to Harry Glickman, May 15, 1959. Abe Saperstein Papers, Box 166/2.
8. Harry Glickman to Abe Saperstein, July 28, 1959. Abe Saperstein Papers, Box 166/2.
9. Abe Saperstein to Harry Glickman,

Chapter Notes—One

August 9, 1959. Abe Saperstein Papers, Box 166/2.
10. Abe Saperstein to Harry Glickman, September 2, 1959. Abe Saperstein Papers, Box 166/2.
11. Abe Saperstein to Harry Glickman, September 8, 1959. Abe Saperstein Papers, Box 166/2.
12. Abe Saperstein to Harry Glickman, October 23, 1959. Abe Saperstein Papers, Box 166/2.
13. Saperstein to Robert E. Smith, undated. Abe Saperstein Papers, Box 166/2.
14. Ibid.
15. Abe Saperstein to Robert E. Smith, January 2, 1960. R. E. (Bob) Smith to Abe Saperstein, January 4, 1960. Abe Saperstein Papers, Box 166/2.
16. Abe Saperstein to Robert E. Smith, February 15, 1960. Abe Saperstein Papers, Box 166/2.
17. R. E. (Bob) Smith to Abe Saperstein, February 16, 1960. Abe Saperstein Papers, Box 166/2.
18. Abe Saperstein to Robert E. Smith, February 27, 1960. Abe Saperstein Papers, Box 166/2.
19. R. E. Smith to Abe Saperstein, March 7, 1960. Abe Saperstein Papers, Box 166/2.
20. Kerkorian, of course, made billions building hotels and casinos in Las Vegas, later buying MGM studios and large percentages of GM and Ford, at various times. He is now worth at least $16 billion.
21. Abe Saperstein to Kirk Kerkorian, July 8, 1959. Abe Saperstein Papers, Box 166/2.
22. Abe Saperstein to Kirk Kerkorian, July 27, 1959. Abe Saperstein Papers, Box 166/2.
23. Abe Saperstein to Kirk Kerkorian, September 3, 1959. Abe Saperstein Papers, Box 166/2.
24. Abe Saperstein to Kirk Kerkorian, et al., March 20, 1960. Abe Saperstein papers, Box 166/2.
25. Handwritten note, March 22, 1960. Abe Saperstein papers, Box 166/2.
26. Abe Saperstein to Bronstein, Kerkorian, and Glickman, March 25, 1960. Abe Saperstein Papers, Box 166/2.
27. Abe Saperstein to Sid Goldberg/Hyman Tatelbaum, March 25, 1960. Abe Saperstein Papers, Box 166/2.
28. Hyman Tatelbaum to Abe Saperstein, May 16, 1960. Abe Saperstein to Hyman Tatelbaum, May 18, 1960. Abe Saperstein Papers, Box 166/2.
29. Sid Goldberg to Abe Saperstein, March 23, 1960, and April 6, 1960. Abe Saperstein Papers, Box 166/2.
30. Harry Glickman to Abe Saperstein, March 29, 1960. Abe Saperstein Papers, Box 166/2.
31. Harry Glickman, "My Comments and Proposals for a New League of Pro Basketball," March 29, 1960. Abe Saperstein Papers, Box 166/2.
32. Abe Saperstein to Harry Glickman, April 4, 1960. Harry Glickman to Abe Saperstein, April 7, 1960. Abe Saperstein Papers, Box 166/2.
33. Abe Saperstein to Harry Glickman, April 9, 1960. Abe Saperstein Papers, Box 166/2.
34. Robert Cromie, "Chicago Gets Basket Team," *Chicago Tribune*, 4/22/60, Pt.F, p.1.
35. Robert Siegel to Abe Saperstein, April 29, 1960. Abe Saperstein Papers, Box 166/2.
36. Abe Saperstein to Robert Siegel, April 29, 1960. Abe Saperstein Papers, Box 166/2.
37. Robert Siegel to Abe Saperstein, May 3, 1960. Abe Saperstein to Robert Siegel, May 8, 1960. Abe Saperstein Papers, Box 166/2.
38. Benjamin Stern to Abe Saperstein, April 4, 1960. Abe Saperstein Papers, Box 166/2.
39. Abe Saperstein to Benjamin Stern, April 5, 1960, and April 20, 1960. Abe Saperstein Papers, Box 166/2.
40. Melvin Davis to Abe Saperstein, April 8, 1960. Abe Saperstein Papers, Box 166/2.
41. Melvin Davis to Abe Saperstein, May 3, 1960. Abe Saperstein to Melvin Davis, May 8, 1960. Abe Saperstein Papers, Box 166/2.
42. Telegram, Seymour Smith to Abe Saperstein, April 21, 1960. Abe Saperstein to Seymour Smith, April 22, 1960. Abe Saperstein Papers, Box 166/2.
43. Norris West to Abe Saperstein,

April 23, 1960. Abe Saperstein to Norris West, April 29, 1960. Norris West to Abe Saperstein, May 17, 1960. Marie Linehan to Norris West, May 23, 1960. Abe Saperstein to Norris West, May 28, 1960. Abe Saperstein Papers, Box 166/2.

44. Abe Saperstein to Harry Glickman, May 8, 1960. Harry Glickman to Abe Saperstein, May 9, 1960. Abe Saperstein Papers, Box 166/2.

45. Harry Glickman to Abe Saperstein, May 17, 1960. Abe Saperstein to Harry Glickman and Harry Lynn, May 18, 1960. Abe Saperstein Papers, Box 166/2.

46. Terry Pluto, *Loose Balls* (New York: Simon & Schuster, 1990), p.41.

47. "Hawaii Chiefs Official Souvenir Program," 1961–62, p.1. Abe Saperstein Papers, Box 166/3.

CHAPTER TWO

1. Don Murphy to Bill?, undated. Abe Saperstein Papers, Box 166/2.

2. See Murry Nelson, *The National Basketball League: A History, 1935–1949* (Jefferson, NC: McFarland, 2009), pp.204, 210, for discussions of Denver's situation in 1948–49.

3. Seymour Smith to Abe Saperstein, April 9, 1961. Abe Saperstein Papers, Box 166/2.

4. Abe Saperstein to Seymour Smith, June 15, 1961. Abe Saperstein Papers, Box 166/2.

5. "New Chicago Basket Team Gets Bellamy," *Chicago Tribune*, 3/20/61, Pt.4, p.2.

6. Constitution of the American Basketball League, Article VII, Section 4. Abe Saperstein Papers, Box 166/2.

7. ABL Constitution, Article XI, and Abe Saperstein to Robert Kline, July 13, 1961. Abe Saperstein Papers, Box 166/2.

8. Allan Bloch to Robert Sturman, July, 10, 1961. Abe Saperstein Papers, Box 166/2.

9. "Agreement," August 3, 1961. Abe Saperstein Papers, Box 166/2.

10. "Estate of A. M. Saperstein, Deceased, Allan R. Bloch and Continental Illinois National Bank and Trust Co. of Chicago, Co-Executors, and Sylvia Saperstein v. Commissioner,"1970 Tax Ct. Memo Lexis 150, 29 T.C.M. (CCH) 916 [1970], p.4.

11. Article XIV, "Distribution of League Revenue" and Article XVI, "Hawaii Transportation Clause," ABL Constitution. Abe Saperstein Papers, Box 166/2.

12. Phil Fox to Abe Saperstein, June 26, 1961. Abe Saperstein Papers, Box 166/2.

13. Ripley decided to not coach the D.C. Tapers, and Stan Stutz was named coach due to the influence of Paul Cohen.

14. Notes, August 2–4. Abe Saperstein Papers, Box 166/2.

15. Phil Fox Summary (n.d.). Abe Saperstein Papers, Box 166/2.

16. American Basketball League Press Release (n.d.). Abe Saperstein Papers, Box 166/2.

17. Phil Fox to Abe Saperstein, August 24, 1961. Abe Saperstein Papers, Box 166/2. One of the "B" referees listed was John Vanka, later corrected as John Vanak of Lansdale, PA, who became a longtime NBA referee, as well as a "jumper" to the ABA.

18. Phil Fox to ABL Referees, October 9, 1961. Abe Saperstein Papers, Box 166/2.

19. Phil Fox to ABL Referees (Memo #2, n.d.). Abe Saperstein Papers, Box 166/2.

20. "Disciplinary Code" (Memo #3, 12/20/61?). Abe Saperstein Papers, Box 166/2.

21. American Basketball League, Playing Rules and Regulations (Memo #4, n.d.). Abe Saperstein Papers, Box 166/2.

CHAPTER THREE

1. Constitution of American Basketball League, Article XIV, in Abe Saperstein Papers, Box 166/2.

2. Phil Fox to Abe Saperstein, June 26, 1961. Abe Saperstein Papers, Box 166/2.

3. Memo, Phil Fox to ABL Referees, October 9, 1961. Abe Saperstein Papers, Box 166/2.

4. Ibid.

5. Phil Fox to Abe Saperstein, August 24, 1961. Abe Saperstein Papers, Box 166/2.

6. Ibid.

Chapter Notes—Three

7. A personal note on this. A family friend, Dave Trager, was the president of the new Chicago Packers franchise, and he very graciously provided complimentary tickets for any Packers game to my mother and me. The only exception was when the Celtics came to town. No free tickets, since the Celtics were supposed to be a big draw. In fact, of the five games the Celtics played in Chicago, there were never more than 3,126 paid at any game, certainly a discouraging and, ultimately, fatal blow to the Chicago Packers.

8. ABL Constitution, Article XI.

9. ABL Constitution, Article XVI.

10. ABL Constitution, Article XXVIII.

11. Roger Kaiser, telephone interview, June 22, 2011.

12. Ken Sears, telephone interview, August 3, 2011.

13. Sears interview.

14. Hal Lear, telephone interview, August 16, 2011.

15. John Barnhill, telephone interview, March 21, 2011.

16. Hand-typed note above letter, George Price to Marie Linehan, June 6, 1962. Abe Saperstein Papers, Box 166/2.

17. "Consumer Income," *Current Population Reports*, U.S. Commerce Department: Washington, D.C., Series P-60, No.41, September 21, 1963.

18. Leonard Koppett, *24 Seconds to Shoot: An Informal History of the National Basketball Association* (New York: Macmillan, 1968), p.137. Oscar Robertson, *The Big O: My Life, My Times, My Game* (Emmaus, PA: Rodale Press, 2003), p.136.

19. Chicago Majors promotional brochure. Abe Saperstein Papers, Box 166/3.

20. David Wolf called the Rens the "best operation in the league." *Foul! The Connie Hawkins Story* (New York: Holt Rinehart & Winston, 1972), p.106.

21. Wolf, *Foul! The Connie Hawkins Story*, p.101. Wolf also said that Jim Palmer was the highest paid Ren with a salary of $10,000, p.106.

22. The Pittsburgh Civic Arena, which was new in 1961, later was known as "the Igloo" and served as the home of the Pittsburgh Penguins of the NHL until May 2010. The Penguins moved across the street to the new Consol Center, and unsuccessful efforts were made to have the Igloo declared a Historic Site to preserve it. Demolition on the arena began in September 2011.

23. "Financial Statements, Pittsburgh Sports Corporation," April 1, 1961, to March 31, 1962. Abe Saperstein Papers, Box 166/3.

24. "Audited Balance Sheet, Cleveland Basketball Club Inc., June 30, 1962," Ernst & Ernst, Auditors. My thanks to Carolyn Hastings for providing this.

25. George M. Steinbrenner III to Stockholders, Cleveland Basketball Club Inc., August 27, 1962. Carolyn Hastings, personal collection, Lakewood, Ohio.

26. Memo to all members of ABL re: "Report and Analysis of 1961–62 Season ...," n.d. Abe Saperstein Papers, Box 166/2.

27. Ibid.

28. George Steinbrenner, preparer, "Proposed SOP for the ABL, 1962–63 Season." Abe Saperstein Papers, Box 166/2.

29. Memo, Marie Linehan to Abe Saperstein, May 3, 1961. Abe Saperstein Papers, Box 166/3.

30. Cablegram, Abe Saperstein to Bill McPhail, May 7, 1961. Abe Saperstein Papers, Box 166/3.

31. Ironically, Dolph became the commissioner of the American Basketball Association (ABA), the successor to the ABL as an alternative to the NBA, in 1969, after nine years as director of *CBS Sports*. One of the great shortcomings of the ABA was its inability to secure a regular network television package.

32. Lester Malitz to Chet Simmons, August 30, 1961. Abe Saperstein Papers, Box 166/3.

33. Benjamin Rader, *In Its Own Image: How Television Has Transformed Sports* (New York: Free Press, Macmillan, 1984).

34. Lester Malitz to Abe Saperstein, December 21, 1961. Abe Saperstein Papers, Box 166/3.

35. See Rader, pp.104–109.

36. Chicago Packers programs printed the television schedule for both the NBA and WGN in each of the game programs.

37. Monty Bancroft to Abe Saperstein, October 9, 1961. Abe Saperstein Papers, Box 166/3. Franklin Mieuli later became

the owner of the Golden State Warriors of the NBA, beginning in 1963, after buying out some other shareholders. He remained as principal owner until 1986.

38. Lester Malitz to Abe Saperstein, October 25, 1961. Abe Saperstein Papers, Box 166/3.
39. Abe Saperstein to Martin Carmichael, December 31, 1961. Abe Saperstein Papers, Box 166/3.
40. Abe Saperstein to Lester Malitz/ Don Taffner/Martin Carmichael, April 21, 1962. Abe Saperstein Papers, Box 166/3.

CHAPTER FOUR

1. David Wolf, *Foul! The Connie Hawkins Story* (New York: Holt Rinehart and Winston, 1972), p.31.
2. Ibid., p.38.
3. Ibid., pp.41–51.
4. Ibid., pp.46–49.
5. Ibid., pp.48–49.
6. Ibid., pp.74–87.
7. http://search.japantimes.co.jp/cgi-bin/sp20090218pv.html (accessed October 10, 2011).
8. Kenny Sears, telephone interview, August 3, 2011.
9. These data come from the St. John's Red Storm website and the Tony Jackson page of "Great Names in St. Johns Basketball History." http://www.redstormsports.com/sports/m-baskbl/spec-rel/stjo-great-names.html.
10. Richard Goldstein, "Tony Jackson, 65, Who Led St. John's Basketball, Dies," *New York Times*, 11/2/2005. http://www.nytimes.com/2005/11/02/sports/ncaabasketball/02jackson.html.
11. Data from Bill Spivey page of Wildcat Basketball, http://www.bigbluehistory.net/bb/statistics/Players/Spivey_Bill.html.
12. Charley Rosen, *Scandals of '51: How the Gamblers Almost Killed College Basketball* (New York: Holt Rinehart, 1978), pp.186–187.
13. Jack Black, J. Michael Kenyon, Bill Hoover, and Robert Bradley, "Bill Spivey Professional Career Highlights," http://www.apbr.org/spivey.html (accessed March 7, 2011).

14. Telephone interviews with Sylvester Blye, June 16, 2011, and Roger Kaiser, June 22, 2011.
15. Kenny Sears, telephone interview, August 3, 2011.
16. Ibid.
17. http://sportsillustrated.cnn.com/vault/article/magazine/MAG1024213/index.htm (accessed October 10, 2011).
18. http://www.usfdons.com/sports/m-baskbl/spec-rel/050600aaa.html.
19. Oscar Robertson, *The Big O: My Life, My Times, My Game* (Emmaus, PA: Rodale Press, 2003), pp.49–51.
20. Sharman v. Longo, 249 Cal.App.2d 948 (April 4, 1967).
21. http://articles.latimes.com/1991-08-12/business/fi-428_1_investment-banking-firm.

CHAPTER FIVE

1. Ben Green, *Spinning the Globe: The Rise, Fall and Return to Greatness of the Harlem Globetrotters* (New York: Amistad Press, 2005), p.55.
2. Green, pp.339 and 353.
3. Basketball Reference.com, Andy Phillip page (accessed March, 2012).
4. Jeff Marcus, *Biographical Directory of Professional Basketball Coaches* (Lanham, MD: Scarecrow Press, 2003.), p.380.
5. Milton Katz, *Breaking Through: John B. McLendon, Basketball Legend and Civil Rights Pioneer* (Fayetteville: University of Arkansas Press, 2007), p.129. Adolph Grundman, *The Golden Age of Amateur Basketball, the AAU Tournament, 1921–1968* (Lincoln, NE: University of Nebraska Press, 2004), pp.214–215.
6. Marcus, pp.46–47.
7. Marcus, pp.268–269; *Chicago Zephyrs Official Program, 1962–63*, p.3.
8. Marcus, pp.381–382; *Kansas City Steers Official Program, 1961–62*, p.3. Abe Saperstein Papers.
9. Marcus, pp.396–397.
10. Rachel Gray, "Basketball Great Maurice King, Dies," *Daily Kansan*, 9/21/2007, http://www.kansan.com/news/2007/sep/21/king.
11. Marcus, pp.363–364.
12. Marcus, pp.194–195.

13. http://guardiansofthecity.org/sheriff/sheriffs/brown.html.
14. Marcus, p.393.
15. Marcus, pp.383–384.
16. Kathryn Conley, *One of a Kind: The Gene Conley Story* (Altamonte Springs, FL: Advantage Books, 2007).

CHAPTER SIX

1. "Estate of A.M. Saperstein, 1970 Tax Court Memo, Lexis 150, 29 T.C.M. (CCH) 916" (1970). Also see "Chicago's a Graveyard for Pro Basketball," *Miami News*, 4/7/63, p.8.
2. See Murry Nelson, *The National Basketball League: A History, 1935–1949* (Jefferson, NC: McFarland, 2009), pp.22–23, for details.
3. This is described in greater detail in Nelson, *The National Basketball League*, pp.68–80. Also see John Schleppi's *Chicago's Showcase of Basketball: The World Tournament of Professional Basketball and the College All-Star Game* (Haworth, NJ: St. Johann Press, 2008), pp.15–23.
4. Again, these seasons are chronicled in Nelson.
5. See Schleppi, pp.82–96, and Nelson, pp.154–157.
6. The history of the Gears is extensively chronicled by Dick Triptow in his self-published volume, *The Dynasty That Never Was* (1997).
7. Seymour Smith, telephone interview, August 24, 2010.
8. There was an open championship from 1908 until 1972, at which time classes were introduced and ended the excitement of the open era. Marshall won again in 1960, led both times by legendary Coach "Spin" Salerio and All-American player, George Wilson, later a star on NCAA champion University of Cincinnati in 1962.
9. "The Chicago Packers Organization," *Chicago Packers Official Program, 1961–62*, personal collection, p.8.
10. At this time, Sara Lee was expanding, acquiring other companies and building a new state-of-the-art production plant, located in Deerfield, Illinois, and right across the street from Briarwood Country Club, where Lubin played at least three times a week in season. Coincidentally, after the plant was razed (outdated by the 1990s), the Chicago Bulls, who began in the NBA in 1966, built a dazzling new practice facility in Deerfield near the site of the former Sara Lee plant.
11. "NBA Packers Get Si Green," *Pittsburgh Post-Gazette*, 11/20/61, p.37. "Podoloff Bars Cage Deal," *Kansas City Times*, 11/21/61, p.26.
12. "Saperstein Gets Chicago Pro Entry," *Chicago Tribune*, 3/19/61, Pt.2, p.6.
13. "The Chicago Packers Organization," p.8.
14. "NBA Club Comes up Short," *Kansas City Times*, 1/19/62, p.17.
15. "ABL Bulletin," May 5, 1961. Abe Saperstein Papers, Box 166/2.
16. "ABL League Bulletin," June 16, 1961. Abe Saperstein Papers, Box 166/2.
17. "New Chicago Basket Team Gets Bellamy," *Chicago Tribune*, 3/20/61, Pt.4, p.2.
18. Fritz Kreisler, "Steers, Tough in Clutch, Take Lead," *Kansas City Times*, 11/13/61, p.21.
19. "Zagar Paces Majors," *Kansas City Times*, 11/14/61, p.14.
20. "Chicago Rally Dumps San Francisco, 94–91," *Pittsburgh Post-Gazette*, 11/18/61, p.10.
21. "ABL Catching On, Saperstein Says," *Kansas City Times*, 11/20/61, p.26.
22. "Spivey Puts L.A. in Gear to Top Rens," *Kansas City Times*, 12/7/61, p.4D. "ABL Bulletin, 11/2/61." Abe Saperstein Papers, Box 166/2.
23. "Steers' Streak Hits 7," *Kansas City Times*, 12/11/61, p.32.
24. Fritz Kreisler, "Steers Streak to 8 Again," *Kansas City Times*, 12/14/61, p.2D.
25. "Steers Still Red Hot," *Kansas City Times*, 12/15/61, p.8C.
26. "Hawaii Trips Majors," *Kansas City Star*, 12/17/61, p.B1. "Majors Win, 102 to 89 for Third in Row," *Chicago Tribune*, 12/23/61.
27. "Majors Keep Moving," *Kansas City Times*, 12/18/61, p.34. "Pipers Rally Late," *Kansas City Times*, 12/20/61, p.18.
28. "Cleveland Bows by 1," *Kansas City Times*, 12/22/61, p.27. "Chicago Bumps

Chapter Notes — Seven

Rens on Rally," *Kansas City Times*, 12/23/61, p.16.

29. "Rens Close Gap on Lead, Trip Majors," *Kansas City Times*, 12/25/61, p.3C. "Full House see Majors Clip Rens," *Kansas City Times*, 12/29/61, p.19. "Rens Surge as Hawkins Scores 31," *Kansas City Times*, 12/30/61, p.12.

30. "Tapers over Chicago," *Kansas City Times*, 1/1/62, p.21.

31. "Pipers Cut off Chicago by 10," *Kansas City Times*, 1/4/62, p.31. "Bridges Saves Steers," *Kansas City Times*, 1/5/62, p.26. "Majors Do Job," *Kansas City Star*, *Kansas City Times*, 1/7/62, p.B6.

Chapter Seven

1. "U.S., Russian Tanks Face Each Other in Berlin," *Los Angeles Times*, 10/28/61, p.1.
2. Forrest Kable, "Report on the American Basketball League," *Sports Review*, Basketball Issue, 22(1), January 1962, p.66.
3. "Jets Drop Opener Before 5,137" *Los Angeles Times*, 10/28/61, Pt.2, p.1.
4. See Murry Nelson, *The National Basketball League: A History, 1935–1949* (Jefferson, NC: McFarland, 2009), especially chap. 12 regarding the 1948–49 season.
5. Jimmy Miller. "Pro Basketball Returns to the City," *Pittsburgh Post-Gazette*, 11/2/61, p.45.
6. Jimmy Miller, "Walt Mangham," *Pittsburgh Post-Gazette*, 10/30/61, p.24.
7. Jimmy Miller, "Rens Drop Majors, 105–90, for 2nd Win," *Pittsburgh Post-Gazette*, 11/8/61, p.25.
8. Jimmy Miller, "Unbeaten Rens Head South for 3 Games," *Pittsburgh Post-Gazette*, 11/9/61, p.43. "Rens Lose First to Hustling Majors, 104–97," *Pittsburgh Post-Gazette*, 11/10/61, p.20. "Rens Make It 2 in a Row over Tapers, 95–84," *Pittsburgh Post-Gazette*, 11/12/61, Sec.4, p.6.
9. Jimmy Miller, "Rens to Fight to Keep Hawkins," *Pittsburgh Post-Gazette*, 11/11/61, p.11. David Wolf, *Foul! The Connie Hawkins Story* (New York: Holt, Rinehart and Winston, 1972), p.109.
10. Jimmy Miller, "Rens' Late Rally Nips Hawaii, 100–99," *Pittsburgh Post-Gazette*, 11/15/61, p.24. Jimmy Miller, "Rens Sweep by Chiefs, 106–93," *Pittsburgh Post-Gazette*, 11/17/61, p.20.
11. Fritz Kreisler, "Tiny Man Rips Steers," *Kansas City Times*, 11/7/61, p.16.
12. "Hawaii Whips Tapers to Win ABL Opener," "Spivey Paces Jets," *Kansas City Times*, 11/8/61, p.14.
13. "Steers Escape Defeat by One," *Kansas City Times*, 11/9/61, p.34. Fritz Kreisler, "Bridges Sparks Steers," *Kansas City Times*, 11/11/61, p.24.
14. Fritz Kreisler, "Steers, Tough in Clutch, Take Lead," *Kansas City Times*, 11/13/61, p.21.
15. "Defense by L.A. Chills Pipers," *Kansas City Times*, 11/14/61, p.14.
16. "Zagar Paces Majors," *Kansas City Times*, 11/14/61, p.14.
17. "ABL Owners Will Discuss Expansion, All Star Game," *Kansas City Times*, 11/16/61, p.48. "ABL Catching on, Saperstein Says," *Kansas City Times*, 11/20/61, p.26.
18. "Steers Risk Lead Tonight," *Kansas City Times*, 11/17/61, p.24.
19. "Pipers Outplay Rens, Win Easily, 137–94," *Pittsburgh Post-Gazette*, 11/27/61, p.28. "L.A. Stops Steers at 8," *Kansas City Times*, 11/27/61, p.26.
20. "Pipers Edge Rens on Fouls, 99–97," *Pittsburgh Post-Gazette*, 11/29/61, p.28.
21. "Hawkins Pulls Rens in with 40," *Kansas City Times*, 11/26/61, p.9B. "Rens' Coach to Undertake Playing Role," *Kansas City Times*, 11/30/61, p.6B.
22. "Steers Shake Off Slump," "Phil Woolpert Fired," *Kansas City Times*, 12/2/61, p.26. Wolf, *Foul!*, p.106.
23. "Tapers Need 3 Overtimes to Nip Hawaii," *Kansas City Star*, 12/5/61, p.28.
24. "Spivey Puts L.A. in Gear to Tip Rens," *Kansas City Times*, 12/7/61, p.4D.
25. "Barnett Testifies He Wasn't Happy with Syracuse," *Kansas City Times*, 12/8/61, p.33.
26. Wolf, p.116–118.
27. Fritz Kreisler, "Steers Will See Rens Often," *Kansas City Times*, 12/13/61, p.25.
28. Fritz Kreisler, "Steers Streak to 8 Again," *Kansas City Times*, 12/14/61, p.2D.
29. "Steers' String Is Ended at 9" *Kansas City Times*, 12/17/61, p.B1.

30. "L.A. Keeps Going over S.F. in L.A.," *Kansas City Times*, 12/17/61, p.B1. "Steers Lose by 4 to Rens Again," *Kansas City Times*, 12/18/61, p.34.
31. "Travel Snarls Steers," *Kansas City Times*, 12/19/61, p.27. "Rens Face Steers for Two Games," *Pittsburgh Post-Gazette*, 12/19/61, p.28.
32. "Jets Sweep Series," *Kansas City Times*, 12/22/61, p.27.
33. "Lynn Not Interested in Tapers' Transfer," *Washington Post*, 12/27/61, p.A20.
34. "Barnett Gets Okay to Play with Pipers," *Kansas City Times*, 12/22/61, p.28.
35. "Ace Scores 49, but Rens Lose," *Kansas City Star*, 12/24/61, p.3D. "Rens Close Gap on Lead, Trip Majors," *Kansas City Times*, 12/25/61, p.3C.
36. "Dees Agrees to Join Rens," *Kansas City Times*, 12/26/61, p.37.
37. "Cleveland Still Easy for Tapers," *Kansas City Times*, 12/27/61, p.16. "Tapers Rally Clicks," *Kansas City Times*, 12/29/61, p.19.
38. Monte Moore, telephone interview, April 10, 2011.
39. "Rens Surge as Hawkins Scores 31," "Pipers Check Skid," *Kansas City Times*, 12/30/61, p.13.
40. Maury Fitzgerald, "Tapers Quit Washington, Transfer to Long Island," *Washington Post*, 1/1/62, p.A20.
41. Ad, *Kansas City Times*, 12/30/61, p.14.
42. "Saints Name Brightman to Coach Club," *Kansas City Times*, 12/27/61, p.16. "Piper Boss Places McClendon [sic] on Spot," *Kansas City Star*, 12/28/61, p.16.
43. "Steers Win it at :02," "Steers Tops in League Travel, Too," *Kansas City Times*, 1/1/61, p.21.
44. *Kansas City Times*, 1/2/62, p.21; 1/3/62, p.23.
45. "Steers Lose to S.F. Late," *Kansas City Times*, 1/4/62, p.31.
46. "Bridges Saves Steers," *Kansas City Times*, 1/5/62, p.26.
47. "Steers Stampede Tapers," *Kansas City Star*, 1/7/62, p.1B. "No Playoffs Here; Steers Play Today," *Kansas City Star*, 1/7/62, p.6B.
48. Fritz Kreisler, "Steers Race in Again," "Pipers Idle San Francisco as Two Star," "Rens Maintain Hold on First as Chiefs Bow," *Kansas City Times*, 1/8/62, p.22.
49. Fritz Kreisler, "Playoff May be Here," *Kansas City Times*, 1/9/62. Fritz Kreisler, "Steers Finally Corral Chicago," *Kansas City Times*, 1/10/62, p.11. "Hawkins Holds Scoring Lead," *Kansas City Times*, 1/10/62, p.11.
50. "Steers' Play-Off Foe Holds the Upper Hand," *Kansas City Star*, 1/11/62, p.20. Fritz Kreisler, "Herd Must Stop Pipers' Speed in Big Series," *Kansas City Times*, 1/12/62, p.20.
51. Fritz Kreisler, "Hot Herd Thunders In," *Kansas City Times*, 1/13/62, p.21.
52. "Pipers Chop up Steers," *Kansas City Times*, 1/14/62, p.S1.
53. Fritz Kreisler, "Steers Nail Down Title," *Kansas City Times*, 1/15/62, p.24.
54. Monte Moore, telephone interview, April 13, 2011.

CHAPTER EIGHT

1. "Steers Hold Hot Pace," *Kansas City Times*, 1/16/62, p.11.
2. "R.C. Owens Plays," *Kansas City Times*, 1/16/62, p.11.
3. "Rumors Grow Jets will Shift L.A. Franchise," *Kansas City Times*, 1/16/62, p.11.
4. "Piper Payroll Late," *Kansas City Times*, 1/17/62, p.12. Milton Katz, *Breaking Through: John B. McLendon, Basketball Legend and Civil Rights Pioneer* (Fayetteville: University of Arkansas Press, 2007), p.142.
5. No N.B.A. Room for Expansion," *Kansas City Times*, 1/17/62, p.12.
6. "Texan Focuses on A.B.L. Team," *Kansas City Times*, 1/17/62, p.12.
7. Roger Kaiser, telephone interview, June 22, 2011.
8. "Pipers Learn from Steers," *Kansas City Times*, 1/12/62, p.13. "Pipers, Nats Will Merge, Paper Says," *Kansas City Times*, 1/18/62, p.37.
9. "Revisions Made in Jets' Games," *Kansas City Times*, 1/18/62, p.37. "Jets Drop Out of Cage Loop," *Kansas City Times*, 1/19/62, p.17. "Jets Go Out of Business," *Los Angeles Times*, 1/19/62, Pt. 4, p.1.

Chapter Notes — Eight

"Steers Feel Effect of Winning Title," *Kansas City Times*, 1/20/62, p.16. "Leader Claims A.B.L. Healthy," *Kansas City Star*, 1/21/62, p.4B.

10. Hal Lear, phone interview, 8/16/11.
11. "Herd Snowballs On," *Kansas City Times*, 1/19/62, p.16.
12. Fritz Kreisler, "Steers Make Point Do," *Kansas City Star*, 1/21/62, p.B1.
13. "Majors' Clamp on 1st Tightens as Rens Falter," *Kansas City Star*, 1/21/62, p.4B.
14. Fritz Kreisler, "Steers Stampede On," "Saints Keep String Alive in A.B.L. Race," "Rollins, Hawkins Star," *Kansas City Times*, 1/22/62, p.16.
15. http://tightwad-hill.blogspot.com/2007/02/sweet-sixteen-11-larry-friend.html (accessed April 16, 2011).
16. "New York Lead Stands," *Kansas City Times*, 1/26/62, p.19. "Jackson Hikes 3-Point Record," *Kansas City Times*, 1/27/62, p.17.
17. Fritz Kreisler, "A.B.L. Has It All ... Except Super Stars," *Kansas City Star*, 1/28/62, p.B2.
18. "Rens Fly as Hawkins Pops in 39," *Kansas City Star*, 1/28/62, p.B3.
19. "Pittsburgh Hex Chills Majors," "Cleveland Bows Again," *Kansas City Times*, 1/29/62, p.20.
20. "Swartz Stars for Tapers, but Rens Win It," *Kansas City Times*, 1/30/62, p.11.
21. "Future Shaky for McLendon," "Pipers Trade Adams for Dierking," *Kansas City Times*, 1/30/62, p.12.
22. Katz, pp.143–146. "Sharman Hired as Cage Coach," *Kansas City Times*, 1/31/62, p.17. "Pipers Hire McLendon Again," *Kansas City Times*, 2/3/62, p.20.
23. Stuart Miller, "Where Steinbrenner and 3-Pointers Started," *New York Times*, 12/25/11, Sports, p.7.
24. "Pipers on Block," *Kansas City Times*, 1/31/62, p.17. "Sale of Pipers Now Complete," *Kansas City Times*, 2/1/62, p.38.
25. "Tapers Win as Swartz Collects 40," *Kansas City Times*, 1/31/62, p.16.
26. "Victory Pulls Chicago Close in A.B.L. Race," *Kansas City Times*, 2/1/62, p.16. "Chicago Goes to Top," *Kansas City Times*, 2/2/62, p.18. "Trotters Pull 20,482 Fans to A.B.L. Tilt," *Kansas City Times*, 2/3/62, p.20.
27. "Steers Bounce Back," *Kansas City Times*, 2/5/62, p.23.
28. "Steers to Finish Road Trip Early," *Kansas City Times*, 2/6/62, p.15. "Saints Win as Francis Finds Range," *Kansas City Times*, 2/7/62, p.11.
29. "Pipers Win: Swartz Hot for Tapers," *Kansas City Times*, 2/8/62, p.28.
30. "Barnett Guns in 43 to Stagger Saints," *Kansas City Times*, 2/9/62, p.18.
31. Fritz Kreisler, "Staverman Scores 35," *Kansas City Times*, 2/10/62, p.22.
32. Fritz Kreisler, "Bill Spivey Isn't Bitter Any More — Much," *Kansas City Star*, 2/11/62, p.B1.
33. "Swartz Shines as Tapers Win," "Pipers Rush Back," *Kansas City Star*, 2/11/62, p.B2.
34. Fritz Kreisler, "Steers Slip By Hawaii," *Kansas City Times*, 2/12/62, p.21.
35. Fritz Kreisler, "Late Rally by Steers," "Saints Get Tough," *Kansas City Times*, 2/14/62, p.10.
36. Fritz Kreisler, "Rens Cool Off Steers," *Kansas City Times*, 2/18/62, p.20. Fritz Kreisler, "Steers Get Up and Go," *Kansas City Times*, 2/19/62, p.23.
37. Fritz Kreisler, "ABL Set to Boot Pipers," *Kansas City Times*, 2/19/62, p.23. Fritz Kreisler, "A.B.L. Action against Cleveland Reflects Solidarity of League, Steers' Official Says," *Kansas City Times*, 2/20/62, p.10. "A.B.L. to Keep Pipers in Loop," *Kansas City Times*, 2/21/62, p.23.
38. "Hawaii Holds On," *Kansas City Times*, 2/19/62, p.23.
39. "Steers Hit Back Again," *Kansas City Times*, 2/21/62, p.23.
40. "A.B.L. Scoring," *Kansas City Times*, 2/21/62, p.23.
41. Fritz Kreisler, "Steers Put on Speed," *Kansas City Times*, 2/22/62, p.35.
42. "Wilt Was Never Headed for A.B.L., Says Leader," *Kansas City Times*, 2/23/62, p.19.
43. "Majors into First," *Kansas City Times*, 2/26/62, p.20. "Tempers and Fouls Gang up on Pipers," *Kansas City Times*, 2/28/62, p.16. "Conley's Fare Helps Tapers Past Pipers," *Kansas City Times*, 3/1/62, p.36.
44. "Majors Grasp Touch to Nip Bid by Pipers," *Kansas City Star*, 3/4/62, p.B4.
45. John Barnhill, telephone interview.

46. Sy Blye, interview, 6/16/2011.
47. Roger Kaiser, interview, 6/22/2011.
48. "Chicago Whips Tapers to Gain Division Lead," *Kansas City Times*, 3/6/62, p.16. "Pipers Finally Get Job Done, Trip S.F. by 2," *Kansas City Times*, 3/9/62, p.22.
49. "Majors Tie for First by Downing Hawaii," *Kansas City Times*, 3/10/62, p.26.
50. Fritz Kreisler, "A.B.L. at Critical Point in Battle for Talent," *Kansas City Star*, 3/11/62, p.3B.
51. "Big Spurt Puts Majors on Top," *Kansas City Times*, 3/12/62, p.23. "Majors Hike Eastern Lead to Full Game," *Kansas City Times*, 3/13/62, p.14.
52. "Warm Barnett Peps Up Pipers," *Kansas City Times*, 3/14/62, p.19. "Jackson Scores 53, but Chicago Bows," *Kansas City Times*, 3/15/62, p.4D.
53. "Chiefs Blow Big Lead," *Kansas City Times*, 3/14/62, p.23. "Hawaii Gets Early Jump on New York," *Kansas City Times*, 3/15/62, p.4D.
54. "Pipers Unload in Last Period," *Kansas City Times*, 3/19/62, p.22. "Jackson Sharp as Majors Edge Chiefs by Four," *Kansas City Times*, 3/20/62, p.16.
55. "A.B.L. to Set Details Later on Play-offs," *Kansas City Times*, 3/21/62, p.20.
56. "Majors Bounce Back," *Kansas City Times*, 3/21/62, p.20.
57. "Pipers Sink When Zagar Hits Big Shot," *Kansas City Times*, 3/23/62, p.25. "Rens Hang on to Take Final on Home Court," *Kansas City Times*, 3/24/62, p.22.
58. "Pipers Slip By on Long Shots," "Long Goals Do Job for Herd," *Kansas City Star*, 3/25/62, p.B1.
59. "Pipers Win to Gain Tie for Pennant," "Steers Pick Area Aces," *Kansas City Times*, 3/26/62, p.22.
60. "A.B.L. Sets up Play-off Plan," *Kansas City Times*, 3/27/62, p.12.
61. "Tapers, Saints Need Overtimes," *Kansas City Times*, 3/29/62, p.2D.
62. "Pipers Battle New York Next," *Kansas City Times*, 3/31/62, p.20.
63. "Cleveland to ABL Final," *Chicago Tribune*, 4/1/62, Sec.2, Pt.2, p.6.
64. "Steers Beat Pipers in ABL Series 126–115," *Pittsburgh Post-Gazette*, 4/2/62, p.23.
65. "Steers Again Beat Pipers," *Pittsburgh Post-Gazette*, 4/4/62, p.26.
66. "Cleveland Wins By 116–114," *Pittsburgh Post-Gazette*, 4/5/62, p.30.
67. "Fifth ABL Tilt Transferred," *Pittsburgh Post-Gazette*, 4/9/62, p.25. "Pipers Beat Steers to Capture ABL Title," *Pittsburgh Post-Gazette*, 4/10/62, p.21.

Chapter Nine

1. "Lucas Agrees to Play for Pipers in NBA," *Chicago Tribune*, 7/17/62, Sports, p.3.
2. "Rens, Pittsburgh Feud Over Terms," *Philadelphia Inquirer*, 7/6/62, p.27.
3. "Cleveland Expected to Get 10th NBA Spot," *Philadelphia Inquirer*, 7/7/62, p.18.
4. "Royals Want Lucas, Oppose Cleveland Bid," *Philadelphia Inquirer*, 7/8/62, Sports, p.6.
5. "Lucas Pact Nullified if Pipers Join NBA," *Philadelphia Inquirer*, 7/10/62, p.24.
6. "NBA Admits Cleveland Pipers Club," *Philadelphia Inquirer*, 7/11/62, p.36.
7. "Reports ABL to Quit," *Philadelphia Inquirer*, 7/11/62, p.36.
8. "Lucas to Ask Hike in Pay to Play for NBA Pipers," *Philadelphia Inquirer*, 7/12/62, p.31.
9. "Sharman Expects to Quit Pipers," *Los Angeles Times*, 7/17/62, Sec.3, p.2.
10. Bill Sharman to Abe Saperstein, July 28, 1962. Abe Saperstein Papers.
11. Marie Linehan to Bill Sharman, July 30, 1962. Abe Saperstein Papers.
12. "Windfall for Hawks," *Philadelphia Inquirer*, 7/12/62, p.34. "Zephyrs Sign Staverman of ABL Steers," *Chicago Tribune*, 7/15/62, Sec.2, p.3.
13. "ABL Owners Ready to Share New NBA Club," *Philadelphia Inquirer*, 7/13/62, p.31.
14. "ABL Won't Fold, Says Saperstein," *Chicago Tribune*, 7/15/62, Sec.2, p.3. "Owners Deny ABL Will Fold," *Philadelphia Inquirer*, 7/15/62, Sports, p.10.
15. Abe Saperstein memo to league owners and league personnel, July 26, 1962. Abe Saperstein Papers.
16. "Saperstein Says ABL Will Try to Keep Going," *Philadelphia Inquirer*, 7/24/62, p.33.
17. Bob Fachet, "ABL Moves Tapers

Chapter Notes — Nine

Here, Threatens Suit Over Pipers," *Philadelphia Inquirer*, 7/26/62, p.34.

18. "Royals' Grace Blasts Podoloff," *Philadelphia Inquirer*, 7/27/62, p.31.

19. "Denies Collapse of Piper Plans to Shift to NBA," *Philadelphia Inquirer*, 7/29/62, Sports, p.5. "NBA Rejects Bid by Pipers, Cites Default on Agreement," *Philadelphia Inquirer*, 7/31/62, p.25.

20. John Barnhill telephone interview, March 21, 2011.

21. "Lane, New Basketball Man, Finds Time to Knock Cubs," *Philadelphia Inquirer*, 7/29/62, Sports, p.5. "McMahon to Sign as Coach of Zephyrs," *Chicago Tribune*, 7/24/62, C1.

22. "Steers Sign King for 2d Season," *Philadelphia Inquirer*, 8/26/62, p.S-3. "Steers Appoint Dee as Coach," *Philadelphia Inquirer*, 8/16/62, p.34.

23. "Pipers Called Through for '62," *Philadelphia Inquirer*, 8/29/62, p.30.

24. Abe Saperstein to Lou Jacobs, August 9, 1962. Abe Saperstein Papers.

25. Harry Kodinsky to Abe Saperstein, 9/14/62. Abe Saperstein Papers.

26. Harry Kodinsky to Abe Saperstein, September 16, 1962. Abe Saperstein Papers. Sparky Adams appears to be the former major league infielder for the Cubs, Cardinals, and Pirates from the period 1922–1934, who was from and lived in Tremont, Pennsylvania, in Schuykill County, 200 miles away.

27. "Ex-Stanford Star Signed by Steers," *Philadelphia Inquirer*, 9/17/62, p.40. "72 Games Slated for ABL Tapers," *Philadelphia Inquirer*, 9/18/62, p.44.

28. Abe Saperstein Memo to League Directors, 9/25/62. Abe Saperstein Papers.

29. "Felix, Hopkins Cut by Chiefs," *Philadelphia Inquirer*, 10/7/62, p.S-5.

30. "Tapers to Stay in Philadelphia, Dicker for Lucas," *Philadelphia Inquirer*, 10/18/62, p.33.

31. Condon, Dave, "In the Wake of the News," *Chicago Tribune*, 10/22/63, p.Sports-1.

32. "Triolo Interested in ABL Franchise," *Philadelphia Inquirer*, 10/25/62, p.40. "A.B.L. Will Announce New Rens Owners Today," *Kansas City Times*, 11/2/62, p.21. "Rens Cage Team to New Owner," *Kansas City Times*, 11/3/62, p.28.

33. "A.B.L. Books 72 Games," *Kansas City Star*, 11/4/62, p.5B.

34. "A.B.L. Teams to Play Two 30-Minute Tilts," *Kansas City Times*, 11/13/62, p.15.

35. Abe Saperstein to Al Abrams, 10/30/62. Abe Saperstein Papers.

36. *Oakland Oaks 1962–63 Official Souvenir Program*, p.10.

37. Bill Sharman to Abe Saperstein, November 15, 1962. Abe Saperstein Papers.

38. Marie to Saperstein, ABL Memo, November 15, 1962. Abe Saperstein Papers.

39. "Steers Edge Oakland," *Kansas City Times*, 11/15/62, p.14C.

40. "Tapers Tip Magic," *Kansas City Times*, 11/15/62, p.14C.

41. "3-Pointers Settle A.B.L. Twin-Bill," *Kansas City Times*, 11/16/24, p.24. Roger Meyer, "American Basketball League 1961–62, 1962–63," in Ken Shouler et al., *Total Basketball* (Wilmington, DE: Sports Media Publishing, 2003).

42. "Majors Trip Rens on Last-Half Surge," *Kansas City Times*, 11/17/62, p.20.

43. "Steers Rapped by Long Beach," *Kansas City Times*, 11/19, 62, p.28. "Steers Tumble to Chiefs for Third Loss in Row," *Kansas City Times*, 11/21/62, p.14.

44. "Steers Swap Jack Audon for Ritter," *Kansas City Times*, 11/22/62, p.8E.

45. "Steers Rise with King," *Kansas City Times*, 11/23/62, p.38.

46. "Steers Fail at Buzzer," *Kansas City Times*, 11/24/62, p.23.

47. "Rens Adept on Line," *Kansas City Times*, 11/28/62, p.20.

48. "Chiefs Keep Slate Clean in Loop Play," *Kansas City Times*, 11/29/62, p.2D. "Long Beach Soars Again for 8 in Row," *Kansas City Times*, 11/30/62, p.24.

49. "Tapers Sign Dayton Ace," *Kansas City Times*, 11/30/62, p.25. Fritz Kreisler, "Crisis in Steers' Camp," *Kansas City Times*, 12/1/62, p.32. "Taper Boss Stands Pat on Playing Dayton Star," *Kansas City Times*, 12/1/62, p.32. "Steers Race on without Coach," *Kansas City Star*, 12/2/62, p.B1. "Dee, Cleary Fulfill Vow in A.B.L. Fuss," *Kansas City Star*, 12/2/62, p.B1. "Dee Leaves for Home in Denver," *Kansas City Times*, 12/4/62, p.18.

50. "Spivey Hot as Chiefs Streak On," *Kansas City Times*, 12/1/62, p.34.

Chapter Notes — Nine

51. "Chiefs Sail on in A.B.L. Breeze," *Kansas City Times*, 12/5/62, p.22. Fritz Kreisler, "Steers Tackle A.B.L.'s Hot Team Tonight," *Kansas City Times*, 12/5/62, p.22. Fritz Kreisler, "Steers Tame Chiefs," *Kansas City Times*, 12/6/62, p.2D. "Tapers Tie Lid on Oaks' Goal," *Kansas City Times*, 12/7/62, p.28.
52. "Hawkins' 34 Guides Rens Past Majors," *Chicago Tribune*, 12/8/62, p.C2.
53. "Chiefs Slip By Rens," *Kansas City Star*, 12/10/62, p.16.
54. "Bridges Pours in 55," *Kansas City Times*, 12/10/62, p.34. "Majors Top Steers," *Kansas City Times*, 12/11/62, p.28.
55. "Bridges, Wilfong Soar," *Kansas City Times*, 12/12/62, p.16. William Richardson, "Steers Beat Pittsburgh," *Kansas City Times*, 12/13/62, p.15C. "Steers Breeze Again," *Kansas City Times*, 12/14/62, p.32.
56. Fritz Kreisler, "A.B.L. to Fine Its Fighters," *Kansas City Times*, 12/15/62, p.36.
57. "Steers Make It 9 in a Row as Tapers Lose, 109–107," *Kansas City Times*, 12/22/62, p.28. Fritz Kreisler, "Steers Win 10th in Row," *Kansas City Times*, 12/24/62, p.10.
58. Fritz Kreisler, "Steers Ready for More Play," *Kansas City Times*, 12/25/62, p.10C.
59. "Oakland Takes Ninth in Row on Home Floor," *Kansas City Star*, 12/28/62, p.16.
60. "Tapers Trip Chicago," *Kansas City Times*, 12/31/62, p.15.
61. Roger Kaiser, telephone interview, June 22, 2011.
62. Frank Dolson, "American Basketball League Collapses," *Philadelphia Inquirer*, 1/1/63, p.24.
63. Frank Dolson, "Cohen Tapers Off on Telephone Calls," *Philadelphia Inquirer*, 1/2/63, p.35.
64. This was the assertion of John Barnhill, Syl Blye, and Monte Moore.

Bibliography

BOOKS

Barry, Rick, with Bill Libby. *Confessions of a Basketball Gypsy*. Englewood Cliffs, NJ: Prentice-Hall, 1972.
Bradley, Robert. *Compendium of Professional Basketball*. Tempe, AZ: Xaler Press, 1999.
Conley, Kathryn R. *One of a Kind: The Gene Conley Story*. Altamonte Springs, FL: Advantage Books, 2007.
Danielson, Michael. *Home Team: Professional Sports and the American Metropolis*. Princeton, NJ: Princeton University Press, 1997.
Graham, Tom, and Rachel Graham Cody. *Getting Open: The Unknown Story of Bill Garrett and the Integration of College Basketball*. Bloomington, IN: Indiana University Press, 2006.
Green, Ben. *Spinning the Globe: The Rise Fall and Return to Greatness of the Harlem Globetrotters*. New York: Amistad Press, 2005.
Grundman, Adolph. *The Golden Age of Amateur Basketball: The AAU Tournament, 1921–1968*. Lincoln: University of Nebraska Press, 2004.
Gruver, Ed. *The American Football League: A Year-by-Year History, 1960–1969*. Jefferson, NC: McFarland, 1997.
Katz, Milton. *Breaking Through: John B. McLendon, Basketball Legend and Civil Rights Pioneer*. Fayetteville: University of Arkansas Press, 2007.
Koppett, Leonard. *24 Seconds to Shoot: A Informal History of the National Basketball Association*. New York: Macmillan, 1968.
Marcus, Jeff. *Biographical Directory of Professional Basketball Coaches*. Lanham, MD: Scarecrow Press, 2003.
McCambridge, Michael. *The Franchise: A History of Sports Illustrated Magazine*. New York: Hyperion Books, 1998.
Meyer, Roger. "American Basketball League 1961–62, 1962–63." In Ken Shouler, Bob Ryan, Sam Smith, Leonard Koppett, and Bob Bellotti, *Total Basketball*. Wilmington, DE, Sports Media Publishing, 2003.
Nelson, Murry. *The National Basketball League: A History, 1935–1949*. Jefferson, NC: McFarland, 2009.
Pluto, Terry. *Loose Balls*. New York: Simon and Schuster, 1990.
Rader, Benjamin. *In Its Own Image: How Television Has Transformed Sports*. New York: Free Press, Macmillan, 1984.
Robertson, Oscar. *The Big O, My Life, My Times, My Game*. Emmaus, PA: Rodale Press, 2003.

Bibliography

Rosen, Charley. *Scandals of '51: How the Gamblers Almost Killed College Basketball.* New York: Seven Stories Press, 1978, 1999.
Schleppi, John. *Chicago's Showcase of Basketball: The World Tournament of Professional Basketball and the College All-Star Game.* Haworth, NJ: St. Johann Press, 2008.
Shapiro, Michael. *Bottom of the Ninth: Branch Rickey, Casey Stengel and the Daring Scheme to Save Baseball from Itself.* New York: Henry Holt, 2009.
Sullivan, Neil. *The Dodgers Move West.* New York: Oxford University Press, 1989.
Thomas, Ron. *They Cleared the Lane: The NBA's Black Pioneers.* Lincoln: University of Nebraska Press, 2002.
Triptow, Dick. *The Dynasty That Never Was.* N.p. : self-published, 1997.
Wolf, David. *Foul! The Connie Hawkins Story.* New York: Holt, Rinehart and Winston, 1972.

JOURNAL ARTICLES

Banks, James P. "N.I.B.L. Makes Some Changes for This Season," *Sports Review*, Basketball Issue, 21(1), January 1961.
"Consumer Income," *Current Population Reports*, U.S. Commerce Department: Washington, D.C., Series P-60, No.41, September 21, 1963.
Kable, Forest. "Report on the American Basketball League." *Sports Review*, Basketball Issue, 22(1), January 1962.

NEWSPAPER ARTICLES

"A.B.L. Books 72 Games," *Kansas City Star*, 11/4/62, p. 5B.
"ABL Catching on, Saperstein Says," *Kansas City Times*, 11/20/61, p. 26.
"ABL Owners Ready to Share New NBA Club," *Philadelphia Inquirer*, 7/13/62, p. 31.
"ABL Owners Will Discuss Expansion, All Star Game," *Kansas City Times*, 11/16/61, p. 48.
"A.B.L. Scoring," *Kansas City Times*, 2/21/62, p. 23.
"A.B.L. Set to Boot Pipers," *Kansas City Times*, 2/19/62, p. 23.
"A.B.L. Sets up Play-off Plan," *Kansas City Times*, 3/27/62, p. 12.
A.B.L. to Keep Pipers in Loop," *Kansas City Times*, 2/21/62, p. 23.
"A.B.L. to Set Details Later on Play-offs," *Kansas City Times*, 3/21/62, p. 20.
"A.B.L. Teams to Play Two 30-Minute Tilts," *Kansas City Times*, 11/13/62, p. 15.
"A.B.L. Will Announce New Rens Owners Today," *Kansas City Times*, 11/2/62, p. 21.
"ABL Won't Fold, Says Saperstein," *Chicago Tribune*, 7/15/62, Sec.2, p. 3.
"Ace Scores 49, but Rens Lose," *Kansas City Star*, 12/24/61, p. 3D.
"Barnett Gets Okay to Play with Pipers," *Kansas City Times*, 12/22/61, p. 28.
"Barnett Guns in 43 to Stagger Saints," *Kansas City Times*, 2/9/62, p. 18.
"Barnett Testifies He Wasn't Happy with Syracuse," *Kansas City Times*, 12/8/61, p. 33.
"Big Spurt Puts Majors on Top," *Kansas City Times*, 3/12/62, p. 23.
"Bridges Pours in 55," *Kansas City Times*, 12/10/62, p. 34.
"Bridges Saves Steers," *Kansas City Times*, 1/5/62, p. 26.
"Bridges, Wilfong Soar," *Kansas City Times*, 12/12/62, p. 16.
"Chicago Bumps Rens on Rally," *Kansas City Times*, 12/23/61, p. 16.
"Chicago Goes to Top," *Kansas City Times*, 2/2/62, p. 18.

Bibliography

"Chicago Rally Dumps San Francisco, 94–91," *Pittsburgh Post-Gazette*, 11/18/61, p. 10.
"Chicago Whips Tapers to Gain Division Lead," *Kansas City Times*, 3/6/62, p. 16.
"Chiefs Blow Big Lead," *Kansas City Times*, 3/14/62, p. 2.
"Chiefs Keep Slate Clean in Loop Play," *Kansas City Times*, 11/29/62, p. 2D.
"Chiefs Sail on in A.B.L. Breeze," *Kansas City Times*, 12/5/62, p. 22.
"Chiefs Slip By Rens," *Kansas City Star*, 12/10/62, p. 16.
"Cleveland Bows Again," *Kansas City Times*, 1/29/62, p. 20.
"Cleveland Bows by 1," *Kansas City Times*, 12/22/61, p. 27.
"Cleveland Expected to Get 10th NBA Spot," *Philadelphia Inquirer*, 7/7/62, p. 18.
"Cleveland Still Easy for Tapers," *Kansas City Times*, 12/27/61, p. 16.
"Cleveland to ABL Final," *Chicago Tribune*, 4/1/62, Sec.2, Pt.2, p. 6.
"Cleveland Wins By 116–114," *Pittsburgh Post-Gazette*, 4/5/62, p. 30.
Condon, Dave, "In the Wake of the News," *Chicago Tribune*, 10/22/63, p. Sports-1.
"Conley's Fare Helps Tapers Past Pipers," *Kansas City Times*, 3/1/62, p. 36.
Cromie, Robert, "Chicago Gets Basket Team," *Chicago Tribune*, 4/22/60, Pt.F, p. 1.
"Dee, Cleary Fulfill Vow in A.B.L. Fuss," *Kansas City Star*, 12/2/62, p. B1.
"Dee Leaves for Home in Denver," *Kansas City Times*, 12/4/62, p. 18.
"Dees Agrees to Join Rens," *Kansas City Times*, 12/26/61, p. 37.
"Defense by L.A. Chills Pipers," *Kansas City Times*, 11/14/61, p. 14.
"Denies Collapse of Piper Plans to Shift to NBA," *Philadelphia Inquirer*, 7/29/62, Sports, p. 5.
Dolson, Frank, "American Basketball League Collapses," *Philadelphia Inquirer*, 1/1/63, p. 24.
Dolson, Frank, "Cohen Tapers Off on Telephone Calls," *Philadelphia Inquirer*, 1/2/63, p. 35.
"Ex-Stanford Star Signed by Steers," *Philadelphia Inquirer*, 9/17/62, p. 40.
Fachet, Bob, "ABL Moves Tapers Here, Threatens Suit Over Pipers," *Philadelphia Inquirer*, 7/26/62, p. 34.
"Felix, Hopkins Cut by Chiefs," *Philadelphia Inquirer*, 10/7/62, p. S-5.
"Fifth ABL Tilt Transferred," *Pittsburgh Post-Gazette*, 4/9/62, p. 25.
Fitzgerald, Maury, "Tapers Quit Washington, Transfer to Long Island," *Washington Post*, 1/1/62, p. A20.
"Full House See Majors Clip Rens," *Kansas City Times*, 12/29/61, p. 19.
"Future Shaky for McLendon," *Kansas City Times*, 1/30/62, p. 12.
Goldstein, Richard, "Tony Jackson, 65, Who Led St. John's Basketball, Dies," *New York Times*, 11/2/2005.
Gray, Rachel, "Basketball Great Maurice King Dies," *Daily Kansan*, 9/21/2007, http://www.kansan.com/news/2007/sep/21/king.
"Hawaii Gets Early Jump on New York," *Kansas City Times*, 3/15/62, p. 4D.
"Hawaii Holds On," *Kansas City Times*, 2/19/62, p. 23.
"Hawaii Trips Majors," *Kansas City Star*, 12/17/61, p. B1.
"Hawaii Whips Tapers to Win ABL Opener," *Kansas City Times*, 11/8/61, p. 14.
"Hawkins' 34 Guides Rens Past Majors," *Chicago Tribune*, 12/8/61, p. C2.
"Hawkins Holds Scoring Lead," *Kansas City Times*, 1/10/62, p. 11.
"Hawkins Pulls Rens in with 40," *Kansas City Times*, 11/26/61, p. 9B.
"Herd Snowballs On," *Kansas City Times*, 1/19/62, p. 16.
"Jackson Hikes 3-Point Record," *Kansas City Times*, 1/27/62, p. 17.

Bibliography

"Jackson Scores 53, but Chicago Bows," *Kansas City Times*, 3/15/62, p. 4D.
"Jackson Sharp as Majors Edge Chiefs by Four," *Kansas City Times*, 3/20/62, p. 16.
"Jets Drop Opener Before 5,137" *Los Angeles Times*, 10/28/61, Pt.2, p. 1.
"Jets Drop Out of Cage Loop," *Kansas City Times*, 1/19/62, p. 17.
"Jets Go Out of Business," *Los Angeles Times*, 1/19/62, Pt.4, p. 1.
"Jets Sweep Series," *Kansas City Times*, 12/22/61, p. 27.
Kreisler, Fritz, "A.B.L. Action against Cleveland Reflects Solidarity of League, Steers' Official Says," *Kansas City Times*, 2/20/62, p. 10.
Kreisler, Fritz, "A.B.L. at Critical Point in Battle for Talent," *Kansas City Star*, 3/11/62, p. 3B.
Kreisler, Fritz, "A.B.L. Has It All ... Except Super Stars," *Kansas City Star*, 1/28/62, p. B2.
Kreisler, Fritz, "ABL Set to Boot Pipers," *Kansas City Times*, 2/19/62, p. 23.
Kreisler, Fritz, "A.B.L. to Fine Its Fighters," *Kansas City Times*, 12/15/62, p. 36.
Kreisler, Fritz, "Bill Spivey Isn't Bitter Any More — Much," *Kansas City Star*, 2/11/62, p. B1.
Kreisler, Fritz, "Bridges Sparks Steers," *Kansas City Times*, 11/11/61, p. 24.
Kreisler, Fritz, "Celt Owner Fails to Faze A.B.L.," *Kansas City Times*, 11/1/61, p. 7C.
Kreisler, Fritz, "Crisis in Steers' Camp," *Kansas City Times*, 12/1/61, p. 32.
Kreisler, Fritz, "Herd Must Stop Pipers' Speed in Big Series," *Kansas City Times*, 1/12/62, p. 20.
Kreisler, Fritz, "Hot Herd Thunders In," *Kansas City Times*, 1/13/62, p. 21.
Kreisler, Fritz, "Late Rally by Steers," *Kansas City Times*, 2/14/62, p. 10.
Kreisler, Fritz, "Playoff May be Here," *Kansas City Times*, 1/9/62.
Kreisler, Fritz, "Rens Cool Off Steers," *Kansas City Times*, 2/18/62, p. 20.
Kreisler, Fritz, "Staverman Scores 35," *Kansas City Times*, 2/10/62, p. 22.
Kreisler, Fritz, "Steers Finally Corral Chicago," *Kansas City Times*, 1/10/62, p. 11.
Kreisler, Fritz, "Steers Get Up and Go," *Kansas City Times*, 2/19/62, p. 23.
Kreisler, Fritz, "Steers Make Point Do," *Kansas City Star*, 1/21/62, p. B1.
Kreisler, Fritz, "Steers Nail Down Title," *Kansas City Times*, 1/15/62, p. 24.
Kreisler, Fritz, "Steers Put on Speed," *Kansas City Times*, 2/22/62, p. 35.
Kreisler, Fritz, "Steers Race in Again," *Kansas City Times*, 1/8/62, p. 22.
Kreisler, Fritz, "Pipers Idle San Francisco as Two Star," *Kansas City Times*, 1/8/62, p. 22.
Kreisler, Fritz, "Steers Ready for More Play," *Kansas City Times*, 12/25/62, p. 10C.
Kreisler, Fritz, "Steers Slip by Hawaii," *Kansas City Times*, 2/12/62, p. 21.
Kreisler, Fritz, "Steers Stampede On," *Kansas City Times*, 1/22/62, p. 16.
Kreisler, Fritz, "Saints Keep String Alive in A.B.L. Race," *Kansas City Times*, 1/22/62, p. 16.
Kreisler, Fritz, "Steers Streak to 8 Again," *Kansas City Times*, 12/14/61, p. 2D.
Kreisler, Fritz, "Steers Tackle A.B.L.'s Hot Team Tonight," *Kansas City Times*, 12/5/62, p. 22.
Kreisler, Fritz, "Steers Tame Chiefs," *Kansas City Times*, 12/6/62, p. 2D.
Kreisler, Fritz, "Steers, Tough in Clutch, Take Lead," *Kansas City Times*, 11/13/61, p. 21.
Kreisler, Fritz, "Steers Will See Rens Often," *Kansas City Times*, 12/13/61, p. 25.
Kreisler, Fritz, "Steers Win 10th in Row," *Kansas City Times*, 12/24/62, p. 10.
Kreisler, Fritz, "Tiny Man Rips Steers," *Kansas City Times*, 11/7/61, p. 16.
"L.A. Keeps Going over S.F. in L.A.," *Kansas City Times*, 12/17/61, p. B1.

Bibliography

"L.A. Stops Steers at 8," *Kansas City Times*, 11/27/61, p. 26.
"Lane, New Basketball Man, Finds Time to Knock Cubs," *Philadelphia Inquirer*, 7/29/62, Sports, p. 5.
"Leader Claims A.B.L. Healthy," *Kansas City Star*, 1/21/62, p. 4B.
"Long Beach Soars Again for 8 in Row," *Kansas City Times*, 11/30/62, p. 24.
"Long Goals do Job for Herd," *Kansas City Star*, 3/25/62, p. B1.
"Lucas Agrees to Play for Pipers in NBA," *Chicago Tribune*, 7/17/62, Sports, p. 3.
"Lucas Pact Nullified if Pipers Join NBA," *Philadelphia Inquirer*, 7/10/62, p. 24.
"Lucas to Ask Hike in Pay to Play for NBA Pipers," *Philadelphia Inquirer*, 7/12/62, p. 31.
"Lynn Not Interested in Tapers' Transfer," *Washington Post*, 12/27/61, p. A20.
"McMahon to Sign as Coach of Zephyrs," *Chicago Tribune*, 7/24/62, C1.
"Majors Bounce Back," *Kansas City Times*, 3/21/62, p. 20.
"Majors' Clamp on 1st Tightens as Rens Falter," *Kansas City Star*, 1/21/62, p. 4B.
"Majors Do Job," *Kansas City Times*, 1/7/62, p. B6.
"Majors Grasp Touch to Nip Bid by Pipers," *Kansas City Star*, 3/4/62, p. B4.
"Majors Hike Eastern Lead to Full Game," *Kansas City Times*, 3/13/62, p. 14.
"Majors into First," *Kansas City Times*, 2/26/62, p. 20.
"Majors Keep Moving," *Kansas City Times*, 12/18/61, p. 34.
"Majors Tie for First by Downing Hawaii," *Kansas City Times*, 3/10/62, p. 26.
"Majors Top Steers," *Kansas City Times*, 12/11/61, p. 28.
"Majors Trip Rens on Last-Half Surge," *Kansas City Times*, 11/17/61, p. 20.
"Majors Win, 102 to 89 for Third in Row," *Chicago Tribune*, 12/23/61.
Miller, Jimmy, "Pro Basketball Returns to the City," *Pittsburgh Post-Gazette*, 11/2/61, p. 45.
Miller, Jimmy, "Rens Drop Majors, 105–90, for 2nd Win," *Pittsburgh Post-Gazette*, 11/8/61, p. 25.
Miller, Jimmy, "Rens' Late Rally Nips Hawaii, 100–99," *Pittsburgh Post-Gazette*, 11/15/61, p. 24.
Miller, Jimmy, "Rens Sweep By Chiefs, 106–93," *Pittsburgh Post-Gazette*, 11/17/61, p. 20.
Miller, Jimmy, "Rens to Fight to Keep Hawkins," *Pittsburgh Post-Gazette*, 11/11/61, p. 11.
Miller, Jimmy, "Unbeaten Rens Head South for 3 Games," *Pittsburgh Post-Gazette*, 11/9/61, p. 43.
Miller, Jimmy, "Walt Mangham," *Pittsburgh Post-Gazette*, 10/30/61, p. 24.
Miller, Stuart, "Where Steinbrenner and 3-Pointers Started," *New York Times*, 12/25/2011, Sports, p. 7.
"NBA Admits Cleveland Pipers Club," *Philadelphia Inquirer*, 7/11/62, p. 36.
"NBA Club Comes Up Short," *Kansas City Times*, 1/19/62, p. 17.
"NBA Packers get Si Green," *Pittsburgh Post-Gazette*, 11/20/61, p. 3.
"NBA Rejects Bid by Pipers, Cites Default on Agreement," *Philadelphia Inquirer*, 7/31/62, p. 25.
"New Chicago Basket Team Gets Bellamy," *Chicago Tribune*, 3/20/61, Pt.4, p. 2.
"New York Lead Stands," *Kansas City Times*, 1/26/62, p. 19.
"No N.B.A. Room for Expansion," *Kansas City Times*, 1/17/62, p. 12.
"No Playoffs Here; Steers Play Today," *Kansas City Star*, 1/7/62, p. 6B.
"Oakland Takes Ninth in Row on Home Floor," *Kansas City Star*, 12/28/62, p. 16.
"Owners Deny ABL Will Fold," *Philadelphia Inquirer*, 7/15/62, Sports, p. 10.

Bibliography

"Phil Woolpert Fired," *Kansas City Times*, 12/2/61, p. 26.
"Piper Boss Places McClendon [sic] on Spot," *Kansas City Star*, 12/28/61, p. 16.
"Pipers Battle New York Next," *Kansas City Times*, 3/31/62, p. 20.
"Pipers Beat Steers to Capture ABL Title," *Pittsburgh Post-Gazette*, 4/10/62, p. 21.
"Pipers Called Through for '62," *Philadelphia Inquirer*, 8/29/62, p. 30.
"Pipers Check Skid," *Kansas City Times*, 12/30/61, p. 13.
"Pipers Chop up Steers," *Kansas City Times*, 1/14/62, p. S1.
"Pipers Cut off Chicago by 10," *Kansas City Times*, 1/4/62, p. 31.
"Pipers Edge Rens on Fouls, 99–97," *Pittsburgh Post-Gazette*, 11/29/61, p. 28.
"Pipers Finally Get Job Done, Trip S.F. by 2," *Kansas City Times*, 3/9/62, p. 22.
"Pipers Hire McLendon Again," *Kansas City Times*, 2/3/62, p. 20.
"Pipers Learn from Steers," *Kansas City Times*, 1/12/62, p. 13.
"Pipers, Nats Will Merge, Paper Says," *Kansas City Times*, 1/18/62, p. 37.
"Pipers on Block," *Kansas City Times*, 1/31/62, p. 17.
"Pipers Outplay Rens, Win Easily, 137–94," *Pittsburgh Post-Gazette*, 11/27/61, p. 28.
"Piper Payroll Late," *Kansas City Times*, 1/17/62, p. 12.
"Pipers Rally Late," *Kansas City Times*, 12/20/61, p. 18.
"Pipers Sink When Zagar Hits Big Shot," *Kansas City Times*, 3/23/62, p. 25.
"Pipers Slip By on Long Shots," *Kansas City Star*, 3/25/62, p. B1.
"Pipers Trade Adams for Dierking," *Kansas City Times*, 1/30/62, p. 12.
"Pipers Unload in Last Period," *Kansas City Times*, 3/19/62, p. 22.
"Pipers Win: Swartz Hot for Tapers," *Kansas City Times*, 2/8/62, p. 28.
"Pipers Win to Gain Tie for Pennant," *Kansas City Times*, 3/26/62, p. 22.
"Pittsburgh Hex Chills Majors," *Kansas City Times*, 1/29/62, p. 20.
"Podoloff Bars Cage Deal," *Kansas City Times*, 11/21/61, p. 26.
"R.C. Owens Plays," *Kansas City Times*, 1/16/62, p. 11.
"Rens Adept on Line," *Kansas City Times*, 11/28/62, p. 20.
"Rens Cage Team to New Owner," *Kansas City Times*, 11/3/62, p. 28.
"Rens Close Gap on Lead, Trip Majors," *Kansas City Times*, 12/25/61, p. 3C.
"Rens' Coach to Undertake Playing Role," *Kansas City Times*, 11/30/61, p. 6B.
"Rens Face Steers for Two Games," *Pittsburgh Post-Gazette*, 12/19/61, p. 28.
"Rens Fly as Hawkins Pops in 39," *Kansas City Star*, 1/28/62, p. B3.
"Rens Hang on to Take Final on Home Court," *Kansas City Times*, 3/24/62, p. 22.
"Rens Lose First to Hustling Majors, 104–97," *Pittsburgh Post-Gazette*, 11/10/61, p. 20.
"Rens Maintain Hold on First as Chiefs Bow," *Kansas City Times*, 1/8/62, p. 22.
"Rens Make It 2 in a Row over Tapers, 95–84," *Pittsburgh Post-Gazette*, 11/12/61, Sec.4, p. 6.
"Rens, Pittsburgh Feud over Terms," *Philadelphia Inquirer*, 7/6/62, p. 27.
"Rens Surge as Hawkins Scores 31," *Kansas City Times*, 12/30/61, p. 13.
"Rens to Fight to Keep Hawkins," *Pittsburgh Post-Gazette*, 11/11/61, p. 11.
"Reports ABL to Quit," *Philadelphia Inquirer*, 7/11/62, p. 36.
"Revisions Made in Jets' Games," *Kansas City Times*, 1/18/62, p. 37.
"Rollins, Hawkins Star," *Kansas City Times*, 1/22/62, p. 16.
"Royals' Grace Blasts Podoloff," *Philadelphia Inquirer*, 7/27/62, p. 31.
"Royals Want Lucas, Oppose Cleveland Bid," *Philadelphia Inquirer*, 7/8/62, Sports, p. 6.
"Rumors Grow Jets Will Shift L.A. Franchise," *Kansas City Times*, 1/16/62, p. 11.
"Saints Get Tough," *Kansas City Times*, 2/14/62, p. 10.
"Saints Name Brightman to Coach Club," *Kansas City Times*, 12/27/61, p. 16.

Bibliography

"Saints Win as Francis Finds Range," *Kansas City Times*, 2/7/62, p. 11.
"Sale of Pipers Now Complete," *Kansas City Times*, 2/1/62, p. 38.
"Saperstein Gets Chicago Pro Entry," *Chicago Tribune*, 3/19/61, Pt.2, p. 6.
"Saperstein Says ABL Will Try to Keep Going," *Philadelphia Inquirer*, 7/24/62, p. 33.
"72 Games Slated for ABL Tapers," *Philadelphia Inquirer*, 9/18/62, p. 44.
"Sharman Expects to Quit Pipers," *Los Angeles Times*, 7/17/62, Sec.3, p. 2.
"Sharman Hired as Cage Coach," *Kansas City Times*, 1/31/62, p. 17.
"Spivey Hot as Chiefs Streak On," *Kansas City Times*, 12/1/62, p. 34.
"Spivey Paces Jets," *Kansas City Times*, 11/8/61, p. 14.
"Spivey Puts L.A. in Gear to Tip Rens," *Kansas City Times*, 12/7/61, p. 4D.
"Steers Again Beat Pipers," *Pittsburgh Post-Gazette*, 4/4/62, p. 26.
"Steers Appoint Dee as Coach," *Philadelphia Inquirer*, 8/16/62, p. 34.
"Steers Beat Pipers in ABL Series 126–115," *Pittsburgh Post-Gazette*, 4/2/62, p. 23.
"Steers Beat Pittsburgh," *Kansas City Times*, 12/13/62, p. 15C.
"Steers Bounce Back," *Kansas City Times*, 2/5/62, p. 23.
"Steers Breeze Again," *Kansas City Times*, 12/14/62, p. 32.
"Steers Edge Oakland," *Kansas City Times*, 11/15/62, p. 14C.
"Steers Escape Defeat by One," *Kansas City Times*, 11/9/61, p. 34.
"Steers Fail at Buzzer ... ," *Kansas City Times*, 11/24/62, p. 23.
"Steers Feel Effect of Winning Title," *Kansas City Times*, 1/20/62, p. 16.
"Steers Hit Back Again," *Kansas City Times*, 2/21/62, p. 23.
"Steers Hold Hot Pace," *Kansas City Times*, 1/16/62, p. 11.
"Steers Lose by 4 to Rens Again," *Kansas City Times*, 12/18/61, p. 34.
"Steers Lose to S.F. Late," *Kansas City Times*, 1/4/62, p. 31.
"Steers Make it 9 in a Row as Tapers Lose, 109–107," *Kansas City Times*, 12/22/62, p. 28.
"Steers' Play-off Foe Holds the Upper Hand," *Kansas City Star*, 1/11/62, p. 20.
"Steers Race on Without Coach," *Kansas City Star*, 12/2/62, p. B1.
"Steers Rapped by Long Beach," *Kansas City Times*, 11/19/62, p. 28.
"Steers Rise with King," *Kansas City Times*, 11/23/62, p. 38.
"Steers Risk Lead Tonight," *Kansas City Times*, 11/17/61, p. 24.
"Steers Shake off Slump," "Phil Woolpert Fired," *Kansas City Times*, 12/2/61, p. 26.
"Steers Sign King for 2d Season," *Philadelphia Inquirer*, 8/26/62, p. S-3.
"Steers Stampede Tapers," *Kansas City Star*, 1/7/62, p. 1B.
"Steers Still Red Hot," *Kansas City Times*, 12/15/61, p. 8C.
"Steers' Streak Hits 7," *Kansas City Times*, 12/11/61, p. 32.
"Steers' String Is Ended at 9," *Kansas City Times*, 12/17/61, p. B1.
"Steers Swap Jack Audon for Ritter," *Kansas City Times*, 11/22/62, p. 8E.
"Steers to Finish Road Trip Early," *Kansas City Times*, 2/6/62, p. 15.
"Steers Tops in League Travel, Too," *Kansas City Times*, 1/1/61, p. 21.
"Steers Tumble to Chiefs for Third Loss in Row," *Kansas City Times*, 11/21/62, p. 14.
"Steers Win it at :02," *Kansas City Times*, 1/1/62, p. 21.
"Swartz Shines as Tapers Win," "Pipers Rush Back," *Kansas City Star*, 2/11/62, p. B2.
"Swartz Stars for Tapers, but Rens Win It," *Kansas City Times*, 1/30/62, p. 11.
"Taper Boss Stands Pat on Playing Dayton Star," *Kansas City Times*, 12/1/62, p. 32.
"Tapers Need 3 Overtimes to Nip Hawaii," *Kansas City Star*, 12/5/61, p. 28.
"Tapers over Chicago," *Kansas City Times*, 1/1/62, p. 21.
"Tapers Rally Clicks," *Kansas City Times*, 12/29/61, p. 19.
"Tapers, Saints Need Overtimes," *Kansas City Times*, 3/29/62, p. 2D.

Bibliography

"Tapers Sign Dayton Ace," *Kansas City Times*, 11/30/62, p. 25.
"Tapers Tie Lid on Oaks' Goal," *Kansas City Times*, 12/7/62, p. 28.
"Tapers Tip Magic," *Kansas City Times*, 11/15/62, p. 14C.
"Tapers to Stay in Philadelphia, Dicker for Lucas," *Philadelphia Inquirer*, 10/18/62, p. 33.
"Tapers Trip Chicago," *Kansas City Times*, 12/31/62, p. 15.
"Tapers Win as Swartz Collects 40," *Kansas City Times*, 1/31/62, p. 16.
"Tempers and Fouls Gang up on Pipers," *Kansas City Times*, 2/28/62, p. 16.
"Texan Focuses on A.B.L. Team," *Kansas City Times*, 1/17/62, p. 12.
"3-Pointers Settle A.B.L. Twin-Bill," *Kansas City Times*, 11/16/24, p. 24.
"Travel Snarls Steers," *Kansas City Times*, 12/19/61, p. 27.
"Triolo Interested in ABL Franchise," *Philadelphia Inquirer*, 10/25/62, p. 40.
"Trotters Pull 20,482 Fans to A.B.L. Tilt," *Kansas City Times*, 2/3/62, p. 20.
"U.S., Russian Tanks Face Each Other in Berlin," *Los Angeles Times*, 10/28/61, p. 1.
"Victory Pulls Chicago Close in A.B.L. Race," *Kansas City Times*, 2/1/62, p. 16.
"Warm Barnett Peps Up Pipers," *Kansas City Times*, 3/14/62, p. 19.
"Wilt Was Never Headed for A.B.L., Says Leader," *Kansas City Times*, 2/23/62, p. 19.
"Windfall for Hawks," *Philadelphia Inquirer*, 7/12/62, p. 34.
"Zagar Paces Majors," *Kansas City Times*, 11/14/61, p. 14.
"Zephyrs Sign Staverman of ABL Steers," *Chicago Tribune*, 7/15/62, Sec.2, p. 3.

INTERVIEWS

John Barnhill
Sylvester Blye
Roger Kaiser
Hal Lear
Monte Moore
Kenny Sears
Bill Sharman
Seymour Smith

ARCHIVAL MATERIAL

Abe Saperstein Papers, The American Basketball League. Briscoe Center for American History, University of Texas-Austin.
"Audited Balance Sheet, Cleveland Basketball Club, Inc., June 30, 1962," Ernst & Ernst, Auditors. Personal collection of Carolyn Hastings, Lakewood, OH.
"The Chicago Packers Organization," *Chicago Packers Official Programs, 1961–62* and *1962–63*. Author's collection.
"Estate of A. M. Saperstein, Deceased, Allan R. Bloch and Continental Illinois National Bank and Trust Co. of Chicago, Co-Executors, and Sylvia Saperstein v. Commissioner," 1970 Tax Ct. Memo Lexis 150, 29 T.C.M. (CCH) 916 [1970], p. 4.

WEBSITES

Article on Kenny Sears from 1954 *SI*, http://sportsillustrated.cnn.com/vault/article/magazine/MAG1024213/index.htm (accessed October 10, 2011).

Bibliography

Article on Larry Friend's investment company, http://articles.latimes.com/1991-08-12/business/fi-428_1_investment-banking-firm.

Association for Professional Basketball Research, http://www.apbr.org.

Black, Jack, J. Michael Kenyon, Bill Hoover, and Robert Bradley, "Bill Spivey Professional Career Highlights," http://www.apbr.org/spivey.html (accessed March 7, 2011).

Cleveland Memory Project of Cleveland State University Libraries site with photos of the Cleveland Pipers, http://images.ulib.csuohio.edu/cdm4/results.php?CISOOP1=exact&CISOFIELD1=subjec&CISOROOT=all&CISOBOX1=Cleveland+Pipers+(Basketball+team).

Kentucky Wildcat Basketball, http://www.bigbluehistory.net.

Larry Friend page of a Cal alum site, http://tightwad-hill.blogspot.com/2007/02/sweet-sixteen-11-larry-friend.html.

Peter Vecsey column from *Japan Times* on Connie Hawkins, http://search.japantimes.co.jp/cgi-bin/sp20090218pv.html (accessed October 10, 2011).

St. Johns Red Storm, http://www.redstormsports.com.

"Sharman v. Longo," 249 Cal.App. 2d 948 (April 5, 1967), http://www.lawlink.com/browse_codes.aspx?caselevel3=44067.

"USF Retires Mike Farmer's Number," http://www.usfdons.com/sports/m-baskbl/spec-rel/050600aaa.html.

Index

ABC Sports 46, 47
Adams, Jack 94, 95, 114, 123, 124, 126, 129
Adams, Ray 98
All-American Football Conference (AAFC) 13
American Basketball Association (ABA) 1, 54, 69, 72–74, 76, 78, 86, 159, 163, 165
American Basketball League (ABL): All-League teams 10; demise 155, 156; financing 37–44; formation 16–34; playoffs 9, 10, 11, 123, 124, 136–138; referees 33–38; rules 4, 10, 33–39, 157, 163; television 45–50
American Football League (AFL) 7, 15, 16
Arledge, Roone 47

Barnett, Dick 7, 9, 10, 11, 31, 41, 45, 61, 64, 65, 74, 75, 117–120, 123, 127, 131, 133, 135–138, 142, 149, 156, 161, 164
Barnhill, John 41, 65, 68, 75, 76, 107, 117, 118, 128, 134, 136, 144, 149, 156, 161
Basketball Association of America (BAA) 16, 34, 77, 78, 100, 111
Beard, Ralph 57, 58
Beatty, Zelmo 69, 136
Beberich, John 92, 137
Bell, Whitey 91, 92, 109
Bellamy, Walt 5, 30, 102, 105
Bloch, Alan 3, 32, 139, 141–143, 145
Blye, Sylvester 59–61, 94, 113, 128, 131, 134, 137, 150
Bolyard, Bucky 89, 108, 113, 117, 134, 142, 150, 156
Braun, Carl 61
Bridges, Bill 10, 31, 41, 81, 84, 113, 114, 116, 117, 122, 123, 125, 127, 128, 130–135, 137, 138, 142, 146, 148, 150, 152, 153, 154, 156, 161, 163, 164
Brightman, Al 78, 91, 121
Bronstein, Isadore 21, 34
Brooklyn Dodgers 13, 14, 16, 67

Brown, Gene 91, 109, 149
Brown, Roger 52
Brown, Walter 3, 68, 159
Brownstein, Phil 100, 143
Burgess, Frank 78, 79, 113, 119, 128, 130, 135

Cable, Barney 102
Carl, Howie 106
Carmichael, Martin 49
CBS Sports 45, 48, 49
Chamberlain, Wilt 47, 62, 77, 85, 133
Chicago American Gears 99
Chicago Coliseum 98, 99, 108
Chicago Duffy Florals 97
Chicago Majors 70–74, 102, 104–109, 112, 123
Chicago Packers 4, 5, 6, 30, 39, 47, 79, 95, 100–105, 108, 118, 122, 128, 142, 149
Chicago Stadium 3, 98–100, 104, 106, 133, 136, 146, 148, 151, 153
Chicago Stags 99, 100
Chicago Studebakers 99
Chicago Zephyrs 81, 82, 85, 108, 142, 144, 146, 148, 156–159
Chmielewski, Bill 96, 151, 152
Cincebox, Jon 89, 90
Cincinnati Royals 24, 139, 144, 159
Cleveland Pipers 74–77, 107, 116, 117, 125, 126, 129, 130, 132, 133, 139, 140, 144, 145
Clifton, Nat 31, 45, 61, 72, 107, 119, 156
Cohen, Jeff 79, 150
Cohen, Paul 2, 7, 60, 96, 121, 143, 147, 151, 155, 156
Coleman, Kelly 72, 73, 106, 107, 115, 135, 150, 151
Conley, Gene 39, 40, 61, 95, 116, 161
Continental League 14, 15, 16, 19
Cooke, Jack Kent 14
Corbosiero, Len 3, 5, 6, 24, 115, 119, 127
Cousy, Bob 67

207

Index

Cox, John 10, 41, 76, 123, 131, 133, 135–137, 149, 156, 161
Crosby, Bing 24
Cullanin, Craig 14
Curtis, Charley 90, 113, 136, 142

Davis, Melvin 25, 26, 116
Davis, Ralph 103, 106
Dee, Johnny 145, 152
Dees, Archie 31, 69, 102, 120, 128, 137, 156, 161
Detroit Pistons 24, 105
Dierking, Connie 11, 31, 43, 69, 77, 95, 112, 126, 131, 136–138, 156, 161, 164
Dolph, Jack 45, 48

Eastern Basketball League (EBL) 21, 26, 31, 59, 60, 72, 73, 96

Farmer, Mike 31, 45, 61–64, 91, 109, 131, 142, 156, 161
Fitzpatrick, Jackie 106–108, 118
Fleer football cards 16
Fox, Phil 21, 24, 25, 33, 34, 35, 36, 37
Francis, Jim 91, 92, 109, 131, 132
Friend, Larry 5, 69, 109, 128

Gibson, Leroy 108, 137
Glickman, Harry 17, 18, 21, 22, 23, 24, 26, 27, 32
Gola, Tom 62
Goldberg, Sid 21, 22
Goldman, Morrie 101
Graboski, Joe 103
Green, Sihugo 103
Groza, Alex 57, 58

Hacken, Joe 53, 54
Hadden, Charlie 80, 150
Hadnot, Jim 93, 149
Halas, George 97, 98
Hale, Bruce 99
Hannum, Alex 25
Hapac, Bill 98
Harlem Globetrotters 1, 2, 3, 5, 6, 16, 18, 19, 28, 29, 35, 37, 44, 54, 58, 70, 72, 79, 98, 105, 106, 109, 112, 114, 121, 130, 133, 137, 150, 151, 157, 160
Harman, Lee 80
Harrison, Les 24
Hatton, Vern 102
Hawaii Kings 77–80, 106, 107, 112, 113, 130
Hawkins, Connie 8, 9, 10, 31, 42, 51–55, 81, 89, 107, 108, 112, 113, 116–120, 123, 125, 128–134, 136, 137, 142, 150, 152–154, 156, 157, 161, 164
Horn, Ron 80, 150–152, 161
Hunt, Lamar 15

International Amphitheatre 4, 101, 104
Ireland, George 100

Jackson, Inman 71
Jackson, Manny 79, 105
Jackson, Tony 7, 9, 10, 30, 31, 52, 55, 56, 72, 108, 115, 123, 127, 128, 133–137, 156, 161
Johnson, Andy 102
Johnson, Edwin 14
Johnson, Rafer 31
Johnson, Rossie 65, 75
Johnston, Neil 8, 34, 54, 87, 89, 116, 141, 157

Kaiser, Roger 31, 39, 40, 60, 94, 95, 115, 116, 120–123, 126, 131, 134, 137, 150, 155, 156
Kansas City Steers 80–86, 106, 107, 113, 116, 119, 123
Karlov, Sam 101
Kautz, Wibs 98
Kennedy, Walter 143
Kerkorian, Kirk 20, 21
Kim, Art 3, 28, 35, 142, 143, 145
King, Maurice 26, 69, 84, 85, 122, 123, 132, 148, 150, 151, 161
Kodinsky, Harry 145, 146
Konysky, Henry 21
Koppett, Leonard 42
Kreisler, Fritz 128, 129, 131, 135
Krueger, Ken 3, 25, 28, 113, 123, 140, 142, 143, 145, 154–156

Lacour, Fred 92, 149
Lane, Frank 144, 145, 156
Lapchick, Joe 55
Lear, Hal 5, 26, 31, 40, 87, 109, 114, 115, 117, 142, 156
Lee, Herb 40, 80, 106, 115, 116, 135, 137
Leonard, Bob 102
Linehan, Marie 21, 26, 37, 45, 71, 141, 142, 149
Litman, Lenny 2, 11, 54, 110, 112, 113, 116, 140–143, 148, 149
Los Angeles Jets 5, 6, 8, 86, 87, 108, 109, 113–115, 126, 127
Lubin, Charlie 101
Lucas, Jerry 43, 75, 139, 140, 144, 145

Index

Ludwig, Arthur 101
Lynn, Harry 2, 7, 28, 119, 121

Madison Square Garden 25, 39, 52, 153
Malitz, Lester 45–49
Mangham, Walt 89, 90, 111, 112, 118, 136
Mann, Henry 101
Mantis, Nick 10, 84, 85, 107, 118, 123, 124, 133, 142, 148, 156, 161
Mays, Willie 13
Mazer, Nathan 52, 53
McCollum, Grady 80, 150, 153
McCoy, Jim 90, 118, 150
McDermott, Bob 99
McGowan, Vince 98
McKeon, George 3, 32, 140–142
McLendon, John 2, 7, 8, 10, 64, 68, 74, 76, 86, 117, 121, 125, 129, 130, 157, 160
McMahon, Jack 3, 8, 34, 77, 80, 81, 85, 141, 144, 157, 159
McPhail, Bill 45, 48
Meyer, Ray 100
Midwest Basketball Conference 97, 111
Mieuli, Franklin 48, 162
Mikan, George 72, 99, 160
Miller, Jimmy 111
Mills, Dave 79, 112
Minneapolis Lakers 17, 100, 104, 119, 160
Moe, Doug 31
Molinas, Jack 59, 60
Moore, Monte 120, 122, 124, 138, 162
Moses, Robert 14
Murphy, Don 29
Musial, Stan 9, 113

National Basketball Association (NBA): attendance 6, 133, 134; history 2, 7, 16–18, 20, 22–24, 31, 34, 35, 46, 47, 49–51, 56, 59, 61, 69, 94, 100–103, 105, 108, 113, 118, 122, 126, 130, 138, 140, 157, 158, 159, 163
National Basketball League (NBL) 29, 34, 55, 97–100, 111
National Football League 47
National Industrial Basketball League (NIBL) 2, 29, 43, 51, 74, 76, 90, 92, 94, 95
Naulls, Willie 61, 62
NBC Sports 46, 47, 104
New York Giants 13, 14, 16
New York Knicks 104, 120
New York Tapers 122
Novak, Mike 98

O'Malley, Walter 14
Osborne, Chuck 100
O'Shea, Kevin 121
Owens, R.C. 125

Palmer, Jim 113, 128
Patrick, Stan 99
Payson, Joan Whitney 14
Perri, Mario 94
Philadelphia Warriors 16, 100, 102, 118, 158
Phillip, Andy 8, 71
Pittsburgh Rens 87–90, 106, 107, 110, 112, 113, 119
Pluto, Terry 29
Podoloff, Maurice 17, 20, 56, 58–60, 103, 132, 140
Pollard, Jim 104
Price, George 40, 106, 116

Rader, Benjamin 46
Rickey, Branch 14, 15
Ripley, Elmer 34
Robertson, Oscar 24, 42, 64, 73, 86
Robinson, Ermer 70, 71, 91, 148, 149, 157, 160
Rocha, Red 8, 77, 78
Rollins, Phil 89, 90, 108, 128
Rupp, Adolph 57
Russell, Bill 47, 63, 67, 117, 157

Saint Louis Hawks 102
San Francisco Saints 78, 90–94, 109, 113, 116, 120–122, 158
Saperstein, Abe: and ABL 1, 5, 6, 11, 16, 17, 21, 22–27, 29, 30–33, 35, 37, 40, 45, 48, 70, 100, 104, 109, 113, 115, 126, 127, 133, 138, 144–147, 149, 155, 157, 162, 163, 165; death 163; and Globetrotters 1, 18, 19, 20, 28, 139, 141
Sauldsberry, Woody 103
Schneer, Morrie 2, 32, 33
Sears, Ken 7, 10, 31, 39, 40, 45, 61–63, 91, 109, 120, 128, 131, 133, 136, 137, 142, 156, 161
Sharman, Bill 3, 5, 8, 9, 40, 45, 61, 67, 69, 86, 109, 116, 128, 129, 141, 149, 156, 157, 159, 160
Siegel, Robert 24
Siegfried, Larry 30, 45, 75, 120, 123, 127, 135, 156, 160, 161, 164
Simmons, Chet 45, 46, 48
Smith, Robert 18, 19
Smith, Seymour 26, 30, 100
Sobie (Sobieszczyk), Ron 72

209

Index

Spivey, Bill 5, 7, 10, 26, 31, 45, 57–59, 78–80, 109, 114–116, 119, 128–134, 137, 150–154
Spraggins, Bruce 96, 150
Staverman, Larry 10, 31, 41, 61, 81–84, 86, 119, 120, 123–125, 127, 130, 131, 137, 138, 142, 146, 149, 152, 153, 156, 161
Steinbrenner, George 2, 8, 9, 10, 11, 43, 121, 125, 126, 129, 130, 138–141, 160, 162
Stern, Benjamin 25
Stoenham, Horace 13, 14
Stutz, Stan 8, 21, 94, 147, 157
Swartz, Dan 5, 9, 10, 87, 94, 114, 116, 117, 119, 120, 122, 128–134, 136, 137, 161
Syracuse Nationals 103, 105, 120, 157, 158

Tatelbaum, Hyman 21, 22
Taylor, Roger 94, 95, 113, 117, 123, 126
Tennessee A&I 74, 117
Todd, Rolland 93, 149
Topps cards 16, 163, 164
Tormohlen, Gene 31, 61, 84, 114, 120, 122, 123, 130, 142, 146, 148, 151, 161
Trager, Dave 4, 6, 100, 101, 105, 145
Triptow, Dick 99
Turner, Herschell 10, 30, 41, 72, 106, 107, 117, 133, 135, 136, 150, 161
Turner, John 92, 149

Uline Arena 28, 120

Vanak, John 162
Vann, Bryce 41, 122

Vaughn, Governor 79, 106, 107, 115, 118, 149

Walker, George Herbert, Jr. 14
Walker, Horace 102
Warley, Ben 65, 68, 69, 75, 76, 80, 113, 114, 116, 117, 121, 123, 131, 150, 152, 153, 156, 161
Washington Tapers 94–96, 108, 112, 113, 120, 121
Wessels, John 30, 41, 72, 74, 106, 108
WGN 47, 104
White, Maurice 99
Whitney, Hank 30, 72, 73, 105, 108, 114, 128, 132, 161
Wilfong, Win 41, 85, 86
Wilkins, Len 69, 87
Wilkinson, Bob 72, 73, 106, 128
Wilson, George 9, 130, 162
Wirtz, Art 3
Wolf, David 116
Wood, Thomas 24
Wooden, John 69, 87, 92
Woolpert, Phil 8, 34, 90, 91, 116, 121

Yardley, George 5, 31, 61, 65–67, 87, 109, 114–116, 122, 128, 156
Yates, Wayne 93, 94, 149

Zagar, Ron 94, 95, 106, 107, 115

www.ingramcontent.com/pod-product-compliance
Ingram Content Group UK Ltd.
Pitfield, Milton Keynes, MK11 3LW, UK
UKHW041958140426
5217IPUK00015B/857